Carson's country

MANCHESTER
1824
Manchester University Press

Carson's army

The Ulster Volunteer Force, 1910–22

Timothy Bowman

Manchester University Press
Manchester and New York

distributed exclusively in the USA by Palgrave

Copyright © Timothy Bowman 2007

The right of Timothy Bowman to be identified as the author of this work has been asserted by him in accordance with the Copyright, Designs and Patents Act 1988.

Published by Manchester University Press
Oxford Road, Manchester M13 9NR, UK
and Room 400, 175 Fifth Avenue, New York, NY 10010, USA
www.manchesteruniversitypress.co.uk

Distributed in the United States exclusively by
Palgrave Macmillan, 175 Fifth Avenue,
New York, NY 10010, USA

Distributed in Canada exclusively by
UBC Press, University of British Columbia, 2029 West Mall,
Vancouver, BC, Canada V6T 1Z2

British Library Cataloguing-in-Publication Data is available

Library of Congress Cataloging-in-Publication Data is available

ISBN 978 0 7190 7372 4 paperback

First published by Manchester University Press in hardback 2007

This paperback edition first published 2012

The publisher has no responsibility for the persistence or accuracy of URLs for any external or third-party internet websites referred to in this book, and does not guarantee that any content on such websites is, or will remain, accurate or appropriate.

Printed by Lightning Source

Contents

List of tables	vi
Acknowledgements	vii
List of abbreviations	x
Map	xii
Introduction	1
1 The origins of Ulster Unionist militancy, 1885–1912	15
2 'An armed democracy'? The social composition and ideological basis of the UVF	45
3 Command, control and military efficiency	76
4 Parades and propaganda: the public face of the UVF	116
5 Arms, equipment and finance	135
6 War and decline, 1914–19	163
7 The revival and demise of the UVF, 1920–22	190
Conclusion	205
Select bibliography	210
Index	227

Tables

2.1	Occupational profile of the Enniskillen Horse	51
2.2	Occupational profile of 1st Fermanagh Regiment	51
2.3	Occupational profile of members of 'H' (Seaforde) Company, 1st South Down Regiment	52
2.4	Occupational profile of officers and men of 5th Tyrone Regiment who attended Baronscourt Camp of Instruction	52
2.5	Occupational profile of members of No. 1 section, 'C' Company, 2nd West Belfast Regiment	54
2.6	Age profile of Derry City Regiment	55
2.7	Age profile of 1st Fermanagh Regiment	56
2.8	Age profile of the Enniskillen Horse	56
2.9	Age profile of 'H' (Seaforde) Company, 1st South Down Regiment	56
2.10	Age profile of two sections of 'J' Company, 4th (Dungannon) Battalion, Tyrone Regiment	57
3.1	The former or current rank of British army officers involved in the UVF	95
5.1	The distribution of rifles and machine guns per county 1917	145
6.1	The strength of battalions of the 36th (Ulster) Division, 3 October 1914	177
6.2	The UVF membership of officers appointed to the 36th (Ulster) Division by January 1915	181

Acknowledgements

This book was largely written during the lengthy apprenticeship period which most British academics are now forced to undertake, between completing my Ph.D. thesis and securing my first permanent academic post. As such, having worked in four universities and five academic departments over the past seven years I have incurred a large number of debts within the academic community.

As an undergraduate at Queen's University Belfast I had the very good fortune to encounter Professor Alvin Jackson. His 'Irish Unionism' module first led me to consider the academic literature on the UVF in detail and it was probably on that wet Thursday morning in Belfast in 1995 when the seminar group argued passionately over what the UVF could have done in July 1914 that the genesis of this book was laid. Professor Jackson has continued to provide helpful advice, criticism and encouragement for which I am indebted.

A number of other individuals have been instrumental in the completion of this work. Professor Ian Beckett, Dr Graham Brownlow, Dr Michael Foy and Timothy Wilson read the manuscript and made a number of useful recommendations. Matthew Jenkinson undertook some preliminary proofreading in a valiant attempt to correct the inadequacies of a progressive school education. Toby Watson provided valuable advice on computing matters. Brenda Clifford and Gregory Muldowney provided a comfortable base for my research in Dublin while Christopher Turley and his family were kind enough to do the same for me in Edinburgh. Elsewhere David Armstrong, Dr Timothy Benbow, Dr John Bourne, Liam Boyle, Dr Mark Connelly, John Crone, Dr Enda Delaney, Dr Robert Foley, Dr Ultan Gillan, Mark Graham, James Hamilton, Dr Neil Fleming, Professor Peter Hart, Dr Andrew Holmes, Professor Keith Jeffery, Dr Karen Jones, Professor Liam Kennedy, Dr Helen McCartney, Dr James McConnell, Professor Ranald

Michie, Dr Alan O'Day, Professor Michael Prestwich, Dr Richard Reid, Dr Simon Rofe, Professor Geoffrey Till, Professor Matthew Uttley, Benjamin Wastnage, Professor David Welch, Dr Michael Wheatley, Dr John Wills and Dr Sarah Wootton provided valuable advice and support.

I would also like to thank those students who studied my courses on Irish history at Queen's University Belfast, the University of Durham, King's College London/Joint Services Command and Staff College and the University of Kent, who provided me with many useful insights and led me to question some of my initial findings more rigorously. Similarly, I would like to thank those who attended research seminars and conference sessions which I addressed at Queen's University Belfast, the University of Birmingham, the University of Durham, JSCSC, National Museum of Ireland, University of Northampton, Trinity College Dublin and University College Dublin for their helpful comments and suggestions.

At Manchester University Press the staff dealt with my manuscript with their customary professionalism, insuring that I met the strict RAE deadline. I would particularly like to thank Alison Welsby and Jonathan Bevan for their patience and assistance. The anonymous reader chosen by MUP also deserves my thanks for providing such a detailed and constructive report in a commendably short period of time.

In terms of finance I have to thank Queen's University Belfast for awarding me one of their Junior Research Fellowships in 2000–1. The Scouloudi Foundation generously financed a research trip to London and Oxford made while I was based in Durham. The Department of History at the University of Durham kindly funded a research visit to Dublin and the Defence Studies Department at KCL/JSCSC provided funding for research trips and photocopying in Oxford and London archives.

Of course, for any historian, a great deal of gratitude must go to those, often anonymous, individuals who provide such excellent service in libraries and record offices. The staff of the Public Record Office of Northern Ireland (PRONI) faced with inadequate accommodation and staffing levels always dealt with my seemingly endless requests for material with courtesy and professionalism. I would particularly like to thank Dr David Huddleston and Ian Montgomery for their valuable advice on the collections. In the context of PRONI, I must also thank the Ulster Unionist Council for permission to view their archive and Lady Sylvia Hermon, MP, for her help in facilitating this. I would also like to thank the Police Service of Northern Ireland for allowing me to view the

Acknowledgements

Ulster Special Constabulary Archive. Elsewhere staff at Belfast Central Newspaper Library, the Bodleian Library, the British Library, Durham Record Office, the House of Lords Record Office, the Imperial War Museum (IWM), Monaghan County Museum, National Archives Dublin, National Archives of Scotland, the National Army Museum (NAM), the National Library of Ireland (NLI), Nuffield College and The National Archives (TNA, formerly Public Record Office), Kew, dealt with my numerous requests in a courteous and professional manner.

Finally, and most importantly, I would like to thank my parents who have again provided endless moral support and a comfortable base in Northern Ireland during the course of my research and writing for this book.

Abbreviations

AAQMG	Assistant Adjutant and Quartermaster General
CI	County Inspector
CO	Commanding Officer
DI	District Inspector
DIG	Deputy Inspector General
DSO	Distinguished Service Order
GOC	General Officer Commanding
GSO	General Staff Officer
HQ	Headquarters
IG	Inspector General
INV	Irish National Volunteers
IPP	Irish Parliamentary Party
IRA	Irish Republican Army
IWM	Imperial War Museum
NAM	National Army Museum
NCO	Non-Commissioned Officer
NLI	National Library of Ireland
OTC	Officer Training Corps
PRON	Public Record Office of Northern Ireland
QMG	Quartermaster General
RIC	Royal Irish Constabulary
RUC	Royal Ulster Constabulary
SR	Special Reserve
TF	Territorial Force
TNA	The National Archives, Kew
USC	Ulster Special Constabulary
UUC	Ulster Unionist Council
UVF	Ulster Volunteer Force
UWUC	Ulster Women's Unionist Council

List of abbreviations

VTC   Volunteer Training Corps
YCV   Young Citizen Volunteers

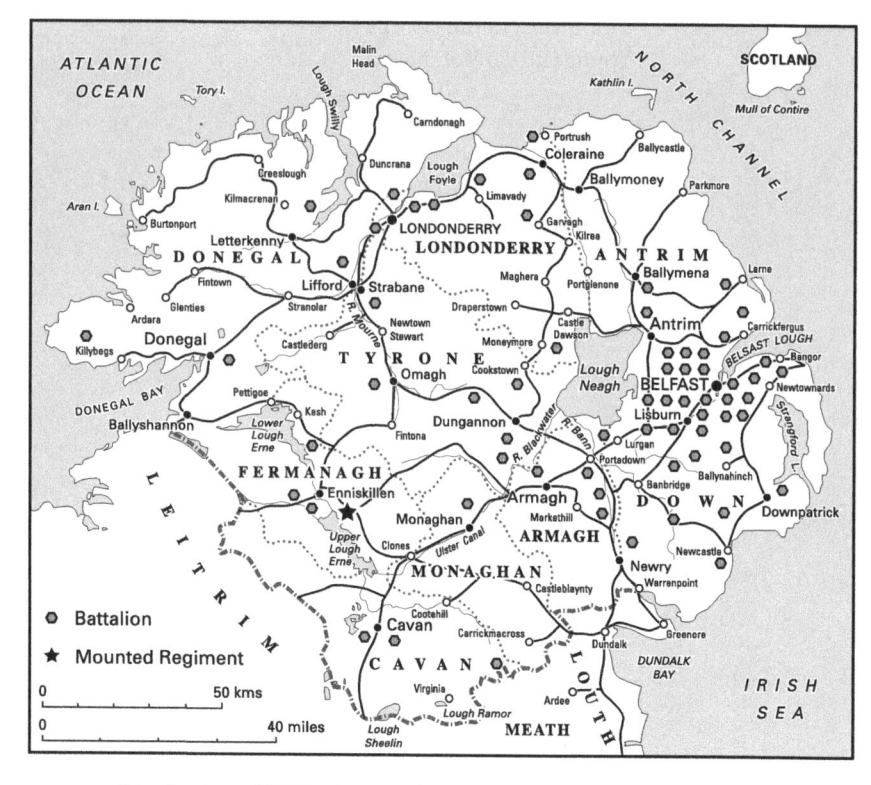

Distribution of UVF units, March 1914. Source: *The Times*, 18/03/1914

For my parents

Introduction

The Ulster Volunteer Force (UVF) remains something of a forgotten army of the Irish revolutionary period. This seems odd, given the size of the movement (possibly as many as 110,000 members at its height in mid-1914) and the roles which it played in the Third Home Rule crisis, Great War, Anglo-Irish War and establishment of the Northern Ireland state. Indeed, given the size of the force and the amount of popular support it attracted, it could be argued that it was the real 'people's army' of the Irish revolution. This neglect seems to be for a number of reasons. Firstly, most of those involved in the UVF seem to have quickly wanted to forget just how close they came to pushing Britain into a civil war. It is noticeable that many British army officers who were involved in the UVF in 1913–14 omitted this information from their *Who's Who* entries in the 1920s and, indeed, reflecting the views of many of their fellow officers, this detail was also omitted from many of their obituaries. Allied to this was the reluctance of UVF members to commit their memories of the movement to print. While Irish Republican Army (IRA) leaders such as Tom Barry and Ernie O'Malley produced popular, well-written works, the only memoirs published by former UVF members (R. J. Adgey, Fred Crawford and Percy Crozier) were little reviewed or noticed, with the exception of Crozier's work and this was largely due to his provocative comments on his experiences in the Great War and Anglo-Irish War, not the pre-war UVF.[1]

Just as important in the neglect of the UVF has been the lack of interest by historians. The IRA has proved of much more interest to historians in recent years; some have certainly been ideological 'fellow travellers' but more important has been the desire to study a true revolutionary movement and the wealth of source material recently released in the Bureau of Military History Archives in Dublin. This has resulted in the production of some excellent work on the IRA, notably by Joost

Augusteijn, Peter Hart and Robert Lynch.[2] A more serious problem in the historiography of the Irish revolution has been the dominance of what Alvin Jackson has termed the 'Trinity school': David Fitzpatrick and the group of historians who have been either taught by him at Trinity College Dublin or deeply influenced by his approaches.[3] While this school has produced excellent works – Fitzpatrick's own work was truly ground-breaking when it appeared in 1977 and Augusteijn and Hart's works are major contributions to Irish history – it has led to two serious problems. The first is an unwillingness to consider Ulster in the revolutionary period. Indeed, it is noticeable that a recently published collection of essays, containing contributions from members of this Trinity school, *The Irish Revolution 1913–1923* included no significant contributions regarding either Ulster or Unionism; Peter Martin's contribution, 'Unionism: The Irish Nobility and the Revolution 1919–23' referring to only a tiny minority of Southern Unionists.[4] The second problem is the tendency for this approach to be applied to an increasing number of the Irish counties which were to become the Irish Free State, leading us into the danger of seeing the Irish revolution through the prism of the 26 Irelands, while ignoring the more useful two Irelands approach and, indeed, of seeing the Irish revolution as a predominantly rural experience.[5] As Fergus Campbell's recent work has shown there is also a serious methodological issue in assuming that one county's experience can be taken as representative of the Irish case as a whole.[6]

This, of course, is not to suggest that the UVF has been entirely neglected by historians. Michael Foy's Ph.D. thesis of 1987 is a well-researched and oft-cited piece of work, its major drawback being the lack of source material which was available to the author at the time of writing.[7] However, there have been methodological problems evident in some of the works produced on the UVF. A. T. Q. Stewart's important, *The Ulster Crisis*, was written in a tradition of Unionist historians with a capital 'U'. To him, the paramilitary route adopted by the Unionist leadership when forming the UVF was broadly justified, given the failure of parliamentary and popular methods to defeat Home Rule.[8] The major problem with Stewart's work in historiographical terms is that it concentrates too much on Buchanesque accounts of the UVF's gunrunning activities. Work by the Marxist writer Michael Farrell suffered from similar ideological problems, with the author's suggestion that the UVF was based on little popular support, being brought into existence by an alliance of Belfast businessmen and British imperialists.[9]

There has also been a tendency for historians of opposition to Home Rule to view the UVF as little more than a supporting cast to the Unionists stars: Sir Edward Carson and Andrew Bonar Law. This has lead to a number of impressive accounts of the high politics of British Unionism in the 1912–14 period which have, unfortunately, tended to view the UVF as simply another of the 'league of leagues' which made up the Edwardian Unionist Party.[10] Similarly Graham Walker's important new work on the Ulster Unionist Party makes scant reference to the UVF and suggests that it was little more than a compliant party auxiliary.[11]

There has recently been a thought provoking discussion regarding the historical period which can be termed the Irish revolution and, indeed, the extent to which the term 'revolution' should be used.[12] In this context something must be said regarding the dates used in this work. The dates 1910 to 1922 have not been selected as absolute beginning and terminal dates for this work. While 1910 saw the first moves towards mass Unionist drilling and arming, it is clear that earlier militant activity had taken place, certainly at the time of the First (1886) and Second (1893) Home Rule Bills. Indeed, a number of UVF members, with some plausibility, identified the force as part of a longer loyalist paramilitary tradition, stretching back to the Irish Volunteers of the 1770s. The date 1922 is even more problematic. It seems that the bulk of the reformed UVF of 1920 gradually assimilated into the Ulster Special Constabulary (USC) and that this process had ended by 1922. However, the fate of the arms of, and funds raised by, the UVF take us into the 1940s, if not the 1960s, and it could be argued that the UVF brought a permanent strain of militancy into the Ulster Unionist community which expressed itself through the USC, Ulster Defence Regiment and Royal Irish Regiment part-time Home Service battalions. Unlike some authors who have written about modern Loyalism it was considered important to choose an early terminal date to confirm the lack of overlap between the UVF of 1910–22 and the UVF of 1966 to date; organisations whose similarity is in little more than name only.[13]

Similarly, there is some discussion over the use of the term 'paramilitary' when discussing the UVF.[14] Peter Hart has freely used this term in his work stating, 'By "paramilitary" I mean unofficial armed and public militias organised along military lines for the ostensible purpose of fighting one another, the police or the official army'.[15] While we should recognise that there are problems in using the term 'paramilitary' in that it provides something of a *Freikorps* or proto-Nazi flavour to the formations being discussed, this work has followed Hart's practice, as the alternatives such as 'political army' or 'political militia' seem equally confusing, especially given the current identification of the term 'militia' with extremist groups in the USA.

Before outlining the structure of this book, it is important to discuss some of the methodological problems involved in studying the UVF in this period. The existing source material means that any study of the movement will inevitably have a bias in favour of rural units, those commanded by members of 'Big House' Unionism and the UVF officer corps. In 1961 when the minds of the members of the Northern Ireland government were turned to the forthcoming fiftieth anniversary of both the Easter Rising and the Battle of the Somme, Lord Brookeborough, the Prime Minister of Northern Ireland, wrote to a number of 'old-established Ulster families prominently identified with the anti-Home Rule movement' asking for material relating to the UVF to be deposited in the Public Record Office of Northern Ireland.[16] Shamefully many of these papers were not catalogued for years, many being unavailable to Michael Foy for his study of the movement completed in 1986.[17] However, the problem of actively seeking accounts from 'Big House' Unionism, while neglecting to target more plebeian accounts appears to have influenced PRONI acquisitions policy up to the mid-1990s. While PRONI did experiment with oral history archives in the early 1970s, those interviewed were, again, prominent figures in the Unionist movement, who in many cases had already deposited detailed collections of papers and diaries. Thus our knowledge of urban 'democratic' UVF units is much more limited than that of rural 'feudal' units, a serious problem given that the UVF's real strength was in urban areas, particularly Belfast. Another major problem in discussing the UVF of 1910–22 is the lack of uniformity in the surviving paperwork. Many UVF units relied on inexperienced commanding officers (COs) and adjutants and, especially in areas where men were well known to each other, it seems that the paperwork kept was minimal

To address these shortcomings in the UVF documents that survive, Royal Irish Constabulary (RIC) and military intelligence reports have been used. However, here there are also problems. The military authorities were particularly keen to find out which serving and retired officers of the British army were involved in the UVF as they could be prosecuted under section 451 of King's Regulations for their political involvement. Most RIC county inspectors were Unionists and this seems to have influenced a number of them when reporting to Dublin Castle on the size and military efficiency of the UVF in their areas.

Introduction 5

There are also problems in using newspaper sources for the UVF in this period. The major problem with the Ulster based press in this period was that it was so politically polarised. While the Unionist press liked to portray the force as composed of fit, determined, intelligent and well-trained men, the Nationalist press liked to present UVF members as misguided youths or drooling geriatrics, dragooned into the movement by their employers or landlords. The other politically divisive issue surrounding the UVF was the demand of the National Service League for conscription in Britain and their condemnation of the limited training carried out in the newly formed Territorial Force (TF). This debate clouded discussions over the efficiency of the UVF as those on the radical right could hardly praise the military performance of the force without, by implication, admitting that a part-time, voluntary force was perfectly adequate for Britain's home defence needs.

The first chapter discusses the origins of Ulster Unionist militancy from 1885–1912. As early as the First Home Rule Bill there was evidence of Ulster Unionists attempting to arm themselves in opposition to government policy.[18] Fred Crawford's writings and some materials on the Lisburn UVF held at PRONI make it clear that in 1892 a militant organisation called 'Young Ulster' and a number of rifle clubs were set up, their members privately equipping themselves with firearms to resist the imposition of the Second Home Rule Bill.[19]

Young Ulster does not seem to have survived the events of 1893; however, as Home Rule again became a possibility (and with the removal of the Lord's veto in 1911 a much more likely one) a number of groups started to drill and arm themselves. Some of this initiative came from the Young Citizen Volunteers of Ireland (YCV), formed in Belfast in September 1912. The YCV was initially started as a non-sectarian organisation (although from the start most members were Unionists) and appears to have been set up as a reaction to the 1908 Haldane Reforms in the British army. While these reforms had left Ireland out of the TF scheme a number of prominent citizens in Belfast seem to have thought that if a military unit was organised, then it would be recognised and adopted by the War Office.

Some previous writers have suggested that the UVF was formed largely out of the Orange Order.[20] While this was the case in many areas, it is now clear that small groups of men started drilling, either independently (for example, Sergeant Osbourne Young, a former member of the Imperial Yeomanry was observed drilling 52 men in Omagh in early 1912) or as part of a club (obviously drilling was popular in the Unionist

Clubs, as Michael Foy has pointed out, but also in organisations as unlikely as the Catch my Pal Temperance Society in Londonderry[21]). It was the popular pressure exerted by this varied grassroots drilling which saw the formation of the UVF in January 1913.

Chapter 2 considers the social composition and political ideology of the UVF. The surviving archival material for the 1913–14 period enables some tentative comments to be made about the composition of the force in the 'classical' UVF period of 1913–14, which appears to have been subject to considerable regional variation. The membership roll of the 1st Fermanagh Regiment seems to show this as an almost 'feudal' rather than 'democratic' unit as it appears to have contained few skilled or lower-middle-class workers, relying on the landed gentry and clergy for its leadership and unskilled labourers for the majority of its rank and file; a very different social mix from that found in the IRA of 1916–23. Surviving membership rolls for West Belfast and Derry City appear to suggest relatively little interest in the force among the middle and upper classes there. Indeed, it is clear that in both Belfast and Londonderry it was difficult to secure officers of what was regarded as appropriate standing to command units. Ironically, where businessmen do appear to have conscripted their workforces into the UVF it seems to have been in rural areas. For example, the Herdmans in Sion Mills, Co. Tyrone and the Andrews in Comber both appear to have enlisted most of the male workers from their linen mills in the UVF units which they commanded.

There will be some discussion here of the formation of UVF units outside Ulster. It is clear that such units existed in Dublin, London, Glasgow and Liverpool and Lord Willoughby de Broke's British League for the Support of Ulster and the Union was certainly active in recruiting ex-officers to serve with the UVF. Unfortunately little paperwork survives about most of these units, but it does seem worth positing why some English, Scottish and Southern Irish Unionists fully supported militant action, while others (notably in Newcastle upon Tyne) refused to.

Assessing the ideology of the UVF membership is no easy task. We should beware of assuming that all UVF members shared identical political views; just as Irish Unionism was, literally and metaphorically, a broad church, so was the UVF. The attitudes of UVF members to key issues such as partition varied considerably by class, region and religion. As became increasingly apparent post 1914, major Protestant landowners in Cavan had different views from industrial workers in East

Belfast about what the UVF had been set up to deliver in political terms. However, there will be some discussion of key political issues relevant to the UVF membership such as the concept of Ulster, an Imperial identity and popular militarism.

The next chapter considers the command structures of the UVF and the force's military efficiency. In terms of command and control, discussion is required of the extent to which the UVF remained under the political direction of Ulster Unionist politicians and, indeed, the Conservative leadership in Britain. Lieutenant General Sir George Richardson was appointed General Officer Commanding GOC of the UVF in September 1913; however his powers of command are unclear. Certainly his appointment suggested that he would have considerable freedom (this is in sharp contrast to the Irish National Volunteers (INV), where the senior military figure involved, Colonel Maurice Moore, was given the post of Inspector General) and Sir Edward Carson was at pains to point out in many public speeches that the UVF was under professional military command. However, Richardson and his staff at UVF headquarters (HQ) in Belfast seem to have exerted little control over the force. Certainly, Richardson appears to have inspected most UVF units at least once, but seems to have had little power over appointing or removing UVF officers.

At the grassroots level it is clear that some Unionist Clubs in South Down and Co. Fermanagh were unwilling to submerge themselves in the UVF and accept officers appointed by the UVF county committees; while at a higher level it is apparent that in Co. Cavan, Colonel Oliver Nugent effectively ignored many of the orders he received from Belfast. There is therefore a serious question to address concerning who did actually command the UVF; was it, in any meaningful sense, Sir Edward Carson or Lieutenant General Sir George Richardson?

Much has been made of the professional expertise of the UVF. While the UVF did, indeed, attract active support from many retired British army officers, they were unequally distributed throughout the force. Thus the 4,000 strong Derry City Regiment appears to have had no experienced military leadership in its first six months of existence while the tiny Greyabbey contingent (with around 100 members) was commanded by a full Major General, W. E. Montgomery, the major local landowner. It is also clear that some of those allocated commands in the UVF, especially in Belfast Regiments, were rarely present with their units. For example, Colonel Fred Crawford's gunrunning activities and Lord Castlereagh's political career kept them away from their UVF commands in Belfast for much of the time. Many of those given senior command positions in the UVF (most notably Colonel G. H. H. Couchman, who had an important role as commander of the Belfast Special Service units) were found wanting when given commands in the British army during the Great War.

Previous works have tended to stress the military effectiveness and efficiency of the force, often citing the Larne gunrunning as an example.[22] This efficiency is, however, highly questionable. Not only is it now clear that the organisation of the Larne gunrunning was far from perfect, but there were few proper contingency plans drawn up for the force in the event of hostilities, and the transport and supply organisation of the UVF was practically non-existent. Charles Townshend has talked of a 'logistical nightmare' for the UVF, in terms of its ammunition supply (the force being armed with rifles of at least four different calibres) but, even more seriously, it appears that UVF regiments had arranged food supplies for their men for little more than two days.[23]

At the lowest level of the UVF, training must be considered to address the question of how effective the UVF actually was as a fighting organisation. Considerable material survives at PRONI and in the local newspapers of the period regarding UVF camps of instruction. It appears that, while most UVF regiments held at least one such camp, attendance at these was much lower than most previous accounts have allowed. This may be partly because they were aimed at potential officers and, perhaps as importantly, because those attending had to pay, at least for their own food, board and travel, and frequently to cover the costs of ammunition and wages of instructors as well. The UVF of 1913–14 was clearly not a well-honed military instrument. However, the force remained capable of over-powering RIC detachments and INV companies in Ulster, which realistically would have been its major military role. Simply as an army in being, the UVF was in a position to put pressure on Asquith's government, especially in the aftermath of the Curragh Incident.

Chapter 4 considers the public face of the UVF. Alvin Jackson has noted that, while UVF attendance for drill and rifle training was often poor, turnouts for major parades were always impressive.[24] Parades were key elements in the experience of all UVF members. In addition to major parades in Belfast, most rural units held at least one major parade, when they were presented with their regimental colours by local worthies and, normally, senior UVF officers and Unionist politicians. The issue of parades is an important one to investigate further in terms of the groups that took part in these parades (there was considerable variation, with UVF members sometimes parading with bands and Orange Lodges) and the focus of the parade (in some rural parades, this was an inspection by a senior UVF officer, while in others the parade ended with a short religious service or reaffirmation of political resolutions against Home Rule).

In terms of wider propaganda, only one brief article has considered this important issue of the public face of the UVF in detail.[25] Unionists seem to have been confused about how to portray the UVF, if at all, in their propaganda. One famous anti-Home Rule postcard, issued c. 1913, shows a women, carrying a rifle, saying 'Deserted, well I can stand alone!' A curious piece, when one considers that this was exactly the period when Unionist political leaders were talking of the military prowess of the UVF. On a wider issue, relating to finance, a number of Unionist Associations (and particularly the Ulster Women's Unionist Council (UWUC)) were unclear whether the aims of Unionism would be best met by raising funds to arm the UVF or using such funds for propaganda work in Great Britain.

The next chapter considers the related issues of finance, arms and equipment. Unfortunately, this, due to the nature of the surviving records, is a somewhat inconclusive chapter. Privileged access was granted to the surviving Ulster Unionist Council (UUC) records regarding the financing of the force. However, these are, perhaps unsurprisingly, incomplete. The UVF clearly used a number of bank accounts in Belfast, London and Paris to conceal their funds from possible RIC seizure, which makes an estimate of UVF funds difficult. Equally, it is clear that some of the sums of money recorded as being in UVF hands were in fact pledges, which would only be given to the force in the event of hostilities.

We can, however, be clear about a number of issues. It is apparent that Belfast businessmen did not bankroll the UVF to the extent that some historians have suggested. Sir Edward Carson berated businessmen for their lack of support (contrasting this with the level of support which he received from working men) and it appears unlikely that major firms in Belfast would have presented bills for relatively small amounts to the UVF if they were providing the organisation with major financial support in other ways. The outgoings of the UVF were also very low; apart from the purchase of the rifles smuggled in at Larne, the major element of UVF expenditure appears to have been the salary of Lieutenant General Sir George Richardson at £1,500 per annum. Indeed, when war broke out in August 1914 it appears that at least one UVF regiment was practically bankrupt. The arming of the UVF has already received considerable attention from historians. However, a number of neglected issues such as the legal framework under which arms were seized by the authorities, the purchases made by local UVF units and the fate of the arms acquired by the UVF will all be examined.

Chapter 6 is entitled 'War and decline, 1914–19'. In this chapter the contribution of the UVF to the 36th (Ulster) Division will be dealt with.[26] While a number of historians have accepted the versions of Colles and Falls that the UVF simply became the 36th (Ulster) Division this requires further explanation.[27] The UVF boasted a strength of 110,000 members by July 1914, yet it is clear that as late as December 1914 the 36th (Ulster) Division (at full strength around 16,000 men) was still 1,200 under-strength.

The UVF at the outset of the war reorganised itself as a home defence force and plans were drawn up to defend Belfast and the coasts of Antrim and Down against a German naval raid. However, most UVF units appear to have gone quickly into decline as officers and reservists were recalled to active service, enthusiasts volunteered for overseas service and the remaining membership was distracted by the lucrative industrial and agricultural employment brought about by the war. Indeed, during the Easter Rising of 1916, the UVF appears to have mobilised less than 2,000 men. The UVF leadership refused to co-operate with the INV for home defence and refused to incorporate their force in either the TF or the Volunteer Training Corps (VTC). It appears that some members of the UVF, especially in Dublin and Lisburn, left the organisation during the war to join the VTC, which they saw as a more effective organisation. In spring 1919, for reasons which remain unclear, Lieutenant General Sir George Richardson resigned as GOC and the UVF was officially disbanded.

The final chapter of this work considers the brief revival of the UVF in 1920 and its amalgamation into the Ulster Special Constabulary. As the Anglo-Irish War escalated, a number of independent Loyalist units were formed and armed from old UVF stocks. These units initially eschewed using the term UVF. Captain Basil Brooke forming his 'Fermanagh Vigilance' avoided the term UVF as he felt it would deter Catholic involvement while Colonel Fred Crawford formed his exotically named 'Crawford's Tigers' from the Tiger's Bay area of Belfast, believing that a small, oath-bound society was needed to deal with the IRA threat. More worryingly for the Unionist leadership a group named the Ulster

Imperial Guards was formed among shipyard workers in Belfast and was seen as having dangerous Socialist leanings.

Faced with these independent units, the Unionist leadership reacted as they had in 1913 by reconstituting the UVF. Colonel Wilfrid Spender (who had served as a staff officer in the original force) was given command of the new force, but it seems to have quickly run into trouble. The pre-war UVF officers were generally unwilling to rejoin the force, the Ulster Imperial Guards were unwilling to surrender their independence, military and police chiefs were convinced that the old UVF battalion and regimental system did not meet current counter-insurgency needs. Ultimately, it seems likely that a number of UVF members faced with the possibility of a 'shooting war' (having in a number of cases recently returned from one on the Western Front) were unwilling to serve in a force which provided no insurance scheme in the event of their injury or death.

The security response to this situation was the USC formed by the British government in late 1920. It was divided into three 'Divisions' and, at its height in 1922/23 consisted of over 40,000 men. 'A' Division, the smallest, was a full-time force, which was mainly composed of mobile, heavily armed platoons. 'B' Division, the largest, was a part-time force and 'C' Division was an emergency reserve. The USC is a force which has aroused fierce historiographical debate. To Michael Farrell, the formation of the USC saw the arming of some of the worst elements of Unionism, who went on to terrorise the Catholic minority in the new Northern Ireland state.[28] Meanwhile, Sir Arthur Hezlet portrayed the force as a group of public spirited individuals who were prepared to work incredibly long hours and risk their lives, with little financial reward, against vicious IRA attacks.[29]

The assumption made by both historians is that the USC relied on former UVF members as its recruiting base and this has been uncritically accepted by other writers. However, it appears that a major group which enlisted in the force may have been 19–20 year olds who thought they had missed the adventure of the Great War and wanted to gain military experience of their own, and 'B' Division operated as something of a patronage machine, as a number of elderly men were enrolled. As a locally raised force, the USC archives are disappointing in that local commanders, enrolling men they knew well, recorded few details regarding occupations or military experience. However, the archives do show that 'A' Division of the USC took a number of recruits from outside Northern Ireland.

Overall the picture that emerges of the UVF is one of regional and local variation. Some UVF units were well trained and well officered, others appear to have been little more than paper formations. The role of the force in the Irish revolution as a whole is a contentious issue. UVF members did not see themselves as 'revolutionary' in 1913–14, arguing that they were defending their constitutional rights as British subjects and as part of the British Empire. The force was counter-revolutionary in the 1920–22 period but was a pale shadow of its former self. It is perhaps worth quoting a contemporary Unionist writer on the role of the UVF in the break up of the United Kingdom: 'If, therefore, Ulster led the way of unconstitutionalism, resistance and rebellion if you will, and if this opened the door to the Rebellion of 1916, as I believe in a measure it did, the fault does not lie at the door of Ulster but is wholly due to the action of the Liberal Government'.[30]

Notes

1 R. J. Adgey, *Arming the Ulster Volunteers 1914* (privately published, Belfast, n.d. but c. 1947), Fred Crawford, *Guns for Ulster* (Graham and Heslip, Belfast, 1947) and F. P. Crozier, *Impressions and Recollections* (T. Werner Laurie Ltd, London, 1930), pp. 142–81.
2 See especially, Joost Augusteijn, *From Public Defiance to Guerrilla Warfare: The Experience of Ordinary Volunteers in the Irish War of Independence 1916–1921* (Irish Academic Press, Dublin, 1996), Peter Hart, *The IRA and its Enemies: Violence and Community in Cork, 1916–1923* (Clarendon Press, Oxford, 1998), Peter Hart, *The I.R.A. at War 1916–1923* (Oxford University Press, 2003) and Robert Lynch, *The Northern IRA and the Early Years of Partition 1920–1922* (Irish Academic Press, Dublin, 2006).
3 Alvin Jackson, 'Unveiling Irish History', *Journal of Contemporary History*, 40, 4, 2005, pp. 785–6. See the seminal, David Fitzpatrick, *Politics and Irish Life 1913–1921: Provincial Experience of War and Revolution* (Gill and Macmillan, Dublin, 1977).
4 Joost Augusteijn (ed.) *The Irish Revolution, 1913–1923* (Palgrave, Basingstoke, 2002).
5 Marie Coleman, *County Longford and the Irish Revolution 1910–1923* (Irish Academic Press, Dublin, 2003) and Michael Farry, *The Aftermath of Revolution: Sligo 1921–1923* (University College Dublin Press, 2000).
6 Fergus Campbell, *Land and Revolution: Nationalist Politics in the West of Ireland 1891–1921* (Oxford University Press, 2005) and Fergus Campbell, 'The Social Dynamics of Nationalist Politics in the West of Ireland 1898–1918', *Past and Present*, 182, 2004.

Introduction 13

7 M. T. Foy, 'The Ulster Volunteer Force: Its Domestic Development and Political Importance in the Period 1913 to 1920', unpublished Ph.D. thesis, The Queen's University of Belfast, 1986.
8 A. T. Q. Stewart, *The Ulster Crisis: Resistance to Home Rule, 1912–14* (Faber and Faber, London, 1967). See also, Alvin Jackson, 'Irish Unionism' in D. G. Boyce and Alan O'Day (eds), *The Making of Modern Irish History: Revisionism and the Revisionist Controversy* (Routledge, London, 1996) pp. 128–9 for a perceptive discussion of Stewart's work.
9 Michael Farrell, *Arming the Protestants: The Formation of the Ulster Special Constabulary and the Royal Ulster Constabulary 1920–1927* (Pluto Press, London, 1983).
10 R. J. Q. Adams, *Bonar Law* (John Murray, London, 1999), E. H. H. Green, *The Crisis of Conservatism: The Politics, Economics and Ideology of the British Conservative Party, 1880–1914* (Routledge, London, 1995), E. H. H. Green, 'The Strange Death of Tory England', *Twentieth Century British History*, 2, 1985, John Kendle, *Walter Long, Ireland and the Union, 1905–1920* (McGill-Queen's University Press, Dun Laoghaire, 1992), Richard Murphy, 'Faction and the Conservative Party and the Home Rule Bill', *History*, 71, 1986, William Rodner, 'Leaguers, Covenanters, Moderates: British Support for Ulster, 1913–14', *Eire-Ireland*, 17, 1982 and Jeremy Smith, *The Tories and Ireland 1910–1914: Conservative Party Politics and the Home Rule Crisis* (Irish Academic Press, Dublin, 2000).
11 Graham Walker, *A History of the Ulster Unionist Party: Protest, Pragmatism and Pessimism* (Manchester University Press, 2004).
12 Peter Hart, 'Paramilitary Politics and the Irish Revolution' in Fearghal McGarry (ed.), *Republicanism in Modern Ireland* (University College Dublin Press, 2003), Peter Hart, 'Definition: Defining the Irish Revolution' in Augusteijn (ed.), *The Irish Revolution, 1913–1923* and Charles Townshend, 'Historiography: Telling the Irish Revolution' in Augusteijn (ed.), *The Irish Revolution, 1913–1923*.
13 David Boulton, *The UVF 1966–73* (Torc Books, Dublin, 1973), Steve Bruce, *The Red Hand: Protestant Paramilitaries in Northern Ireland* (Oxford University Press, 1992) and I. S. Wood, *God, Guns and Ulster: A History of Loyalist Paramilitaries* (Caxton Editions, London, 2003).
14 I am grateful to Professor Charles Townshend and the members of the History Research Seminar at the University of Northampton for their interesting thoughts on this topic.
15 Peter Hart, 'Paramilitary Politics and the Irish Revolution' in McGarry (ed.), *Republicanism in Modern Ireland*, pp. 23–4.
16 PRONI, *Report of the Deputy Keeper of the Records for the Years 1960–1965* (HMSO, Belfast, 1968), p. 20.
17 Foy, 'The Ulster Volunteer Force'.
18 *Weekly Dispatch*, 16/05/1886.

19 Crawford, *Guns for Ulster*, pp. 9–11 and PRONI, D.845/1. Jenkins papers, enrolment forms for Lisburn UVF, which asked members to state if they knew the whereabouts of rifles from 1886 or 1893.
20 P. Gibbon, *The Origins of Ulster Unionism: The Formation of Popular Protestant Politics and Ideology in Nineteenth-Century Ireland* (Manchester University Press, 1975) p. 9.
21 Little is more controversial in Ireland that the naming of Ulster's second city. The convention I have followed is that I have used 'Derry' when writing about the city and 'Londonderry' when writing about the county. However, this is complicated by the fact that contemporaries, including UVF officers, for whom the politicisation of the name was not an issue, used the term 'Derry' for both.
22 See, for example, Ian Maxwell, 'The Life of Sir Wilfrid Spender, 1876–1960' unpublished Ph.D. thesis, The Queen's University of Belfast, 1991, pp. 45–79, Patrick Buckland, *Irish Unionism 2: Ulster Unionism and the Origins of Northern Ireland, 1886–1920* (Gill and Macmillan, Dublin, 1973) p. 61.
23 Charles Townshend, *Political Violence in Ireland: Government and Resistance since 1848* (Oxford University Press, 1984) p. 255.
24 Alvin Jackson, 'Unionist Myths, 1912–1985', *Past and Present*, 136, 174, 1992.
25 Michael Foy, 'Ulster Unionist Propaganda Against Home Rule 1912–1914', *History Ireland*, 4, 1, 1996.
26 This issue has already been covered in some depth in Timothy Bowman, 'The Ulster Volunteer Force and the Formation of the 36th (Ulster) Division' *Irish Historical Studies*, 32, 128, 2001.
27 See, Ramsay Colles, *The History of Ulster from the Earliest Times to the Present Day* (Gresham Publishing, London, 1920), p. 246 and Cyril Falls, *The History of the 36th (Ulster) Division* (McCaw, Stevenson and Orr, Belfast, 1922), p. 2.
28 Farrell, *Arming the Protestants,* especially pp. 7–54.
29 Sir Arthur Hezlet, *The 'B' Specials: A History of the Ulster Special Constabulary* (Tom Stacey Ltd, London, 1972), pp. 1–48.
30 H. S. Morrison, *Modern Ulster: Its Character, Customs, Politics and Industries* (H. R. Allenson Ltd, London, 1920), p. 159.

1

The origins of Ulster Unionist militancy, 1885–1912

In traditional Unionist accounts of the Third Home Rule crisis, militancy was a measured and controlled response by Ulster Unionists to the actions of the Liberal government. To Ronald McNeill, Ian Colvin and A. T. Q. Stewart, Ulster Unionists only resorted to drilling and arming on a large scale following the mass rally held on 23 September 1911 at James Craig's house, Craigavon, in East Belfast.[1] As McNeill and Colvin, but curiously not Stewart, acknowledged, there had been some drilling among Ulster Unionists before this rally; however, in these accounts this was stated as being purely among a small contingent of Orangemen from Co. Tyrone. In McNeill's words:

> The Craigavon meeting led, almost by accident as it were, to a development the importance of which was hardly foreseen at the time. Among the processionists who passed through Captain Craig's grounds there was a contingent of Orangemen from County Tyrone who attracted general attention by their smart appearance and the orderly precision of their marching. On inquiry it was learnt that these men had of their own accord been learning military drill. The spirit of emulation naturally suggested to others to follow the example of the Tyrone Lodges. It was soon followed, not by Orangemen alone, but by members of the Unionist Clubs, very many of whom belonged to no Orange Lodge. Within a few months drilling – of an elementary kind, it is true – had become popular in many parts of the country.[2]

County Inspector Edward Pearson of the Crime Special Branch observed the Craigavon demonstration and noted:

> it was observed that by far the greater number of the men who marched in procession carried themselves as men who had been drilled, particularly the members of the Unionist Clubs and the Orangemen from the Counties of Tyrone and Armagh.

It has been ascertained that about 100 of the Armagh Contingent, when going to and returning from the Railway Station at Armagh on this occasion, 'fell in' in two ranks, numbered off, formed fours, and marched off at the word of Command of a retired Army Sergeant named Walker. These men were all young, and it is believed that they had previously learned drill in the Yeomanry, Militia or in the Boys' Brigades. The majority of the Orangemen, however, took no part in this display, but went and returned in the usual way.³

In the same report, Pearson noted that Thomas Nelson, a 22-year-old former Boys' Brigade member had drilled about 50 young men in Killylea Orange Hall and had arranged to drill others elsewhere, with the aim of providing a contingent of 1,000 drilled men from Armagh for the demonstration at Belfast on Easter Monday. He also stated that, 'many of the Orangemen have served in the County Militia Regiments' and noted, 'We have no definite information that rifles are being obtained, or collected in suitable places, in the Northern Counties'.⁴ Pearson's account is therefore a useful corrective to the traditional Unionist descriptions of this rally. Clearly Pearson was convinced that drilling was fairly widespread by September 1911. While it certainly seems likely that the Craigavon demonstration provided a fillip to Ulster Unionist militancy, it would be wrong to suppose either that this provided the first evidence of Unionists clearly involved in military training for political ends or that such drilling as occurred between 1911 and 1912 was carried out under the respectable leadership of the Orange Order and Unionist Clubs.

It seems indisputable that the Unionist drilling and arming of 1910–14 built on earlier precedents, witnessed during the First and Second Home Rule Bill debates. The UVF should also be seen as the early twentieth-century incarnation of what D. W. Miller has termed the 'Protestant volunteering tradition' in Ireland.⁵ This tradition encompasses the militia formed periodically from 1666 onwards, the Irish Volunteers of 1777–92 and the Yeomanry of 1796–1834.⁶ Certainly the UVF had much in common with the Irish Volunteers of the 1770s and the Yeomanry in terms of its recruiting base, regional strength and leadership. However, while reference was often made to Irish Volunteer links this was not the case with the Yeomanry. Probably this is because the Yeomanry was almost exclusively Anglican before 1798 and, indeed, in the Battles of Ballynahinch and Saintfield in the 1798 Rebellion, locally raised Anglican Yeomanry had fought against local Presbyterian United Irishmen. It is therefore not surprising that UVF leaders concerned about awaking such unhappy and politically inconvenient memories did not make any comparisons between the Yeomanry and their own units.

Curiously, information on the militant aspects of the Unionists campaigns of 1886 and 1893 is sparse. Reviewing the situation in February 1911 a senior RIC officer stated, 'I have been unable to trace any papers on the question of the importation and distribution of arms in Ireland in 1886 or 1893'.[7] Drilling certainly took place at Richill, Co. Armagh in 1886 and, as discussed later in this chapter, the government's failed attempt to prosecute those participating in this drilling seriously curtailed the Liberal administration's ability to act against the more widespread drilling of 1913–14. A maximum of 50 men appear to have been drilled in the Demesne and Temperance Hall at Richill, through most of 1886. This drill was led by Edwin Best, a solicitor and Charles McCallum, who was described by the RIC as a 'gentleman'. Of those being drilled 29 were identified by the RIC and the occupations of 26 given. This shows a fairly wide cross section of rural society at this time with 15 being labourers, three farmers, two servants, two drivers, two shoe-makers, one merchant and one carpenter.[8]

Some drilling also took place in 1893. In Co. Fermanagh small groups of men were drilling at Castle Irvine, Ballinamallard, Killadeas, Magheraha and Carrickreagh. Most of this drilling seems to have been organised by Major Gerard Irvine, although in Ballinamallard it appears that it was led by a former sergeant of the Fermanagh Militia and a local shoemaker. The local District Inspector of the RIC approached Captain D'Arcy Irvine (later to be involved in the UVF) in the hope that he could stop his father continuing with this drilling. Facing the dilemma which was to confront Unionist leaders much more starkly in 1914, D'Arcy Irvine stated that, 'he could not tell his followers it should altogether be abandoned. He would not like to loose his influence with them'. The Inspector clearly thought that Gerard Irvine was beyond reason, describing him as, 'an obstinate, self-opinionated man, who likes to make himself of importance'. The RIC believed that no more than 200 men had been drilled and none of them had practised with anything but dummy rifles. The RIC felt that a prosecution would serve no useful purpose but would simply 'play into the hands of Major Irvine'. The Deputy Inspector General, RIC, noted that Major Irvine's followers consisted of 'farmer's sons and labourers'.[9]

During the Second Home Rule Bill's passage through Parliament, Fred Crawford, later to become famous for his gunrunning activities of 1910–14, formed the Young Ulster movement. This was a secret society, members of which had to possess a Martini rifle, Winchester rifle or a .45 revolver and operated under the guise of a gymnastic club. Crawford also claimed to have established several rifle clubs and revived the North of Ireland Rifle Club's range to allow Unionists to practice shooting. It appears that the Young Ulster movement petered out as Crawford became worried that his arrest was increasingly likely and of course the Second Home Rule Bill was defeated in the House of Lords.[10] It is likely that military training and drill in the 1886 and 1893 periods extended further than police reports suggest. In 1913, men enrolling for the UVF in Lisburn were asked if they knew where rifles issued during 1886 and 1893 were being kept.[11]

With regard to the Third Home Rule crisis period, it seems that Ulster Unionists began drilling and arming as early as December 1910, when the Orange Order was preparing its members for military training, although it appears that this information did not come into the possession of the RIC until April 1911. This perhaps suggests that Orange commitment to military action was much slower to manifest itself than previous works have allowed or may simply be a reflection of the ability of members of Orange Lodges to drill secretly in Orange halls. In December 1910 Colonel R. H. Wallace, the Grand Master of the Orange Order, sent a circular letter to Lodges noting, 'Already steps are being taken to enrol men to meet any emergency. Orangemen must set the example to other Unionists by volunteering their services'. Details were to be taken of Orangemen's names, addresses and previous military service, if any, on a form which they were then asked to sign, although it did not clearly commit them to any course of action.[12] By April 1911 it was clear that Orange Lodges in parts of Co. Fermanagh had started to drill.[13] By December 1911 Orange Lodges in the Co. Armagh area had ordered rifles from the Midland Gun Company, Birmingham and on 5 December 1911, 24 Martini-Henry rifles and 1,000 rounds of ammunition had arrived at Garvagh.[14] Of course not all drill instruction being carried out in Orange Lodges was of a high standard, in Magherafelt the police reported that 22 Orangemen had begun to drill, noting, 'The Instructor is Robert Hamilton of Rainey Street. He was a Private in the Inniskilling Fusiliers, and was invalided on account of insanity. He does not belong to the Army Reserve'.[15]

It is clear that, in some areas, the Orange Order only came to predominance after drilling had already been started either by Unionist Clubs or independently. Captain Watt, the Grand Master of the Orange Order in Co. Londonderry, proposed a resolution in Coleraine on 8

January 1912 calling for Unionists to resist Home Rule, if needs be, by force of arms. This resolution was passed by a Unionist meeting as a whole, rather than simply by the local Orange Order and, indeed, there was little evidence of Orange Order militancy in this area before this meeting was called.[16] Nevertheless, by May 1912, the RIC had definite information that ten Orange Lodges (Tyrooney, Coalisland, Mountjoy, Lisonelly, Dromore, Gortnamuck, Tandragee, Allistragh, Glentimon and Artigarvan) throughout Ulster had been receiving instruction in military drill.[17]

In late 1910 Lord Templetown was asked, by the Ulster Unionist Council, to reform the Unionist Clubs, as a focus for Unionist opposition to the Third Home Rule Bill. These clubs had originally been formed in 1893 but had been suspended in 1896, although as late as September 1895 it appears that the Unionist leadership wanted them to remain intact for future use.[18] A general meeting was held of the surviving members of the Council of the Unionist Clubs of Ireland in April 1911. Many of those present were later to become prominent in the UVF and the Unionist Clubs were soon to develop as the organisational basis for much Unionist drilling. However, not all members of the Unionist Clubs should be seen as supportive of the drive to militancy. Many members of Unionist Clubs highlighted the importance of the movement for propaganda work in Great Britain.[19] Some of the Southern Unionists who formed clubs in places like Kingston and Cork presumably saw the movement as an all-Ireland one, which would serve the interests of Southern not just Ulster Unionists.

The minute books of just one individual Unionist Club, Fortwilliam from North Belfast, survive. This was probably atypical of most in that it was urban, organised a wide range of activities for its members, was administratively well organised and seems to have had a large membership. Certainly the social activities were many and varied; military activities such as route marches (the first recorded in April 1912) and drilling (taking place twice weekly from November 1912) certainly occurred, but were complimented by smoking concerts and church parades. The Club was also active in forming links with other Clubs in Ulster and with Unionist Associations in Great Britain, especially in Glasgow. The Club maintained good relations with the local Orange Order, contributing £1 for the 12 July arch in 1912 and, indeed, a number of its parades and marches were very Orange in tone, being accompanied by the Castleton Pipe Band.[20]

The Unionist Clubs movement developed very quickly. By mid-December 1911 there were 164 Clubs in existence, by the end of February

1912 there were 232 Clubs and by mid-August 1912 there were 316 Clubs; all but ten of them in the nine counties of Ulster.[21] However, the establishment of Unionist Clubs occurred in an *ad hoc* manner which may, partly, be explained by Alvin Jackson's view that Unionism was able to manifest itself through existing organisations in some areas.[22] The County Inspector for Tyrone noted in February 1911, 'movement to re-establish Unionist Clubs started but so far not much enthusiasm has been manifested in the matter'.[23] By contrast, in March 1911, it was noted that Unionist Clubs had been formed in most of the major towns of Co. Antrim and that they were now being established in rural areas, whereas in Armagh it was noted that Unionist Clubs had been formed in 'a few places' only.[24] It seems that by April 1911 the regional variations in Unionist commitment were already evident. It was noted that in Belfast 'a number of Unionist Clubs are being revived and new ones formed', while Armagh was still seen as largely inactive.[25]

Michael Foy has suggested that Unionists in counties Cavan, Donegal and Monaghan were very slow to mobilise. Indeed, he has suggested that it was only in the aftermath of the Curragh Incident and Larne gunrunning that Unionists in these counties resorted to militant action in significant numbers.[26] However, it is clear, as Foy acknowledges, that early drilling was not confined to the Unionist heartlands of North East Ulster. The County Inspector for Cavan reported in April 1911 that seven Unionist Clubs had been recently established in the county.[27] In September 1912 the Glasslough and Clones Unionist Clubs, both in Co. Monaghan had begun to drill.[28] Somewhat surprisingly, one of the 'hawks' within the Unionist Clubs was Lieutenant Colonel J. C. Madden of Clones Unionist Club. At the AGM in March 1913 he, 'suggested the advisability of distributing six rifles to each Club for instructional purposes'.[29]

The Unionist Clubs were designed to have a wide membership base; they were, 'established to enrol all Unionists over 16 years of age, whether electors or not'.[30] Portaferry Unionist Club explicitly stated that it wanted to 'bring in young men' who were not members of either the Orange Order or North Down Voters' Association.[31] Other Clubs restricted their membership in some way; the Annahoe Club for example restricted its membership to farmers and labourers, the only exception being their chairman, Rev. Thomas Adderley.[32] John Gordon MP felt that the Clubs would be most useful in getting artisans involved in the Unionist movement.[33] There also seem to have been some hopes that the Ulster Clubs would attract some Catholic support, with the *Irish Times* noting that they were 'absolutely non-sectarian' and the Ballynakelly Unionist Club passing a resolution that, 'all those holding Unionist principles are eligible as members irrespective of creed or party and whether voters or non-voters'.[34]

While some Unionist Clubs (including the Ballynakelly one) met in Orange Halls others choose different buildings. This may represent an attempt to define the Unionist Clubs as something very different from the Orange Order or may simply have been based on a practical desire to utilise the most suitable building locally available. Thus in Lambeg meetings were held in the schoolhouse; in Hillsborough, in the courthouse and in Newtownards, in the Town Hall.[35] Uniquely it seems, the Ballywalter Unionist Club met in a public house, the Dunleath Arms, presumably reflecting the strength of the temperance movement among Ulster Protestants in this period.[36]

Drilling by Unionist Clubs had come to the attention of the RIC by early 1912. By May 1912 the RIC had received information that 11 Unionist Clubs (Balmoral (Belfast), Carrickfergus, Carricklea, Castlecaulfield, Upper Glenanne, Whitehead, Mossley Mill, Newcastle, Newbliss, Artigarvan and Seaforde) spread throughout Ulster had been witnessed drilling.[37] It is clear that by August 1912 most clubs were involved, at least by association, in militant action. A miniature rifle competition had been organised for the clubs and a challenge cup presented by Lloyd Campbell to the winning team from Bangor. At the following AGM Thomas Greer of Stewartstown 'Urged the necessity for uniformity in drill taught in different clubs'.[38] In late 1912 T. J. Smith, the Chief Commissioner of Belfast was becoming concerned at Unionist Club activity, noting that on 26 August, 260 members of the North East Unionist Club had marched through the city. On 2 September 200 members of the Crescent Unionist Club had done the same.[39]

A number of Unionist Clubs formed rifle clubs through which to pursue their military training.[40] One of the first was Irvinestown Unionist Club in May 1912. Indeed, it is worth noting that the meeting which agreed to establish this club was presided over by Major D'Arcy Irvine, who had been seen as a restraining influence over his father who had drilled men in the same area in 1893.[41] A number of these became affiliated to the National Rifle Association or Society of Miniature Rifle Clubs as this meant both that members did not require gun licences (which at 10s each where a relatively heavy financial commitment) as long as they merely used rifles on club premises and did not carry them to and from their club and that miniature rifles could be obtained cheaply. This was one area of militant Unionist activity that the government did seek to curtail. In January 1913 new regulations came into force which meant that clubs in Ireland had to reaffiliate to the Society of Miniature Rifle Clubs each year and that a list of members had to be provided for both the society and for the Irish Executive. An article in the *Belfast Evening Telegraph* noted, indignantly, that no similar requirements were necessary for clubs in Great Britain.[42] It is clear from the index of the Chief Secretary's Office Registered Papers that the Dublin Castle Administration did carefully scrutinize the future applications from rifle clubs and, indeed, attempts to obtain arms for youth movements.[43] Unfortunately the files to which these indexes refer no longer survive.

With the formation of the UVF proper in January 1913 the military function of the Unionist Clubs supposedly ceased. However, as will be discussed in greater detail in chapter 3, many Unionist Clubs were unwilling to merge into the UVF. The surviving functions of the Unionist Clubs were hotly debated by the Clubs themselves and, at least in some areas, the Unionist Clubs were viewed, as the Orange Order was by the Yeomanry in the 1790s, as a home guard which would remain to police and defend Unionist areas when UVF units were mobilised and sent elsewhere. As late as August 1913 it was seen that the Unionist Clubs were, in many areas, refusing to co-operate with the UVF. Writing in a circular letter Captain Frank Hall, secretary of the Unionist Clubs of Ireland and a senior staff officer in the UVF, stated:

> With reference to Sir Edward Carson's letter forwarded to you last week asking your Club to assist in the immediate organisation of the UVF, the following points may be of value to your Committee in obtaining that end.
> 1. The existing Clubs organisation, complete as it is, has not gone far enough in the actual formation of a purely military force, which will be absolutely essential when the crisis comes.
> 2. To meet this difficulty the Ulster V. F. has been formed, and enrolment has already proceeded apace. All Unionists who are willing to assist in defending themselves, their homes, and their neighbours should enrol irrespective of whether they are already members of Clubs, or Orange Lodges.
> 3. The details of organising this are in the hands of 'County Committees'...
> 4. You will understand that there is no idea or intention of breaking up the existing Clubs Organisation, and where drill has been carried on systematically to the satisfaction of the County Committee, such drill will continue and be utilised to the full extent by the UVF.

The Clubs will continue to exist and all such work as education on the Home Rule question, linking with Clubs across the water, speakers and canvassers classes etc. must be kept going and encouraged by them in view of the possibility of a General Election before the actual passage of the Home Rule Bill, and the consequent outbreak of hostilities.[44]

Many of the early manifestations of Ulster Unionist militancy occurred outside the formal structures of the Orange Order and Unionist Clubs. In considering these, it is perhaps worth thinking of four models of UVF units: the feudal, politicised society, civic and friendship group. Historians considering the Rifle Volunteer movement in Great Britain have commented on its neo-feudal nature in a number of rural areas.[45] It is perhaps not surprising that some of the earliest forms of armed Unionism during the 1910–14 period took a similar form and, indeed, this neo-feudalism was to survive in the UVF proper between 1913 and 1914, as will be discussed further in chapter 3. Drilling was used by some gentry to emphasise their own importance, especially in the context of their political decline given the reform of local government in Ireland in 1898 and economic decline in the wake of the Land Acts, and may have been part of a wider rural patronage network. Alvin Jackson suggests that by about 1910 the debate over the land issue had cooled within Unionism and, certainly in the case of Armagh, he believes that, 'there was a return to the old modes of deference within the Unionist movement. Certainly landlords played a prominent role in opposing the Third Home Rule Bill, both as figureheads, and as local organisers of the Ulster Volunteer Force. But the renaissance of the political landlord … should not be exaggerated: if landlords were partially restored, then it was to a local political arena where the distribution of power was more diverse and complex than hitherto'.[46]

In Fermanagh traditional gentry leadership quickly exerted itself. In July 1912 Major D'Arcy Irvine was witnessed drilling 36 men in an enclosed yard at Castle Irvine, Irvinestown.[47] In the same month, it became clear to the RIC that small-scale drilling was also being carried out at Crom Castle, the seat of the Earl of Erne at Newtownbutler.[48] Meanwhile, in Co. Down, Major W. G. Forde had started to drill Seaforde Unionist Club in March 1912.[49] More problematically, Lord Dunleath eagerly organised drill for members of the Orange Lodges in Ballywalter, Carrowdore and Greyabbey. Dunleath was the major landowner in Ballywalter and had close family connections in Carrowdore, and his organisation of drilling there was seen as perfectly natural. However, the Montgomerys were the major landowners in

Greyabbey and, as the local RIC District Inspector noted, 'I believe General Montgomery did not view favourably an incursion by Lord Dunleath's people into his own territory'.[50] Indeed, in this landed dispute over territory one can discern faint echoes of the disputes between the Downshire and Londonderry interests over control of the Co. Down Militia in the 1793–1802 period.[51]

The civic unit covers two regiments which were formed in advance of the formation of the UVF proper in January 1913: the Enniskillen Horse and the Young Citizen Volunteers of Ireland (which despite its name never extended beyond Belfast) both formed in September 1912. Both units were, in some ways, expressions of civic pride, although this is much more marked in the case of the YCV, which was founded under the patronage of the Lord Mayor of Belfast. The Enniskillen Horse appears to have been fairly quickly assimilated into the UVF in early 1913; however, the YCV did not join the UVF until spring 1914 and then only after a bitter split between their governing council and the unit's CO.

William Copeland Trimble, the proprietor of the *Impartial Reporter* newspaper, formed the Enniskillen Horse in September 1912 to provide a mounted escort for Sir Edward Carson when he visited the town.[52] Writing in a circular letter on 3 September 1912, Trimble encouraged his fellow Unionists to establish a mounted escort for Sir Edward Carson, stating, 'Other places may have their meetings. Enniskillen must have one great distinctive feature of its own … This Escort will be the greatest feature of the day'.[53] Explaining his vision in more detail, Trimble observed, 'As the Enniskillen meeting will be the first to be addressed by Sir Edward Carson in this campaign, unusual importance attaches to it, and newspapers will be represented from all parts of the globe. It is, therefore, all the more incumbent on us that our mounted escort be no childish affair with clumsy men and unmanageable horses, but a fine turn out of smart soldierly-looking men, well-groomed horses, and all showing the effects of organisation and discipline'.[54] At this Unionist demonstration on 18 September, 200 mounted men assembled, although only 40 gathered on 'Ulster Day' on the 28th of that month.[55]

Trimble's efforts do not appear to have met with approval from a number of Unionists in the area. The RIC noted that, when the unit was formed, 'the prominent people disapproved of the thing altogether'.[56] Indeed, police officers stressed that the force was composed largely of local farmers.[57] However, when the Enniskillen Horse had become an established unit, the local landlords appear to have lent it their backing. As early as December 1912 the regiment was training at Castlecoole

Demesne and at land at Lurganbrea belonging to Colonel Doran.[58] By October 1913, in the very different context of the Enniskillen Horse being the only cavalry regiment in the entire UVF, Major Viscount Crichton, a serving officer of the Royal Horse Guards and grandson of the Earl of Erne was prepared to be publicly identified with the corps, addressing one of its parades.[59]

Initially, the military expertise available to the regiment on its formation appears to have been minimal and what was available seems to have been badly misused. This was particularly the case with C. S. M. Baines of the North Irish Horse's permanent staff based in Enniskillen.[60] Baines, as an experienced non-commissioned officer (NCO) with a Special Reserve (SR) unit, would have been ideally placed to provide useful military instruction to the Enniskillen Horse. However, when attending their parade on 10 September 1912 he appears merely to have sat in a cart, representing Sir Edward Carson as the regiment planned their escort duties.[61] Baines may have been wary of taking on a more active role, although even this limited involvement was noted by the RIC or Trimble, who, afraid of having his military deficiencies exposed, may have relegated Baines to this task which, if pointless militarily, did make his presence visible to all members of the Enniskillen Horse.

The YCV of Ireland was formed at a public meeting in Belfast City Hall on 10 September 1912. Surprisingly, given its later high-profile involvement in the UVF the YCV was formed as a non-political organisation. Many different ideas went into the formation of the corps. Some regarded it as a senior unit for those who had been members of the Boys' Brigade, Church Lads' Brigade and Boy Scouts to pass into when they became adults. The YCV was also seen as fulfilling an important role in providing a basis for the amateur military tradition given the failure of the 1908 Haldane reforms to extend the TF scheme to Ireland.

The corps seems to have owed its origins to the Belfast Citizen's Association which was, effectively, a body representing concerned ratepayers.[62] The first 'Volunteer Executive' consisted of 70 members. This read as something of a roll call of Ulster Unionism, with the President of the Executive being R. J. McMordie MP, the Lord Mayor of Belfast. Other notable members of this committee were Major Fred Crawford, later to become famous for his gunrunning activities, Councillor Frank Workman of the Workman and Clark shipyard and James Mackie, owner of Mackie's Foundry.[63] No prominent Nationalist was a member of this committee but despite this Unionist dominance, the constitution of the YCV stated that the organisation was to be 'strictly non-sectarian and non-political' and this was reinforced by the rules committee's edict that the battalion band should not play party tunes.[64] The constitution stated that the objects of the corps were:

> (a) To develop a spirit of responsible citizenship and municipal patriotism by means of lectures and discussions on civic matters.
> (b) To cultivate, by means of modified military and police drill, a manly physique, with habits of self control, self respect, and chivalry.
> (c) To assist as an organisation, when called upon, the civil power in the maintenance of the peace.[65]

The bye-laws of the YCV went even further, noting that, 'Members shall not, as such, take part in any political meeting or demonstration; nor shall they wear the uniform of the Corps if attending any political meeting'.[66]

The President of the YCV, R. J. McMordie, also stated that the corps had been formed as, 'the young men of our country have been seriously handicapped in the past in not having any general organization capable of continuing the good work done by the Boys' Brigade, Church Lads' Brigade, and Boy Scouts' Movements'.[67] The early plans show that it was hoped that companies could be formed from old boys of the 9th and 37th companies of the Boys' Brigade.[68] Indeed, in giving his inaugural address to the YCV, F. C. Forth, the Principal of Belfast Municipal Institute, stated, 'I learn from your secretary that many of the members of the Young Citizen Volunteer Corps were formerly associated with the Boys' Brigade'.[69] The *Northern Whig* welcomed the formation of the YCV largely as it would enable those that had been in the Boys' Brigade, Church Lads' Brigade and Boy Scouts to continue in this 'warm comradeship of the ranks'.[70]

In a letter to prospective financial supporters it was also noted that the corps would cultivate a manly physique and instil habits of self-control, self-respect and chivalry.[71] The *Northern Whig* fully endorsed this aim, noting the United Kingdom's poor performance in the Olympic Games.[72] At the inaugural meeting, F. T. Geddes encouraged membership by noting, 'Their [YCV] halls would form a splendid training ground for athletes of all sorts'.[73]

McMordie went on to lament the fact that TF units had not been established in Ireland following the Haldane Reforms of 1906–8, stating, 'If our young men had the advantage of the Volunteer Acts in Great Britain, or the opportunity of becoming Territorials in Ireland, a very considerable Government grant would be made'.[74] Indeed, the committee appears to have been surprised when the Army Council refused to provide the YCV with obsolete rifles for drill purposes.[75] R. H. Kinahan, head of the Boys' Brigade in Belfast, raised what were to be proved false hopes by suggesting at the inaugural meeting that the War Office would fully equip the YCV, especially as the existing youth organisations had largely refused to become cadets.[76] F. C. Forth, when providing his inaugural address to the YCV, proudly mentioned his own previous membership of the Rifle Volunteers, thus clearly intending to locate the unit in this tradition. Developing other important themes, he made reference to men's duty to their employer, city and empire.[77]

Outlining a definite military role for the corps, a correspondent of the *Northern Whig* stated, 'We can picture it [the YCV] in the event of a threatened foreign invasion guarding the shores of Belfast Lough and bringing to that duty the discipline of Landweher [sic] and the enthusiasm of sons of the empire'.[78] Frank Workman, speaking at the inaugural meeting of the YCV, similarly made reference to Germany and the benefits of conscription.[79] However, not all Belfast opinion was enthusiastic about turning the YCV into a full military unit; one newspaper correspondent noted approvingly that there were no plans to teach the men how to use rifles and that militarism would not be taken 'beyond the review stage'.[80]

However, from the outset, the YCV was organised along military lines. Indeed, the local Unionist press noted approvingly that the YCV would act as special police and assist the Lord Mayor in the event of rioting or breaches of the peace, taking the place of regular troops in such a crisis.[81] The Nationalist *Irish News and Belfast Morning News* believed that this was the real reason for the formation of the force, suggesting, with memories of the bitter dock strike in Belfast in 1907, that it was being formed mainly to suppress industrial strikes. This newspaper's headline also referred to the 'Utterly misleading statement as to the powers of the new "corps"' but, unfortunately, did not elaborate on this further.[82]

The YCV were to be formed in companies of 50 strong, each commanded by a captain. Initially, it seems to have been hoped that a number of battalions would be formed and complicated arrangements existed for the appointment of officers by a mixture of their superior officers, a battalion executive and the central volunteer executive. It was certainly hoped that a battalion would be formed in Derry.[83] However, the movement did not extend beyond Belfast, possibly due to the costs of membership.[84]

In a perhaps conscious attempt to emulate the system which operated in some of the more exclusive Territorial battalions of the London Regiment, each member of the YCV was expected to pay 2s 6d on enrolment and a further 6d each month and, more significantly, to pay a total of £1 10s for his uniform in monthly instalments.[85] It appears that the members of the corps were making regular payments for their uniforms (the minutes note only one man who refused to either return his uniform or keep up the payments for it) but the heavy financial outlay seems to have lead the YCV into serious financial difficulties from an early stage.[86] Indeed, it is worth noting that in the exclusive 14th London (Scottish) Regiment the financial outlay expected from recruits was an entrance fee of 10s and an annual subscription of 10s, with no payment expected for uniform except khaki trews, which demonstrates the high financial outlay that was expected from YCV members.[87]

The choice of a light grey uniform also appears an unusual one and the minutes of the uniform committee provide no details as to why this colour was chosen.[88] It may have been an attempt to emulate the Rifle Volunteers of the late 1850s who, when choosing their uniforms had generally avoided the adoption of the red, blue or green of the regular army and militia.[89]

At the outset, the Lord Mayor of Belfast appealed for a capital sum of £1,500 to purchase uniforms, which members of the corps would pay off in instalments, and an annual running cost of £500.[90] The financial outlay of the YCV was low (apart from the purchase of uniforms) but four permanent staff appear to have been employed, ex-Sergeant Bentley as chief instructor (at £1 per week, rising to £1 15s from 1 January 1913), ex-Sergeant Elphick, as his assistant from December 1912 at £1 10s per week, Mr Stevenson as general secretary (who appears to have served on a voluntary basis) and Miss Morrison as typist (at 9s per week).[91] Nevertheless, the YCV faced perennial financial difficulties, despite these low overhead costs, largely due to the failure of Belfast businessmen to provide monetary support. It is clear, from the minutes of the finance committee, that a number of major businesses in the greater Belfast area were approached when the corps was formed. Some of the firms approached, such as Dunville's Distillery, William Ewart & Son Ltd and Gallaher's Tobacco, were closely associated with Unionism but one must conclude that these approaches yielded little. Indeed, of the firms initially approached it appears that only three, the York Street Flax Spinning Company, Inglis's Bakery and William Ewart & Son Ltd made contributions, and these of just £25, £5 and £10 respectively. Dunville's Distillery 'assured the Lord Mayor that the movement had their sincere sympathy' and, perhaps, most embarrassing of all Frank Workman, the YCV honorary treasurer, claimed that he had to discuss any contribution from Workman and Clark Shipbuilders with his business partner.[92] However, it is clear that by early 1914 Workman was, effectively, underwriting the YCV, having settled the corps overdraft with the Northern Banking Co. Ltd. Although as joint guarantor with the by then deceased R. J. McMordie he had little choice in this matter.[93]

These financial difficulties led to F. W. L. May, a 'captain' in the unit, writing to the volunteer committee on behalf of himself and the other officers. He noted that most of the activities carried out by the YCV were supported by monies raised from the NCOs and men of the corps. May also felt that, as the corps was not receiving government recognition, a strong effort should be made to secure alternative funds. In particular he felt that funds would be needed to provide the men with more serviceable uniforms and greatcoats, stating, 'I am to add that the Officers think there should be no difficulty found by such an influential Committee in obtaining ample subscriptions from the general public'. Indeed, May felt that could such monies be secured, this would greatly facilitate government recognition and he suggested that a delegation be sent to London to meet the Secretary of State for War with this in mind.[94]

By January 1914 the financial position of the YCV was desperate. The credit on the current account was just £11 and there was a debit of £389 on the uniform account. Curiously, the finance committee felt that the political situation made it less rather than more likely that they would be able to solve these difficulties, noting, 'no further effort be made at present owing to the difficulty experienced in raising money for other than political purposes'.[95]

The YCV evidently had some difficulty in securing a CO. A Major Ferrar was initially approached, but appears to have declined. Colonel R. Spencer Chichester, a member of a prominent Belfast family, was then secured, who presumably caused some concern to the committee by insisting on a 'free hand with regard to the military side of the Organisation', an expansion in the size of the companies (which, strangely, had been limited to a maximum of 50), the early purchase of rifles and the appointment of additional instructors.[96] Chichester did, however, help the ailing funds of the YCV by initially contributing £100 to it and paying for the instruments for the band.[97] Ultimately, he was to donate £260 6s 8d to the corps.[98]

Chichester also wanted an approach to be made to the Secretary of State for War, pointing out the defenceless state of Belfast, and offering the services of the YCV to remedy this situation. It was agreed, by the volunteer council, that a resolution should be passed by the city corporation, Harbour Board and Chamber of Commerce, supporting this measure; but this seems to have come to nothing.[99] It appears that Chichester did ultimately seek recognition from the War Office; presumably hoping that the YCV would become a unit of the TF, with him retaining command.[100]

The activities planned for the YCV evidently extended beyond purely military pursuits. In December 1913 it was proposed that a lecture on the history of Belfast should be given to the corps by Mr Robert Meyer.[101] It was suggested to hold an open air fete and a fancy dress ball, largely to raise funds, in May 1913 but this was not endorsed by the volunteer committee.[102] The Lord Mayor did, however, gain the support of the committee for his proposal that the corps would attempt to find 'suitable employment' for its members. 'It was decided on the suggestion of Councillor Riddell that the attention of the employers should be drawn to the fact that eligible young men could be recommended by their Officers to fill vacancies occurring'.[103] Captain May and a number of the other officers of the corps felt that in return for their subscriptions, members of the corps should have the use of a central club room where they could play billiards and obtain refreshments.[104] It was, of course, the provision of social facilities such as tennis and badminton courts that made membership of exclusive London TF units so attractive.[105]

Given the financial problems faced by the YCV, the death of their first president, R. J. McMordie MP in early 1914 and the political inclinations of its CO, it was, perhaps inevitable that the corps would become ever more closely associated with the UVF. However, when the YCV did become part of the UVF, the volunteer committee appears to have dissolved in some chaos. At the volunteer council meeting of 2 April 1914 a resolution was proposed by Mr Geddes and seconded by Captain Mitchell, 'That the Office Bearers and Council of the YCV of Ireland deeply regret that they were not consulted prior to the recent amalgamation of the 1st Battalion YCV, with the Ulster Volunteer Force, and they take this opportunity of informing the public that it was done without their authority and consent'. However, Captain May raised the point that the council was not now in office, as an AGM should have been held in December.[106] Only two further committee meetings were held. At one in April 1914 Frank Workman reported that he had spoken to Colonel Chichester without any satisfactory result. Some committee members, while committed to the UVF, were disappointed at Chichester's decision. Leon McVicker, the managing director of Cantrell & Cochrane's large aerated water production plant in Belfast apologised that he would be unable, for business reasons, to attend this meeting and stated, 'altho.[ugh] I am a member of the U. V. F., I am not in favour of the Y. C. V. being "turned over", especially so, remembering the object – "Non Pol[itical]" + "Non Sec.[tarian]". My idea was to grant men leave of absence during the present crisis. By being taken over it completely destroys for ever the Y. C. V. + leaves the organisation open to criticism'.[107] This penultimate meeting also heard of the utterly dire state of the corps' finances, there was only £24 1s 6d available and the uniform fund was £383 15s 0d in deficit.[108] The final committee meeting held was of a special subcommittee which met in May 1914. It was noted that Colonel Chichester has refused to respond to any letters from the committee regarding the merger of the YCV with the UVF, although he was willing to discuss finance. The subcommittee briefly considered taking legal action against Chichester, but decided to reconvene in two weeks when one of its members had reviewed the legal position; it never did.[109] It seems that the 400 or so Catholic members who had been with the corps left at this point, unwilling to remain as a separate unit. The unhappy history of the YCV provides useful insights into both the ideological concepts and financial problems that were evident in the UVF as a whole in 1913–14.

The third model of a UVF unit, the 'politicised society', covers a number of organisations. Perhaps not surprisingly, the Protestant militarised youth organisations, the Boys' Brigade and Church Lads' Brigade, quickly became identified with Unionism in this period. J. B. Lonsdale was led through the City of Armagh by a procession of Orangemen and members of the Boys' Brigade in July 1911 to celebrate his recent baronetcy and the Church Lads' Brigade and Boys' Brigade both paraded in Armagh City on Ulster Day in 1912. Reflecting on the comparatively late development of the Boy Scouts in Co. Armagh, Jackson states, 'Indeed, it is possible, given the effective limitation of overtly Unionist youth movements like the Young Citizens' Volunteers to Belfast, that organisations such as the Scouts were consciously regarded as filling a gap in rural protestant mobilization'.[110] In Derry City the Church Lads' Brigade provided very concrete help to local militant Unionists, in the form of their dummy rifles, and James Harvey, one of their officers, acted as drill instructor to Londonderry Unionist

Club.[111] The Catch My Pal temperance movement was a useful mobilising agent for Unionism as it was designed to be exclusively Protestant in its membership.[112] Indeed, in Magherafelt, the local branch of this organisation provided an early focus for military training as its members were drilling twice weekly by May 1912.[113]

The 'friendship group' covers the number of small units which seem to have sprung up under the command of retired other ranks or officers who were not simply enrolling their tenants in 'feudal units'. It is impossible to estimate how many of these groups existed in the 1910–12 period. Perhaps they came to undue prominence as their drills were generally held in the open, whereas members of the Orange Order or Unionist Clubs often had halls to drill in; but conversely, one could argue that Belfast's shipyards, heavy engineering works and linen mills contained many storerooms where drill could have been practiced away from the prying eyes of RIC officers or, given the employment patterns of Edwardian Belfast, Nationalists. In Omagh, Osbourne Young, a former Sergeant in the Imperial Yeomanry who had served in the South African War, took it upon himself to drill nine mounted men.[114] In Lack, Co. Fermanagh men were being drilled at the rectory of Rev. S. Anderson by Private Bob Evers of the North Irish Horse.[115] In September 1912 the *Belfast Evening Telegraph* carried a major story, accompanied by two photographs. The caption read, 'Ulstermen's Opposition to Home Rule' and the article went on to explain how Major McCammon, Captain James Craig MP and Colonel Wallace had been teaching a group of men how to drill and shoot.[116]

By the end of 1912 the attitude of a number of army officers towards Ulster's planned resistance was therefore becoming obvious and they were making their views known to various Unionist groups. Sergeant J. English of the RIC observed Lieutenant A. M. Alexander of the 2nd Royal Inniskilling Fusiliers addressing an Orange Lodge in Carrickmore on 23 December 1912. Alexander refused to complete a UVF membership form along with the others, 'He explained to the meeting that he could take no part in the proceedings while serving in the Army; but, added that as soon as the Home Rule Bill becomes law he will sever his connection with it'. At the same meeting a letter was read from Colonel Sir Hugh H. Stewart of the 3rd Royal Irish Fusiliers. He likewise stated that he would resign his commission as soon as the Bill became law.[117]

The responses of the RIC and Dublin Castle administration to early Unionist militancy must now be discussed. RIC County Inspectors' reports reveal that there was little evidence of a 'rush to the colours' among Unionists. A report, prepared by the RIC Crime Special Branch, noted in September 1911 that the lack of restrictions on the sale of firearms meant that many Unionists possessed cheap revolvers or shotguns, although there was no evidence of the systematic import of large numbers of firearms. This report went on,

> As regards drilling, the officers are unanimous in stating that there has been nothing of the sort out of doors. No locality is so exclusively Protestant or Unionist as to be free from scattered Nationalists who jealously watch the doings of the Orange Lodges and Unionist Clubs.
>
> Drilling inside the Orange Halls may possibly be carried on to the extent of teaching men to handle a rifle and explaining how to use it. Information has been received that this is going on near Coleraine and Aghadowey, but nothing really definite has leaked out and it has proved impossible to verify the statement.[118]

The County Inspector of Antrim expressed his view that Unionists, 'are confident that a Home Rule Bill will not become law for many years, if ever, and consequently they believe that it is not necessary to prepare for armed resistance, but that should such a measure become law they believe that by passive resistance to taxation, followed by active resistance if necessary, the operation of such a scheme would be rendered unworkable'.[119] It must have been immensely reassuring for the senior officers of the RIC to hear the views of the District Inspector for the notoriously Orange Portadown area that, 'There is no such thing as the drilling of men going on here in my District that I can hear of, and no Army Reserve men have been employed for this purpose'.[120]

As late as July 1912 the British authorities felt that Ulster Unionist threats would amount to little real military activity. On 13 July the Deputy Inspector General of the RIC noted that the only positive information he had received regarding the illegal importation of arms concerned 200 rifles sent from Hamburg to Belfast. The name of the consignee was indicated only by initials and, as soon as police surveillance was discovered, these had all been returned to Hamburg.[121] However, the Inspector General of the RIC clearly felt that a number of his officers were making few attempts to uncover Unionist arms caches. In September 1912 he sent County Inspector Holmes of the Crime Special Branch to interview 34 officers in Ulster. Holmes was armed with a special minute, shown to these interviewees, which ominously read:

> There appears to be a general impression that rifles are being collected in large quantities in the North of Ireland, and that they are being hidden away so as to be ready for use if required.

I have directed Co. Inspector Holmes to show this minute to each officer he may consult on the subject, and I desire to impress on every officer who reads it the very grave personal responsibility which devolves on him in the matter – I would ask him to carefully consider the position in which he would be placed if, hereafter, it transpired that arms and ammunition had been collected and hidden away, in his county or district, unknown to him.[122]

In February 1912 Sir David Harrell, a former Under Secretary for Ireland, prepared what was to prove a highly optimistic assessment of Ulster Unionist resistance. In this he noted:

So far the Ulster man, bearing in mind that he has not a House of Lords as of old, conceives it to be his duty to fight every inch of the way, to demonstrate and to protest, and so to influence the electorate of Great Britain. In all this I believe him to be quite serious, and in a general, far off way he may be thinking of a time when it may come to a fight in the open, but he is too shrewd and practical to place himself outside the law upon hypothetical data. I do not believe there is any purposeful arming or drilling. There are unquestionably quantities of rifles, guns, and revolvers in the country, and in the event of local disturbances and riots these may be used, but I cannot think that platform speeches will materialise into deliberate and armed resistance to authority ... My idea is that the whole question will be kept within the bounds of political warfare, if the financial proposals be generous, and if the guarantees for equitable distribution and against unfair and oppressive taxation be of a tangible as distinguished from a statutory or paper character.[123]

Augustine Birrell, the Chief Secretary for Ireland, remained blasée regarding Ulster Unionist intentions and as late as July 1913 he was mainly concerned with the 'grave possibilities of riots'.[124] Indeed, Birrell was happily disregarding the warnings of impending militant action in RIC reports stating, 'You must remember that they are all obviously onesided. Sir Neville Chamberlain [Inspector General, RIC] himself is a true Blue + the majority of the Reporting Officers (probably) would be themselves Covenanters, were they not policemen'.[125] As it transpired, Dublin Castle's failure to tackle isolated Unionist drilling in 1910–12 left it in a very weak position in 1912–14.

The pre-1913 period is worthy of investigation as it was at this time that the legal precedents under which the government could, and indeed would, deal with the UVF proper were established. In June 1886 the government was forced into an embarrassing climb down when an attempt to try Edwin Best, Charles McCallum and Robert Mitchell for drilling 50 or more Unionists (and to try six others for attending the drill) at Richill Demesne, Co. Armagh, on 2 June 1886 failed completely, when magistrates refused to send the case for trial.[126] Apparently such drilling had been going on for some time and following this legal victory by the Unionists, drilling continued in the Temperance Hall in Richill.[127] Reflecting on this debacle, the then Attorney General, Sir Samuel Walker, stated:

> The magistrates appear to have arrived at the conclusion that the men were not being drilled in military movements and evolutions. This was a question of fact and they were competent to arrive at the opinion that there was not a case to send for trial on such a charge. I myself do not see how they arrived at it. But as the Magistrates, including the experienced R.M., have arrived at that conclusion, I do not think on this case at all events any further action can be taken by the Executive.[128]

In late 1912 the problems involved in trying those Unionists drilling under the 1819 legislation (one of the so called Six Acts, introduced to curb the activities of the Chartists) became increasingly apparent. Having received a report from Sergeant J. R. Hunter regarding drilling, conducted by two army reservists, Nixon and Totten, in Glasslough, Co. Monaghan, W. A. O'Connell, the Deputy Inspector General of the RIC responded, 'It should be stated whether the police can give evidence as to these drillings and whether they can prove of their own knowledge whether Nixon and Totten acted as instructors'. Sergeant R. Callaghan stated in response to this, 'as the drilling takes place in the Orange Hall the police cannot give evidence of their own knowledge'.[129] In this early period, most drilling seems to have taken place in closed premises: demesnes, Orange Halls, Temperance Halls, hotels and even public houses, which made observation by RIC officers virtually impossible.[130]

Quickly, other problems in mounting prosecutions under the existing legislation became apparent. Writing of drilling in Ballywalter, W. A. O'Connell noted:

> Under 60 Geo. III, c.1, the unlawful training to military exercises or training to the use of arms is forbidden, but the Act provides that such training may be legalised by two of the County Magistrates or by the Lieutenant of the County. We have no means of knowing whether any such authority has been given in this instance.
>
> The party which was drilled in the Dunleath Arms Hotel did not carry arms.
>
> It is presumed that it would have to be set out in any charge to be framed that the drilling was being carried out to the terror of His Majesty's

peaceable subjects. The drill instruction in this case was given by the rector, and there is nothing to show that he has any special knowledge of military training.

The Magistrates would inevitably refuse informations in a case such as this, and it is quite probable that legal proceedings would only result in a political advertisement for the rector and his men.[131]

The Attorney General addressing the Ballywalter example stated:

> By Geo. III, cap. 1, meetings and assemblies of persons for the purpose of being trained in or practising military exercises are prohibited unless held under the authority of the Lieutenant or two Justices of the County. Offenders against the Act are liable to be indicted and punished by imprisonment.
>
> At common law drilling is not necessarily but may be unlawful. If it is carried on for a seditious purpose it is an act of sedition for which all who take part in it are liable to be indicted.
>
> Whether the drilling is a seditious act is a question to be decided by the evidence of surrounding circumstances. The storing of arms, inflammatory speeches, etc., side by side with drilling would go to show that the latter was carried out for a seditious purpose.
>
> I think that it would be a mistake to institute any prosecution under the Statute above referred to. The prosecution could be defeated by the production of an authority from two Justices.
>
> Of course no Justice could legally give authority to carry on drilling for an illegal purpose, but once illegal purpose is established there is the common law offence.[132]

Provided with such confusing legal advice the RIC, quite naturally, never attempted to prosecute those involved in drilling under either the 1819 legislation or common law. The other option for the government was to prosecute officers, or those on the reserve, who had been observed drilling men under King's Regulations; however, again the government decided not to act against these officers. Outlining the situation in May 1912, V. P. Le Fanu (Augustine Birrell's private secretary) noted:

> The question then arises of the purpose of this drilling. It cannot with any show of veracity be contended that it has a purely educational object, as in the case of the boy scouts. The object may be seditious resistance to constituted authority as has often been openly stated; but it does not need either statute or regulation to condemn any action taken with such an object as contrary to the first duty of a soldier.
>
> An officer who takes part in meetings for such a purpose (political demonstrations) at all events in Belfast or any of the towns where soldiers are quartered, would appear to come within Clause 451 of the King's

Regulations, by which an officer or soldier is forbidden to institute or take part in any meetings, demonstrations or processions for party or political purposes in barracks, quarters, camps or their vicinity. At all events, there would not seem to be any objection to asking those officers who have taken part in drilling in any places which can be held to come within the Regulations how they explain their conduct.[133]

This issue was resolved by another memorandum of May 1912 stating, 'Col. Seely [Secretary of State for War] discussed with Mr. Birrell the question raised in these enclosures. It has been decided that nothing shall be done for the present as the evidence is not sufficiently conclusive against any of the officers on the enclosed list; but the matter will be closely watched by the Irish Office'.[134]

There was also concern regarding the attitude of the military to the Solemn League and Covenant. An RIC District Inspector stated, 'I find that it is perfectly true that a large number of Sergeants and Privates of the R.[oyal] I.[nniskilling] Fusiliers stationed at Omagh have signed the "Covenant". A number of the non-commissioned officers were in plain clothes in the town here on Saturday 28th ultimo. Amongst these were Colour-Sergeant Young and Sergeants Hanna, Williamson, Eames and Holmes ... There are a number of other non-commissioned officers who are believed to have signed'.[135]

It is clear that early in the Third Home Rule crisis Unionists were quite clear about their legal rights in both carrying arms and drilling. At a speech made at Coleraine in January 1912, the unlikely 'hawk' William Moore MP stated that a man carrying a gun, without a firearms licence could be prosecuted but he then went on:

> if the time came for organised defence against invasion of their constitutional rights as citizens of the United Kingdom, no one was going to have time to ask for gun licences then ... as regards drilling; there was an old statute passed about a hundred years ago which forbade it with or without arms. But twenty-five years ago the good people in County Armagh in a crisis like the present took the lead ... in adopting defensive measures and began to drill. The Crown took proceedings against them. There were a dozen or so as respondents, but they were very ably defended by a junior barrister, brought down from Dublin, who argued before the Court that the statute was obsolete and, in the end the Court including a resident magistrate, refused informations ... under the Act itself drilling could be carried on with licence from two justices.[136]

The wide dissemination of Moore's advice is perhaps shown by the attitude of Rev. S. Anderson, drilling men at Lack Rectory in Co.

Fermanagh in July 1912, who stated to an observant police officer, 'that they were going to have some drill this evening that all these were Orangemen that they had the authority of two Magistrates for to drill'.[137] However, in Bangor, Co. Down, it appears that members of the Unionist Club there were at some pains to stress that their drilling was solely to enable them to parade properly in the demonstration at Balmoral showgrounds in Belfast on Easter Tuesday 1912.[138]

The period 1885–1912 is an important one in discussing the development of the UVF proper in 1913–14. This period demonstrates the general timidity with which the Liberal government dealt with Unionist militancy. Wishful thinking about Unionist intentions, combined with a much too liberal interpretation of the rights of the citizen to drill and own firearms, lead to the escalation of the crisis in 1913–14. The examples of the Enniskillen Horse and the YCV provide us with a foretaste of the financial and command problems which were to dog the UVF itself. Finally, the roles of the Orange Order and Unionist Clubs in Unionist militancy, as has been demonstrated, were not absolute. However, in some areas the UVF struggled to identify itself as a separate entity to these longer established Unionist organisations.

Notes

1 Ronald McNeill, *Ulster's Stand for Union* (John Murray, London, 1922), pp. 46–52; Ian Colvin, *The Life of Lord Carson* (Victor Gollancz Ltd, London, 1934), p. 82 and Stewart, *The Ulster Crisis*, pp. 47–8.
2 McNeill, *Ulster's Stand for Union*, pp. 56–7.
3 TNA, CO904/28/2, report by CI Edward Pearson, undated but October 1911.
4 TNA, CO904/28/2, report by CI Edward Pearson, undated but October 1911.
5 D. W. Miller, 'Non-professional Soldiery, c. 1600–1800' in Thomas Bartlett and Keith Jeffery (eds), *A Military History of Ireland* (Cambridge University Press, 1996), p. 331.
6 On these bodies see also, Allan Blackstock, *An Ascendancy Army: The Irish Yeomanry 1796–1834* (Four Courts Press, Dublin, 1998) and P. D. H. Smyth, 'The Volunteer Movement in Ulster: Background and Development, 1745–85', unpublished Ph.D. thesis, The Queen's University of Belfast, 1974.
7 TNA, CO904/28/1, '1886–1913 Arms Importation + Distribution', memorandum, W.M.C. to Under Secretary, 20/02/1911.

8 TNA, CO904/28/1, '1886–1913 Arms Importation + Distribution', memorandum, George Hazlett, Sessional Crown Solicitor, Lurgan to Chief Secretary, 11/06/1886. See also CO904/182, 'Prosecution for Illegal Drilling in June 1886'.
9 All details on this 1893 drilling are taken from TNA, CO904/28/1, '1886–1913 Arms Importation + Distribution', reports by CI, Fermanagh, 22/09/1893, DI, P. R. Slacker, 21/07/1893 and DIG, A. Gambell, 18/03/1893 and the *Donegal Vindicator*, 12/05/1893.
10 Crawford, *Guns for Ulster*, pp. 10–11.
11 PRONI, D.845/1, Jenkins papers, enrolment forms for Lisburn UVF.
12 TNA, CO904/28/2, report from Belfast Detective Department, RIC, 04/04/1911 and TNA, CO904/182, letter, Colonel R. H. Wallace to Masters of Orange Lodges, ?/12/1910.
13 TNA, CO904/182, report by DI J. McMahon, 06/04/1911.
14 *Northern Whig*, 01/12/1911 and *Irish Times*, 07/12/1911. See also TNA, CO904/28/1, '1886–1913 Arms Importation + Distribution', report by Inspector E. S. Cary, 11/12/1911.
15 TNA, WO141/26, 'Miscellaneous Papers Regarding "Drilling" by Civilians in Ulster', report by Inspector J. Willband, 21/09/1912.
16 TNA, CO904/182, report by DI W. S. Irwin, 11/01/1912.
17 TNA, WO141/26, 'List of Army or Militia Officers Who Have Taken Part in Drill at Unionist Clubs or Orange Lodges' and 'List of Members of Rank and File of ARMY RESERVE Who Have Taken an Active Part in Drilling in Orange Halls, Unionist Clubs, & c.', 1913–14.
18 PRONI, D.1327/1/1, 'Minutes re. Unionist Clubs'. See especially the entry for 11/01/1911.
19 *Northern Whig*, 01/04/1911.
20 All details taken from PRONI, D.1327/1/9, 'Minute Book of Fortwilliam Unionist Club'.
21 PRONI, D.1327/1/1, 'Minutes re. Unionist Clubs', minutes of special meetings, 15/12/1911, 23/08/1912 and AGM 29/02/1912.
22 Alvin Jackson, 'Unionist Politics and Protestant Society in Edwardian Ireland', *Historical Journal*, 33, 4, 1990.
23 TNA, CO904/83, report by CI, Tyrone to IG, February 1911.
24 TNA, CO904/83, IG, RIC to Under Secretary, Dublin Castle, March 1911.
25 TNA, CO904/83, Inspector General's reports for April 1911, CO904/83.
26 Foy, 'The Ulster Volunteer Force', p. 117.
27 TNA, CO904/83, Inspector General's report for April 1911.
28 TNA, WO141/26, 'Miscellaneous Papers Regarding "Drilling" by Civilians in Ulster', reports by Sergeant J. R. Hunter, 04/09/1912 and 20/09/1912 and report by Inspector M. J. Egan, 12/09/1912.
29 PRONI, D.1327/1/1, 'Minutes re. Unionist Clubs', minutes of AGM, 05/03/1913.

30 *Irish Times*, 25/01/1911.
31 *Belfast News Letter*, 06/02/1911.
32 *Belfast News Letter*, 15/02/1911.
33 *Northern Whig*, 01/04/1911.
34 *Irish Times*, 02/03/1911 and *Northern Whig*, 11/03/1911. The Randalstown Unionist Club publicly expressed similar sentiments, *Northern Whig*, 31/05/1911.
35 *Belfast News Letter*, 21/02/1911, 25/02/1911, 13/03/1911.
36 *Northern Whig*, 16/05/1911.
37 TNA, WO141/26, 'List of Army or Militia Officers Who Have Taken Part in Drill at Unionist Clubs or Orange Lodges' and 'List of Members of Rank and File of ARMY RESERVE Who Have Taken an Active Part in Drilling in Orange Halls, Unionist Clubs, & c.', 1913–14.
38 PRONI, D.1327/1/1, 'Minutes re. Unionist Clubs', minutes of special meeting, 23/08/1912 and AGM 05/03/1913.
39 TNA, WO141/26, 'Miscellaneous Papers Regarding "Drilling" by Civilians in Ulster', report by T. J. Smith, Chief Commissioner, Belfast, 06/09/12.
40 TNA, CO904/182, RIC Crime Special Branch, 'Importation of Arms and Secret Drilling in Ulster', 08/09/1911 and PRONI, D.1327/1/2, 'Minutes of the Meetings of the Executive Committee of the Unionist Clubs Council', minutes, 03/12/1912.
41 TNA, WO141/26, 'Miscellaneous Papers Regarding "Drilling" by Civilians in Ulster', report by Constable W. P. Lapsley, 01/06/1912.
42 *Belfast Evening Telegraph*, 22/01/1913.
43 See indexes for National Archives, Dublin, CSORP, 9711, 18231, 1324 and 4606; 1913.
44 PRONI, D.1518/3/8, Lyle papers, circular letter from Captain Frank Hall to Unionist Clubs, 25/08/1913.
45 I. F. W. Beckett, *Riflemen Form: A Study of the Rifle Volunteer Movement 1859–1908* (The Ogilby Trusts, Aldershot, 1982), pp. 52–3 and David French, *Military Identities: The Regimental System, the British Army and the British People c. 1870–2000* (Oxford University Press, 2005), p. 211.
46 Jackson, 'Unionist Politics and Protestant Society in Edwardian Ireland', p. 850.
47 TNA, CO904/27/1, report by Constable W. P. Lapsley, 20/07/1912.
48 TNA, CO904/27/1, report by DI J. McMahon, 05/07/1912.
49 TNA, WO141/26, 'List of Army or Militia Officers Who Have Taken Part in Drill at Unionist Clubs or Orange Lodges', 15/03/1912 and 'Miscellaneous Papers Regarding "Drilling" by Civilians in Ulster'.
50 TNA, CO904/182, 'Drilling in Ballywalter', report by Inspector D. Murnane, 31/01/1912.
51 Sir Henry McAnnally, *The Irish Militia 1793–1816* (Eyre and Spottiswoode, London, 1949).

52 TNA, CO904/27/1, 'Enniskillen Horse', memorandum, O'Connell, DIG to Under Secretary, 25/04/1913.
53 TNA, WO141/26, 'Miscellaneous Papers Regarding "Drilling" by Civilians in Ulster', circular letter from W. C. Trimble, 03/09/1912.
54 TNA, WO141/26, 'Miscellaneous Papers Regarding "Drilling" by Civilians in Ulster', circular letter from W. C. Trimble, 30/08/1912.
55 TNA, CO904/27/1, 'Enniskillen Horse', report by CI, 04/10/1912.
56 TNA, CO904/27/1, 'Enniskillen Horse', report by CI, 04/01/1913.
57 TNA, CO904/27/1, 'Enniskillen Horse', report by Inspector P. A. Marriman, 15/06/1913.
58 TNA, CO904/27/1, 'Enniskillen Horse', reports by Acting Sergeant Reilly, 03/01/1913 and Sergeant J. Taggart, 06/12/1912.
59 *Irish Times*, 18/10/1913.
60 The North Irish Horse was a part-time regiment which, since 1908, had been part of the SR. The involvement of its members in the Enniskillen Horse and UVF more widely is discussed in chapters 2 and 3.
61 TNA, CO904/27/1, 'Enniskillen Horse', report by DI C. E. Armstrong.
62 *Northern Whig*, 11/09/1912.
63 NAM, 8210–88, *Annual Report of the YCV of Ireland, 1912–1913*.
64 PRONI, D.1568/3, Constitution and Bye-Laws of the YCV of Ireland and PRONI, D.1568/2, minutes of YCV rules committee, 21/10/1912.
65 PRONI, D.1568/3, Constitution and Bye-Laws of the YCV of Ireland.
66 PRONI, D.1568/3, Constitution and Bye-Laws of the YCV of Ireland.
67 NAM, 8210–88, circular letter from R. J. McMordie asking for subscriptions (undated, but late 1912) and *Northern Whig*, 11/09/1912.
68 PRONI, D.1568/2, minutes of YCV advisory committee, 30/10/1912.
69 PRONI, D.1568/5A, printed booklet, 'Inaugural Address by F. C. Forth, A.R.C.Sc.I., Principal of Belfast Municipal Institution', 10/12/1912.
70 *Northern Whig*, 10/09/1912.
71 PRONI, D.1568/7, circular letter, no date.
72 *Northern Whig*, 10/09/1912.
73 *Belfast News Letter* and *Belfast Evening Telegraph*, 11/09/1912.
74 NAM, 8210–88, circular letter from R. J. McMordie asking for subscriptions (undated, but late 1912).
75 PRONI, D.1568/2, minutes of YCV volunteer council, 29/08/1912 and finance committee, 27/01/1913.
76 *Belfast Evening Telegraph*, 11/09/1912.
77 PRONI, D.1568/5A, printed booklet, 'Inaugural Address by F. C. Forth, A.R.C.Sc.I., Principal of Belfast Municipal Institution', 10/12/1912.
78 *Northern Whig*, 10/09/1912.
79 *Belfast News Letter*, 11/09/1912.
80 *Northern Whig*, 10/09/1912.
81 *Northern Whig*, 11/09/1912.

82 *Irish News and Belfast Morning News*, 11/09/1912.
83 *Northern Whig*, 10/09/1912.
84 PRONI, D/1568/3, Constitution and Bye-Laws of the YCV of Ireland.
85 NAM 8210–88, Constitution and Bye-Laws of the YCV of Ireland and circular letter from R. J. McMordie asking for subscriptions (undated, but late 1912).
86 PRONI, D.1568/2, minutes of YCV finance committee, 21/04/1913 and 24/11/1913.
87 *Standing Orders of the 14th (County of London) Battalion, The London Regiment (London Scottish)* (McCorquadale & Co. Ltd, London, 1912), pp. 32 and 67.
88 PRONI, D.1568/2, minutes of the uniform committee, YCV, 07/10/1912.
89 Examples of YCV uniforms can be seen at the Royal Ulster Rifles Museum, Belfast.
90 NAM 8210–88, circular letter from R. J. McMordie asking for subscriptions (undated, but late 1912).
91 PRONI, D.1568/2, minutes of YCV volunteer council, 08/10/1912, advisory committee, 30/10/1912 and finance committee, 29/10/1912 and 12/12/1912.
92 PRONI, D.1568/2, minutes of YCV finance committee, 29/10/1912, 04/11/1912 and 28/11/1912.
93 PRONI, D.1527/1, printed statement of YCV accounts 5/11/1912 to March 1914.
94 PRONI, D.1568/10, letter, Captain F. W. L. May to acting adjutant, 1st. Bn. YCV of Ireland, 17/11/1913.
95 PRONI, D.1568/2, minutes of finance committee, 26/01/1914.
96 PRONI, D.1568/2, minutes of YCV volunteer council, 08/10/1912 and 28/11/1912.
97 PRONI, D.1568/2, minutes of YCV finance committee, 28/11/1912 and 21/04/1913.
98 PRONI, D.1527/1, printed statement of YCV accounts, 05/11/1912 to March 1914.
99 PRONI, D/1568/2, minutes of YCV volunteer council, 07/05/1913.
100 PRONI, D/1568, minutes of finance committee, 24/11/1913.
101 PRONI, D/1568/2, minutes of YCV volunteer committee, 12/02/1913.
102 PRONI, D/1568/2, minutes of YCV volunteer committee, 07/05/1913.
103 PRONI, D/1568/2, minutes of YCV volunteer committee, 07/05/1913.
104 PRONI, D/1568/10, letter, Captain F. W. L. May to acting adjutant, 1st. Bn. YCV of Ireland, 17/11/1913.
105 *Standing Orders of the 14th (County of London) Battalion, The London Regiment (London Scottish)*, pp. 64–5.
106 PRONI, D/1568, minutes of YCV volunteer council, 02/04/1914.
107 PRONI, D/1568/14, letter, Leon McVicker to Mr Stevenson [general secretary of the YCV], 02/04/1914.

108 PRONI, D/1568/2, minutes of YCV volunteer council, 20/04/1914.
109 PRONI, D/1568/2, minutes of subcommittee, 19/05/1914.
110 Jackson, 'Unionist Politics and Protestant Society in Edwardian Ireland', p. 860.
111 Reports by CI C. G. Cary, 31/07/1912 and Sergeant B. Daagan, 29/07/1912, 'Miscellaneous Papers Regarding "Drilling" by Civilians in Ulster', WO141/26.
112 Jackson, 'Unionist Politics and Protestant Society in Edwardian Ireland', p. 858, citing R. J. Patterson, *Catch-my-pal: A Story of Good Samaritanship* (privately published, London, 1912).
113 TNA, WO141/26, 'Miscellaneous Papers Regarding "Drilling" by Civilians in Ulster', report by Inspector J. Wilband, 24/05/1912 and report by Constable W. P. Lapsley, 01/06/1912.
114 TNA, WO141/26, 'Miscellaneous Papers Regarding "Drilling" by Civilians in Ulster', report by Constable T. Hynes, 10/10/1912.
115 TNA, WO141/26, 'Miscellaneous Papers Regarding "Drilling" by Civilians in Ulster', report by Sergeant M. Cleary, 27/07/1912.
116 *Belfast Evening Telegraph*, 10/09/1912.
117 TNA, CO904/27/2/I, report by Sergeant J. English, 27/12/1912.
118 TNA, CO904/182, RIC Crime Special Branch, 'Importation of Arms and Secret Drilling in Ulster', 08/09/1911.
119 TNA, CO904/182, RIC Crime Special Branch, 'Importation of Arms and Secret Drilling in Ulster', 08/09/1911.
120 TNA, CO904/182, RIC Crime Special Branch, report by DI S. Hanna to IG, 05/05/1911.
121 TNA, CO904/28/2, report by W. H. O'Connell to the Under Secretary, Dublin Castle, 13/07/1912.
122 TNA, CO904/28/2, minute by Lieutenant Colonel N. Chamberlain, 01/09/1912.
123 Bodleian Library, Oxford, Asquith 38, 'Memo. for the Use of the Cabinet' prepared by Sir David Harrell, ?/02/1912.
124 Bodleian Library, Oxford, Asquith 38, letter, Birrell to Asquith, 24/07/1913.
125 Bodleian Library, Oxford, Asquith 38, letter, Birrell to Asquith, 20/08/1913.
126 For a full account of these legal proceedings, see *Morning News*, 18/06/1886 and *Ulster Gazette*, 19/06/1886.
127 *Ulster Gazette*, 19/06/1886 and TNA, CO904/28/1, '1886–1913 Arms Importation + Distribution', report by Sergeant William Dreissmand, 10/06/1886.
128 TNA, CO904/182, 'Legal Opinion on Drilling, c.1870–1914', note by Attorney General, 20/06/1886.
129 TNA, WO141/26, 'Miscellaneous Papers Regarding "Drilling" by Civilians in Ulster', reports by Sergeant J. R. Hunter, 04/09/1912, query by W. A. O'Connell, DIG, 24/09/1912, reply by Sergeant R. Callaghan, 27/09/1912.

130 TNA, CO904/182, reports by DI D. Murnane, regarding drilling in various towns in Co. Down, 30/01/1912 and 31/01/1912.
131 TNA, CO904/182, memo, 'Drilling at Ballywalter', W. A. O'Connell, DIG to Under Secretary, 07/02/1912.
132 TNA, CO904/182, 'Illegal Drilling: Opinion of the Attorney General', 10/02/1912.
133 TNA, WO141/26, 'Miscellaneous Papers Regarding "Drilling" by Civilians in Ulster', memorandum by V. P. Le Fanu, 17/05/1912.
134 TNA, WO141/26, 'Miscellaneous Papers Regarding "Drilling" by Civilians in Ulster', memorandum, 15/05/1912. See also TNA, CO904/182, memorandum by J.M., 17/05/1912.
135 TNA, WO141/26, 'Miscellaneous Papers Regarding "Drilling" by Civilians in Ulster', report by DI B. Conlin, 02/10/1912.
126 *Belfast News Letter*, 09/01/1912.
137 TNA, CO904/27/1, 'Enniskillen Horse', report by Sergeant Michael Gleary, 24/07/1912.
138 TNA, CO904/182, 'Drilling in Bangor' reports by CI F. C. Wallace, 30/01/1912 and DI D. Murnane, 31/01/1912.

2

'An armed democracy'? The social composition and idelogical basis of the UVF

The title of this chapter comes from Charles a la Court Repington's article in *The Times* in which, as the paper's military correspondent, he wrote of the UVF as, 'a democratic army'.[1] He went on to state that the UVF had an enrolled strength of 110,000 men stating, 'Almost every Protestant man and boy in the Province will fight if fighting begins'.[2] Repington's opinion was echoed by H. S. Morrison who noted the wide class basis of the UVF and its popularity among Presbyterians noting that it was certainly not based around, 'the old ascendancy gang trying to regain their power'.[3] However, assessing the actual social composition of the UVF, even in the 1913–14 period, is no easy task for the historian. As discussed in the introduction, the Public Record Office of Northern Ireland failed to cast its net very wide in searching for UVF material. Insufficient interest was taken in UVF materials relating to Belfast and Derry City with the result that there is a rural as well as gentry bias to the materials surviving in PRONI. Some assumptions must therefore be made about the social composition of the UVF in Belfast based on a very small sample. In addition to this, the paperwork completed by UVF units did not fit a uniform pattern. This is, undoubtedly, a reflection of the lack of experience among unit adjutants and, indeed, a wider reflection of the difficulty some urban units had in securing suitable officers at all and the laxity of UVF HQ in failing to keep centralised membership records. Thus for the Derry (so called) City Regiment of the UVF we have a complete roll, which gives us the names, ages, addresses and previous military experience but, frustratingly, not the occupations of the 3,428 members of the force there. By contrast, for the 'H' (Seaforde) Company of the 1st South Down Regiment we have full details of men's addresses, occupations, military experience, ages and attendance at drill.[4] More unusual is the evidence for the social composition of the Enniskillen Horse. When it was first formed in late 1912, the RIC took a keen interest in it and a police report detailed the occupations and ages of its members. By late 1913, when around 100,000 men had enrolled in the UVF the RIC had, understandably, desisted from making such reports.[5] We should also be conscious that the material regarding serving and ex-British army officers involved in the UVF is exceptionally strong. Partly this was due to government interest, as for a time it appeared that such officers would be prosecuted under section 451 of King's Regulations, which prohibited officers from participating in political meetings. This is also a reflection of the arrangements made over the formation of the 36th (Ulster) Division, when UVF HQ appears to have been guaranteed the services of officers who had served in the UVF for this new formation – this was the incentive needed for UVF HQ to produce a detailed list of such officers.

Another major problem for historians is that journalistic coverage of the UVF tended to reflect the polarised and partisan political opinions of the newspapers concerned. Thus to Liberal and Nationalist organs the UVF was composed of impressionable youths and senile old men, easily lead astray by Carson's rhetoric.[6] Whereas the Conservative and Unionist press tended to locate the UVF firmly in the British amateur military tradition, comparing its personnel favourably with English TF and National Reserve units and commenting favourably on the discipline and determination of the force.[7]

Finally there is the problem with the existing historiography, namely that, with little evidence, historians have commented on the composition of the UVF. A. T. Q. Stewart blithely wrote of the UVF as a, 'citizen army, commanded by landowners and businessmen and later by retired British army officers'.[8] Meanwhile, Marxist historians (such as Michael Farrell and Belinda Probert) have suggested that the UVF was founded with little real popular support, relying on the finance and machinations of Belfast businessmen and the Orange Order.[9]

Initially it seems a number of local leaders were identified by the UUC and asked to enrol men for the UVF. The original instructions asked them

> To enrol a force of men for self-preservation and mutual protection of all Loyalists in and adjoining their own Districts, and generally to preserve the Peace ... To only enrol persons who from personal knowledge, or after careful enquiry, are capable and willing to perform the duties above mentioned and
> 1. are between the ages of 18 and 60.
> 2. have signed the Covenant.
> 3. Will sign a Declaration upon volunteering.[10]

However, there were marked local differences over how these orders should be interpreted. In Co. Down, which had a large Unionist majority, the county committee felt that, 'only those who had drilled or were willing to drill + to bear arms should be enrolled'.[11] By contrast in Co. Tyrone, where Unionists were in a minority, Lord Northland appears to have attempted to conscript all male Protestants over 14 years old, living in Dungannon, into his UVF battalion.[12] E. C. Herdman, the CO of the 1st (North) Tyrone Regiment took a similar view when he issued his first battalion orders in January 1913 making it quite clear who should be targeted by his officers, 'You will receive herewith circulars for the UVF meeting in your district. It is most important that these should be well distributed in good time for the meeting. One should be placed in every Protestant house in which there is a man – or boy over 14 – This, I think, would be best done by your Sectional Leaders and members of your [Unionist] clubs'.[13] Furthermore, Herdman instructed that a printed handbill be circulated in October 1913. This reproduced Carson's call for all able-bodied Unionists to join the UVF and went on, 'every man who has signed the Covenant is expected to attend'.[14] On 1 August 1914 for reasons which are not clear General Adair threw open recruiting for the UVF in Co. Antrim but stated, 'Care must be taken to impress upon all recruits that they will probably never be armed'.[15] Thus local commanders ensured that the UVF was much less selective than the UUC had intended, in terms of its recruiting base, particularly as regards age.

Historians of the British auxiliary forces have commented on their feudal nature in rural areas. David French has stated, 'In rural areas with scattered settlement patterns Volunteer units sometimes resembled bands of feudal retainers. But most rural units were centred on small towns and recruited their rank and file from tradesmen, artisans, and craftsmen who were in full-time employment'.[16] Meanwhile, Ian Beckett has noted, 'the historian of the Volunteer Movement in rural areas can only be struck by the marked resemblance of some units to bands of neo-feudal retainers'.[17] Not surprisingly this pattern appears to have been common in the UVF and was, perhaps, given an added impetus by the decline in landlord power witnessed in Ireland in the wake of the Land War, establishment of peasant proprietorship under the Land Acts and establishment of democratic local government in 1898.[18] Lord Castlereagh, a former captain in the Royal Horse Guards and MP for Maidstone, was involved in drilling his family's tenants and estate workers at Mountstewart in Co. Down.[19] In Co. Monaghan there was a definite feudal aspect to the UVF, which was organised mainly by large landowners and, it seems, recruited extensively from among their estate workers and tenants.[20] Certainly John Madden enrolled his family's estate workers in the Monaghan UVF battalion which he commanded.[21]

However, the picture is not a simple one and we should be wary of assuming that all members of the gentry pushed themselves into command positions. Indeed, Dooley's study of big house Unionism in Cavan, Donegal and Monaghan concedes that while gentry support was widespread in Cavan and Monaghan, this was much less the case in Donegal.[22] The Seaforde Company included Major William George Forde, J.P., D.L., the major landowner in the village, and his sixteen-year-old son, Thomas William Forde, in its ranks but the company was actually commanded by Alexander McMeekin, the Forde's coachman. Indeed, the enlistment dates suggest that McMeekin may have been the driving force behind establishing the UVF in that part of South Down as he was one of the first to enrol in the Seaforde UVF on 20 January 1913, while Major Forde did not join until 27 September 1913 after not only his coachman but also his butler and gamekeeper had joined the UVF.[23] Similarly, in Newtownbutler, Lord Crichton attended the local UVF drills but not in a position of command.[24] Therefore we should be wary of seeing tenants as merely following the lead of their landlords.

Elsewhere there seems to have been some dissatisfaction that local gentry did not become more involved in the UVF. This was certainly the case in Florencecourt, Co. Fermanagh, where members of the local Unionist Club complained that Lord Cole did not take more interest in their drilling.[25] This may also be the reason why in August 1913 South Down Unionist Clubs choose to hold an inspection in a field near the entrance to Murlough House, the home of the Marquess of Downshire, who had refused to become involved with the force as he spent most of his time in England.[26] However, in some areas the involvement of gentry was seen as of little benefit by UVF senior officers. For example, at Lisnaskea it was noted that the presence of Lords Crichton and Lanesborough at drills proved of little benefit as training was, 'Coming along very slow here [and the rank and file] don't seem too interested'.[27]

Shane Leslie, when depositing his father's papers in the PRONI in the late 1960s, suggested that some gentry were not terribly enthusiastic about taking command of UVF units, noting, 'Sir John Leslie and Lord Farnham took command of the Monaghan and Cavan regiments chiefly to keep hot heads in order'.[28] Elsewhere, Desmond Murphy believes that in Co. Donegal and Co. Londonderry the gentry and Protestant clergymen were practically obliged to take command of UVF units as local businessmen were concerned that they would be boycotted if they accepted leadership roles.²⁹

Curiously, perhaps, it was the *noveaux riches* of Ulster society, especially those industrialists who effectively owned industrial villages, who seem to have instituted the most compulsion on their workforces to join UVF units which they commanded. E. C. Herdman, as part owner of the linen mills, which provided the majority of employment at Sion Mills, Co. Tyrone, seems to have effectively conscripted the local Protestant population into his UVF unit.³⁰ This also seems to have been the situation in the Comber West Company of the UVF, where the prominent local businessman, John M. Andrews, who owned the local distillery and linen mill, styled himself as 'Captain', despite never having held any rank whatsoever in the British army. His company included 89 men in four sections but a reserve of 64 and 23 in the 'night work section', which suggests that those who worked for Andrews were also expected to enlist, in some capacity, in his UVF company.³¹ However, not all Unionist industrialists were so enthusiastic about their workers playing an active part in the UVF. J. Milne Barbour, later to be Minister of Commerce in the Northern Ireland government from 1925–41, was very concerned about the situation in his linen firm based in Hilden near Lisburn, stating, 'I have been making enquiries and find that in the Works of the Linen Thread Company it so happens that a good many of the volunteers are in groups in different departments, and in some small departments of great importance, such as the Boiler House and Engine Drivers, possibly the whole staff are in the volunteers, so any extensive scheme of mobilisation would have a very disturbing effect, and I think it is a very important matter just now that workpeople should be kept employed as much as possible. This is just as important from a political standpoint as for any commercial reason'.³²

In only a small sample of units can we come to any definite conclusions about the social composition of the UVF membership. In rural areas, the composition of the Enniskillen Horse, 1ˢᵗ Fermanagh Regiment, 'H' (Seaforde) Company of the 1ˢᵗ South Down Regiment and, effectively, the officer and NCO corps of the 5ᵗʰ Tyrone Regiment, are detailed in Tables 2.1–2.4, based on surviving membership records. In large part these rolls tend to confirm the view of elements of the UVF as partly feudal in nature as, of those involved in the Seaforde Company, 19 seem to have worked for the Fordes, again invoking the client–patron relationship evident in the Comber West Company.³³ Having noted this, it is worth drawing attention to the high number of farmers and farmers' sons involved in these units, who in the wake of the 1903 Land Act were likely to be farm proprietors rather than tenants.

It is clear from these membership roles that many UVF units were reliant on fairly minimal military expertise. In the 5th Tyrone Regiment Lieutenant Colonels Mayhew and Twigg and three former other ranks were all listed as instructors and specifically were not given command of any specific subunits; none of those listed as officers in the battalion had any previous military experience. Similarly, the Enniskillen Horse could, at least initially, draw on the experience of very few professional soldiers. Three of the squadron commanders had served in the army, two in cavalry regiments, but only it seems as private soldiers, while one of the troop commanders had served in the South African Constabulary.[34] However, Trimble later suggested that Major W. F. Martin of the Leicestershire Yeomanry acted as his second in command, Captain Wailes of the York [sic] Yeomanry commanded his 'B' Squadron and Lieutenant Hugh Wansey of the East Kent Yeomanry acted as his adjutant, suggesting considerable, though one suspects rather temporary, support for the Enniskillen Horse from English TF officers.[35] The number of ex-soldiers available to serve as NCOs in the UVF also seems to have been rather limited. This was a reflection of the unpopularity of long-term regular service in late Victorian and Edwardian Ulster, as the 1911 census returns for the province showed that only 807 army pensioners lived in it.[36]

The UVF officer corps in rural areas came from landed gentry and rural Ulster's small professional and middle classes. This is very clear in the 5th Tyrone Regiment where the CO was Thomas MacGreger Greer, a landed proprietor, and the adjutant was John Byers, a solicitor, while the company commanders were: Thomas Hegan, a farmer; William Leeper and Hugh Duff, both mill owners; Viscount Charlemont and Thomas Greer, both landed proprietors; Rev. C. A. B. Millington (one of three clergymen holding a rank in this battalion); and William Weir, a publican. Of the section commanders a number were labourers and factory workers, suggesting that there was class consciousness in appointing 'officers'; the section commander being viewed as an NCO. As in the 5th Tyrone Regiment, clergymen formed a key element in the professional element of the 1st Fermanagh Regiment as five of these professionals were clergy although, very unusually, Rev. W. A. Stack seems to have been an army officer before taking holy orders. In terms of the social structure of the rural units as a whole, Jack Sears (the county instructor for Co. Fermanagh) comment that the units at Hollymount, Tomlaght and Garvary were composed of the 'Country class of men' is supported by the profile of the 1st Fermanagh Regiment.[37]

Table 2.1 Occupational profile of the Enniskillen Horse

Occupational group	Numbers	%
Farmer/son	170	87
Farm labourer	0	0
Un/semi-skilled	10	5
Skilled	7	4
Shop assistant/clerk	2	1
Professional	3	2
Merchant/son	4	2
Student	0	0
Gentry/son	0	0
Other	0	0
TOTAL	196	

Source: This is based on a RIC report on the Enniskillen Horse, TNA, CO904/27.

Table 2.2 Occupational profile of 1st Fermanagh Regiment

Occupational group	Numbers	%
Farmer/son	363	57
Farm labourer	160	25
Un/semi-skilled	26	4
Skilled	39	6
Shop assistant/clerk	13	2
Professional	13	2
Merchant/son	26	4
Student	2	0.3
Gentry/son	0	0
Other	0	0
TOTAL	642	

Source: This is based on PRONI, D.1267/1, adjutant's roll of 1st Fermanagh Regiment.

Table 2.3 Occupational profile of members of 'H' (Seaforde) Company, 1st South Down Regiment

Occupational groups	Numbers	%
Farmer/son	61	41
Farm labourer	35	23
Un/semi-skilled	19	13
Skilled	28	19
Shop assistant/clerk	2	1
Professional	2	1
Merchant/son	0	0
Gentry/son	2	1
Student	1	1
Other	0	0
TOTAL	150	

Source: This is based on a roll book held in PRONI, D.1263/3.

Table 2.4 Occupational profile of officers and men of 5th Tyrone Regiment who attended Baronscourt Camp of Instruction

Occupational group	Numbers	%
Farmer/son	61	54
Farm labourer	0	0
Un/semi-skilled	13	12
Skilled	11	10
Shop assistant/clerk	8	7
Professional	8	7
Merchant/son	2	2
Gentry/son	6	5
Student	0	0
Other	4	4
TOTAL	113	

Source: This is based on a return in PRONI, D.1132/6/7A.

In heavily urban UVF units we can be less certain about the social composition of those involved, which is somewhat ironic as Belfast was so dominant in terms of UVF personnel. An insight into the social composition of one of the Belfast UVF regiments is provided by

Repington, who wrote, 'Lord Castlereagh commands the North Belfast Regiment of six battalions and a strength of over 8,000 men. The regiment is recruited from a district that is mainly occupied by artisans of the skilled type – shipwrights, engineers, Queen's Island workers, the very strongest of Belfast Unionists. Other classes, too, must be represented in the regiment for a certain part of North Belfast is purely suburban'.[38] By contrast, Lilian Spender highlighted the low social status of members of the West Belfast Regiment, 'The West Belfast Regiment is the poorest of all, I mean its men are of a lower class than the others, as they are all in Devlin's constituency, which is the slummiest in the city. Many of the men looked just the type you see loafing about public houses, and were no better dressed, but they marched every bit as well as the others, and looked just as keen and determined'.[39] Conversely, the YCV appear to have been a self-conscious 'class corps'. A contemporary noted, 'This was a body composed largely of young business men ... In general type it closely resembled units of the standing of the London Scottish or the Artists' Rifles; and a very large number of its members subsequently obtained commissions [in the British army during the Great War]'.[40] The existence of the YCV served to deprive a number of other Belfast UVF units of middle-class membership and probably also contributed to the officer shortage evident in the city.

With regard to the Derry City Regiment it is clear that this unit had very little military expertise upon which to draw. Just ten of its almost 3,500 members had previous military experience and none of these were officers. Indeed, the closest thing which the unit had to a British army officer was T. E. Hastings of Templemore Park who was a student at the University of Edinburgh and a member of the Officer Training Corps (OTC) there. Beyond this of the nine former soldiers involved only two had been NCOs: John Rooks and James Porter Robinson who had both been sergeants in the Royal Inniskilling Fusiliers. There was little middle-class involvement in the Derry City Regiment with no doctors or reverends and no gentry from outlying areas initially involved.[41] As discussed below, this officer shortage was also a problem in Belfast, where units relied disproportionately on a small number of officers from Great Britain provided through the British League for the Support of Ulster and the Union.

In occupational terms it is worth contrasting the composition of the UVF with that of the IRA and of British amateur military units. Both Joost Augusteijn and Peter Hart have shown that in the IRA farmers dominated its rural membership.[42] This was certainly also the case in the

Table 2.5 Occupational profile of members of No. 1 section, 'C' Company, 2nd West Belfast Regiment

Occupational group	Numbers	%
Un/semi-skilled	13	52
Skilled	11	44
Shop assistant/clerk	1	4
Professional	0	0
Other	0	0
TOTAL	25	

Source: This is based on a section commander's roll in PRONI, D.3692/8.

Enniskillen Horse, where the criteria for membership seems to have involved the ownership of a horse, and in the sample of the 5th Tyrone Regiment, which was effectively the officer and NCO corps of this battalion. However, farmers were less dominant in the other rural UVF units sampled. Similarly farm labourers, who were under-represented in the IRA, were well represented in UVF units, appearing to be over-represented in the 1st Fermanagh Regiment, given the number of farm labourers in the county in the 1911 census.[43] The number of shop assistants and clerks, professionals and merchants and their sons was much smaller in the rural UVF than in the IRA and this was also, apparently, the same in Belfast UVF units, which consisted largely of skilled and unskilled workers (for example, see Table 2.5). In social terms the typical UVF member was likely to be from a more socially inferior group than an IRA member, suggesting that the UVF was much more of a mirror of Irish society and the real 'people's army' of the Irish Revolution. It also seems likely that the UVF in Belfast should, in terms of social composition, be viewed largely as an element of the British amateur military tradition. As Ian Beckett has shown, shortly before its incorporation in the TF in 1908, the Rifle Volunteers were dominated by artisans (35.5 per cent of the total membership) and factory hands (12.9 per cent).[44]

The age profile of the UVF can be assessed rather more clearly than its social composition, as UVF officers who did not think it was worthwhile recording the occupations of their men obviously felt that their ages should be noted (see Tables 2.6–2.10). Repington was most flattering regarding the age profile of the UVF stating, 'an inspection of any Volunteer battalion will show that the units are composed in the main of men in the flower of their age and that they are a much more level lot than one would anticipate. The physique is decidedly good and in many cases remarkable'.⁴⁵ Writing more specifically of the North Belfast Regiment he noted, 'The average age of the recruits was, as far as I could observe, between 25 and 30, but I noticed, too, some of those quite old men who join the Volunteers for sentiment's sake'.⁴⁶ In rural areas, the situation seems more varied. Jack Sears, a retired NCO and UVF county instructor, who cycled furiously throughout Co. Fermanagh in 1913–14, inspecting, drilling and training units noted that rural volunteers in Co. Fermanagh were largely middle aged. However, he also noted that in some parts of the county a disproportionate number of boys were enrolled, presumably to increase the size of units, where Unionists were heavily outnumbered. Thus he noted that in Bellagh, Co. Fermanagh, of 16 UVF members present at one drill five were boys.⁴⁷ The oldest member of the Derry City Regiment may have been David McCauley who was 77 years old in 1914; however, a number of men, for example John H. Foster, where simply noted as 'aged' and may have been even older.⁴⁸ The youngest member of the UVF may have been Lionel Leslie, the youngest son of Lieutenant Colonel John Leslie, who recruited him into the Monaghan Regiment which he commanded, when Lionel was still a young boy.⁴⁹

As with the IRA, the bulk of UVF members appear to have been in the 20–29 age bracket. However, the proportion over 29 years was much higher in the UVF than in the IRA; indeed the over 40 years group, which was tiny in the IRA, was a significant percentage of the UVF. If, as Peter Hart has argued, membership of the IRA was a result partly of a rebellion of youth, then membership of the UVF seems to have been more likely a result of a mid-life crisis.⁵⁰

Table 2.6 Age profile of Derry City Regiment

Age group	Numbers	%
16–19	577	17
20–29	1039	30
30–39	800	23
40–49	576	17
50–59	346	10
60–69	82	2
70–79	8	0.2
TOTAL	3428	

Source: PRONI, D.3054/4/12, J. M. Harvey papers, roll book of the Derry City Regiment.

Table 2.7 Age profile of 1st Fermanagh Regiment

Age group	Numbers	%
12–19	113	16
20–29	268	37
30–39	189	26
40–49	101	14
50–59	44	6
60–69	5	1
70–79	1	0.1
TOTAL	721	

Source: This is based on a roll book held in PRONI, D.1267/1.

Table 2.8 Age profile of the Enniskillen Horse

Age group	Numbers	%
15–19	15	8
20–29	93	47
30–39	51	26
40–49	30	15
50–59	6	3
60–69	1	1
TOTAL	196	

Source: This is based on a RIC report on the Enniskillen Horse, TNA, CO904/27.

Table 2.9 Age profile of 'H' (Seaforde) Company, 1st South Down Regiment

Age group	Numbers	%
16–19	30	20
20–29	62	42
30–39	29	20
40–49	20	14
50–59	5	3
60–69	1	1
70–79	0	0
TOTAL	147	

Source: This is based on a roll book held in PRONI, D.1263/3.

'An armed democracy'?   57

Table 2.10 Age profile of two sections of 'J' Company, 4th (Dungannon) Battalion, Tyrone Regiment

Age groups	Numbers	%
17–19	8	13
20–29	15	25
30–39	14	23
40–49	13	22
50–59	7	12
60–69	3	5
70–79	0	0
TOTAL	60	

Source: This is based on a roll book held in PRONI, D.1132/6/17.

The officer corps of the UVF is one component of the force about which a great deal of evidence survives. The RIC took a keen interest in the activities of officers who were involved in drilling and training the UVF as did the War Office; particularly in the case of serving officers, against whom legal action was considered for some time.[51] Local newspapers were also keen to emphasise the involvement of army officers, with the implication that they were able to turn the UVF into a professional force. The officers involved fall into five main categories: long service professional officers who had retired and lived in Ireland; those who had served in the regular army briefly; those who were serving in the regular forces; those who had served or were serving in Special Reserve (i.e. part-time) units based in Ulster; and officers from outside Ulster, who, in most cases seem to have been recruited through the actions of the British League for the Support of Ulster and the Union. Overall, it appears that the UVF had, at one time or another, just over 130 former or serving British army officers serving with its units.

The long service professional soldiers, men such as Colonel Oliver Nugent, who had retired from the King's Royal Rifle Corps in early 1914 and was living on his family's estate in Co. Cavan, or Captain Ambrose Ricardo, who had left the Royal Inniskilling Fusiliers in 1906 to manage his family's linen business in Sion Mills, Co. Tyrone, tended to dominate the county and regimental commands in the UVF.[52] A number of those with battalion commands in the UVF, such as Viscounts Acheson and Northland, had retired from the regular army after serving for a relatively short space of time.[53] This reflected the widespread practice of the sons of wealthy men serving as officers for only a short period of time in their late teens and early twenties before resigning their commissions when they inherited their family's estate.[54] Some officers, home on leave, took a considerable risk of being court martialled by training UVF units while serving officers in the British regular army. Prominent examples of this included Captain Basil Brooke, who was involved in drilling his family's estate workers in Co. Fermanagh while on leave from the 4th Queen's Own Hussars, and Major J. B. Scriven of the 21st Empress of India's Lancers, who served as a member of UVF HQ staff in early 1914.[55] Overall it appears that seven serving regular officers were involved in the UVF in this way.

Those who had served or were serving in SR units were another group. In social background, these men were often not that different from the two noted above, for example Lieutenant Colonel T. V. P. McCammon of the 5th Royal Irish Rifles was independently wealthy and described himself as a 'gentleman' on his UVF enrolment form.[56] There was some overlap between the short service regular group of officers and the SR; for example, Lord Farnham had served briefly in the 10th Prince of Wales's Own Royal Hussars, retiring as a lieutenant, but had then joined the North Irish Horse, in which he was a major by 1914.[57] The SR did still provide a vehicle through which industrialists could establish themselves in county society, as was the case of Captain W. E. H. Workman, 3rd Royal Inniskilling Fusiliers, who was a family member of the shipyard concern, Workman and Clarke. Seventeen officers serving in SR units based in Ulster, six from the North Irish Horse alone, took up commands in the UVF, although a larger number of retired militia and SR officers, such as James Craig (who had retired as a captain in the 5th Royal Irish Rifles in 1908) and Colonel R. H. Wallace (who had retired from the same unit in 1912), were involved in the UVF.[58]

The UVF also secured a large number of officers from outside Ulster, some of whom were passionate supporters of the Unionist cause, while others primarily seem to have wanted to supplement their military pensions. A few senior officers, notably Lieutenant General Sir George Richardson, the GOC of the UVF, and Colonel George William Hacket Pain, his Chief of Staff, seem to have been recruited directly by the Ulster Unionist leadership. Some British army officers also seem to have served in the UVF at their own expense and possibly only for short periods of time. Thus Lieutenant R. C. Orr of the 3rd Somerset Light Infantry was seen drilling men in Ballymena in July 1913 and Captain A. F. Penny of the 5th Royal Fusiliers was involved in the Belfast Division of the UVF by

July 1914.[59] The British League for the Support of Ulster and the Union secured the services of at least seven and possibly nine officers for service in either UVF HQ or the Belfast Regiments.[60] Most of these seem to have had perfectly conventional army careers: however, Captain F. P. Crozier, Colonel J. H. Paterson and Charles St. Aubyn Wake had decidedly unusual military backgrounds and Paterson was seen as bringing some glamour to the Unionist cause.

F. P. Crozier, who was from an Anglo-Irish military family, worked as a rubber planter in Malaya, before enlisting in Thorneycroft's Mounted Infantry during the South African War. He served with distinction there, being rewarded with a commission in the Manchester Regiment. He went on to serve in the West African Frontier Force but he had been forced to resign from the 2nd Manchester Regiment in 1908 for issuing a dishonoured cheque in payment of his mess bill. Crozier became, by his own admission, an alcoholic while serving in Africa but on leaving the army he became a teetotaller and emigrated to Canada, where he may have been involved in raising the Saskatchewan Light Horse. He returned to Britain in 1913 and, through the auspices of the British League, was soon in Belfast commanding the Special Service Section of the West Belfast Regiment. Crozier was able to reinvent himself in the UVF and went on to command the 9th Royal Irish Rifles in 1915 and commanded a brigade in the 38th (Welsh) Division by the end of the Great War. In 1920 he returned to Ireland but as commander of the Auxiliary Division of the RIC rather than in the reformed UVF.[61]

Charles St. Aubyn Wake had an even more exotic military career. The son of Admiral Charles Wake he had served briefly in the merchant marine, before enlisting in the Dorsetshire Regiment, in which he served during the Nile Relief Expedition of 1885. He then served as a lieutenant in the Zanzibar Protectorate Force (1893–95) where he lost a leg while storming a stockade and was then appointed Vice Consul at Mombassa. In 1896, at his own request, he rejoined the army and was appointed a garrison adjutant in the East African Rifles in which he served with distinction during the Uganda mutiny, receiving the (Distinguished Service Order (DSO). He left the King's African Rifles in 1903, becoming a captain in the Devon Militia. He retired from the militia in 1907 and served as the recruiting officer for Bristol for four years. He resigned from this post to serve as an officer in the Turkish army, serving in the Libyan War (1911–12) against Italy. Through the UVF he received a commission in the 14th Royal Irish Rifles in 1914 and ended the war as a major in the Royal West Kent Regiment.[62]

Colonel J. H. Patterson was already a well known military figure by the time he came to Belfast to command the West Belfast Regiment. He was famous to contemporaries as the author of *Man-Eaters of Tsavo*, in which he recounted how, while an engineer building the Mombassa to Uganda railway line in 1898, he had successfully stalked and killed two lions, which had killed a number of the labourers working on the line.[63] Patterson was born in Co. Longford and enlisted in the 3rd Dragoon Guards in 1885; he left the army in 1897 having reached the rank of sergeant and been involved in a number of construction projects in India. At the outbreak of the South African War Patterson rejoined the army and was gazetted a second lieutenant in the 76th Company, Imperial Yeomanry. He served with distinction in South Africa, was awarded the DSO and by January 1902 was a lieutenant colonel. In 1908 Patterson was forced to leave the army when he was accused of killing his wife's lover while on a safari. Between 1908 and 1913 he seems to have been involved in engineering projects and safaris in Africa. His return to Britain in 1913 to take up a command in the UVF was, in the words of his biographer, 'on a professional basis and, as such, just a "job"'. However, Patterson was to be an advocate of other extreme causes: having dallied with Unionist militancy in 1913–14 he became a Zionist and formed the Zionist Mule Corps, which he commanded at Gallipoli, and later he commanded the Jewish battalion of the Royal Fusiliers, which served in the Middle East.[64]

This chapter has concentrated up to this point on the men involved in the UVF, but there were also a significant number of women involved in the UVF, perhaps as many as 5,000. Some ladies – and this term is used advisedly as UVF HQ seems to have been willing to provide drill facilities for middle- and upper-class women while denying them to their working-class sisters – did engage in military drill. Lilian Spender, whose husband Wilfrid was a UVF staff officer, obtained the services of Jack Scriven, a regular cavalry officer employed at UVF HQ, to drill herself and a small group of female friends shortly after her arrival in Belfast.[65] Generally, however, women were relegated to the roles which they performed in the British army in the Great War, largely in the UVF nursing corps.[66] It is therefore hard to reconcile women's service in the UVF with Viviana Marsano's view that, 'The UVF has never been recognised as an organisation which cut across the gender divide and helped to change the position of Protestant Ulster women during the early years of the twentieth century'.[67] Indeed, Carson and others felt that the UWUC should confine its work to political propaganda campaigns in Great Britain.[68]

It seems that the UVF was fortunate in obtaining some skilled nurses, capable of teaching first aid. Lilian Spender was very complimentary about the instruction she received, stating that her practical nursing course was run by, 'Miss Ketch, an Army nurse, who has had 15 years Red Cross work in India, and is used to training ordinary Tommies for ambulance work at a moment's notice, so to speak, and so is exactly what we want'.[69] However, it is evident that, as with other aspects of the UVF, there was considerable regional variation. As late as February 1914 it was felt that the North Belfast nursing division was 'dismally behind in its organisation' and by late March 1914 it was clear that a nursing corps had not been properly organised for Co. Antrim.[70] Indeed, it seems likely that women were disproportionately enlisted into the UVF in counties where Unionists were in a small minority, largely to swell the numbers parading at UVF inspections. It is noticeable that there was no attempt made to revive the women's sections of the UVF in 1920.

Clearly UVF units were formed outside Ulster. As early as September 1913 the British army's Irish Command understood that the UVF had organised two battalions with over 2,000 members in Dublin. Supposedly these men had made arrangements to send their families to England in the event of civil war and would then operate as a reserve for the UVF in Ulster.[71] More curiously, a UVF unit seems to have been formed in Co. Leitrim by early 1914.[72] UVF membership in Britain was largely connected with the British League for the Support of Ulster and the Union, which began putting together lists of 'the actual number of able-bodied men in Great Britain who will be willing and able personally to join the loyalists of Ulster at the last emergency' from May 1913.[73] The British League was confronted by apathy in Britain and the hostility of some members of UVF HQ who believed that the UVF required arms, not untrained or semi-trained personnel.[74]

The British League claimed to have 5,000 volunteers in Liverpool by spring 1914, although its main purpose, as discussed below, seems to have been to enlist ex-officers who would serve with the UVF in Ulster.[75] There is little evidence of UVF units having been formed in Britain. Dan Jackson and Don MacRaild have found no evidence of the formation of UVF units among the immigrant Ulster Unionist communities in Liverpool and Newcastle.[76] The only case of a UVF unit parading in Britain was when the Glasgow UVF battalion was inspected by General Sir Reginald Pole-Carew on 10 July 1914. Interestingly, the UVF in Glasgow appears to have drilled initially under the cover of being athletics clubs attached to Orange Lodges.[77] It seems that a UVF unit existed in London as three men applying for commissions in the 36th (Ulster) Division claimed to have served in the English Ulster Volunteers; namely Eric Crawley from Blackheath, Frank Quicke from Hounslow and H. M. Allom, who was normally resident in South Kensington.[78]

The British League also seems to have been active in recruiting Southern Unionists for work in North East Ulster; Gerald Madden of the prominent Co. Monaghan Unionist family noted that he had been approached by the secretary of the League in June 1913 asking him to spend a week inspecting the drill of Unionist clubs.[79] Some members of the British League made their own arrangements. A. A. Somerville, a master at Eton College, wrote directly to J. C. Madden, the CO of the Monaghan Regiment, stating that while Somerville was committed to serving in Southern Ireland he would provide the expenses and pay for one year for a captain in the Maidenhead National Reserve, who was a South African War veteran in reduced circumstances, to serve in Madden's unit.[80]

David Fitzpatrick has made much of the 'fraternities' that he thinks were crucial in Irishmen's decisions to enlist in the British army in the Great War and it is worth investigating the importance of such groups in the formation of the UVF.[81] Curiously, unlike the British army, which fostered the 'Pals' concept when forming the New Armies in 1914–15 enabling battalions to be based on specific workplaces, sporting clubs, etc., the UVF did not advocate a similar policy.[82] While in many rural areas UVF companies may have been virtually indistinguishable from Orange Lodges or Unionist Clubs, in the two major cities it appears that these groups were broken up. In Belfast UVF units were initially based on workplaces, notably in the case of the shipyards; however, Richardson, when he took over as GOC, seems to have insisted that UVF units were enrolled by street. This was certainly the manner in which the UVF was formed in Derry. While rugby clubs in Ulster cancelled their fixtures in 1914, urging their members to drill, it appears that they did not carry out drill as clubs or form club-based UVF companies.[83]

Obviously, the UVF was only one of a number of Unionist organisations and many UVF members belonged to the Orange Order and Unionist Clubs. Unfortunately the Orange Order archives are practically non-existent for this period and the existing histories are unsatisfactory, but it would appear that Orange Order links were particularly strong in Co. Fermanagh as no men turned up to a UVF drill meeting in February 1914 as it coincided with an Orange meeting.[84]

Beyond the obvious Orange Order and Unionist Clubs, there were a variety of other groups. The 6th South Belfast Regiment appears to have been dubbed 'University', at least initially as it recruited from the undergraduate body at The Queen's University of Belfast.[85] Some men also enlisted through family connections; for example, in the Seaforde Company four brothers of the Larmour family aged between 17 and 24 years and John Donnelly and his two sons, Samuel and William, were all members of the same unit.[86]

For some officers there were regimental associations. Most of the officers of the North Irish Horse seem to have been involved in the UVF though few from the SR battalions of the Royal Inniskilling Fusiliers, Royal Irish Rifles and Royal Irish Fusiliers. There were also a significant number of officers from the Royal Fusiliers, whose regimental journal, coincidentally named *The Red Hand*, noted that five former officers were serving in the UVF and continued, 'Much has been written about the Ulster Volunteer Force and it only remains for me to record in this journal the share taken in this unique and democratic movement by retired Officers of the Royal Fusiliers. The Regiment may claim to have provided more Officers than any other Regiment in the service'.[87] More surprisingly, it seems that some of the former British army officers in the UVF may have become friends due to their secondments to the Egyptian army. Colonel T. E. Hickman, the UVF's Inspector General and Conservative MP for Wolverhampton, had commanded the 15th Battalion of the Egyptian army at the same time that Colonel G. W. Hacket Pain had been the army's Assistant Adjutant General. It is also possible that the Captain R. L. Moore, who was noted as a UVF regimental officer, was the same officer who had served on secondment with the Egyptian army between 1901 and 1908.[88] With regard to other ranks, there were also previous regimental connections. The Irish Command noted of the Enniskillen Horse, 'It is believed that with the exception of half a dozen men the men belong to N.[orth] Irish Horse (S.[pecial] R.[eserve])'.[89]

Ulster Unionists are often portrayed as little more than religious extremists with a curiously strong attachment to the concept of the United Kingdom, but this is to grossly over-simplify the ideology behind the UVF. Sheer religious bigotry and an apartheid-style view of planter superiority is insufficient to explain the complex ideological views held by over 100,000 people.[90] Of course, the UVF, like Ulster Unionism generally, was a broad church containing Presbyterians and Anglicans, employers and employees, men and women, those from areas with solid

Unionist majorities and those from areas with small Unionist minorities. As such there was no single UVF doctrine on issues such as women's suffrage or the roles of trade unions. The standard work on Ulster Unionist doctrine, D. W. Miller's *Queen's Rebels*, seems to make a persuasive case in arguing that Ulster Unionists saw their political allegiances in a contractual framework, holding that their loyalty was ultimately to the sovereign not to a government that they believed was subverting the British Constitution.[91] It could, indeed, be claimed that by signing the Solemn League and Covenant (which every UVF member had to do, even if it was retrospectively) this was the one doctrine that UVF members could agree on. The extent to which UVF officers still saw their force as loyal, throughout the Third Home Rule crisis, is shown by an incredible confidential document written by Major General W. T. Adair in which he stated:

> It is anticipated that on, or after, the Third reading of the Home Rule Bill in the House of Commons the Nationalist party may make some demonstrations of rejoicing which may prove provocative to Unionists.
>
> You are to confer with the local District Inspector of the Royal Irish Constabulary and offer the services of the Battalion under your command to assist the RIC in whatever measures they may take to preserve the peace, previous to calling out the troops for that purpose.[92]

Not surprisingly, the RIC County Inspector declined such promised support, providing his thought that the mobilisation of UVF units would hardly serve to prevent trouble.[93] In this section other key themes of an Ulster identity, religion, popular militarism, imperialism, historical connections, the role of women and the economy will be discussed.

It would be thought that the term 'Ulster' in the title of the UVF would have been a key element in the ideological views of all UVF members. The mass volunteering of 1913–14 could be seen as creating an Ulster identity in the way that Linda Colley argues the mass volunteering of the 1790s created a British identity.[94] There had also been a long (and arguably still ongoing) attempt to create the concept of an 'Ulster Scots' identity in Ulster arguing that religiously, economically, historically and linguistically Ulster was an entity separate from the rest of Ireland, and speaking in the House of Commons in July 1913 Bonar Law made much of the Scottish character of Ulster.[95] However, some UVF members were uncomfortable with this 'Ulster' identity; Colonel Oliver Nugent stressed that Co. Cavan was, 'geographically and politically isolated from North East Ulster'.[96] By contrast other members of the UVF in the peripheral

Ulster counties became concerned that the Ulster Unionist leadership would accept an unsatisfactory compromise over partition. Gerald Madden, a prominent Co. Monaghan Unionist wrote, 'I hope there is no talk in Belfast of accepting Churchill's hint of withdrawing only the 4 N.[orth] E.[astern] Counties, that would be betraying the rest of Ulster, who are Covenanters like themselves, and any separation should be resisted at all costs'. In the same letter Madden made it clear that he would rather serve in his brother's unit in 'a humble command' in the Monaghan Regiment rather than take command of a battalion elsewhere in Ulster.[265] However, Lilian Spender, writing from the perspective of a British Unionist living in Belfast, felt 'relieved' that Asquith's partition offer, with a time limit of six years, made Unionists' course 'perfectly plain', suggesting that in 1914 permanent six county exclusion would have proved attractive to many UVF members.[98] As discussed further in chapter 7, when the crisis came very few UVF members were prepared to take up arms to preserve a nine county Ulster as a political entity, whatever the niceties of the Covenant had pledged them to do. By contrast to members of the British League for the Support of Ulster and the Union, who were closely allied with the UVF, the cause of Ulster became a test case for wider issues; writing in May 1913 their assistant secretary noted, 'I desire to point out that it is quite clear that the men of Ulster are not fighting only for their own liberties. Ulster will be the field on which the privileges of the whole nation will be lost or won'.[99]

Religion was certainly an important aspect of many UVF members' ideological framework and, as discussed in chapter 4, church parades were a frequent display of local UVF activity. H. S. Morrison recounted attending a Presbyterian special sermon preached by the Rev. R. Moore to the Ulster Volunteers of Leck, Ballinteer and Coleraine. In his sermon, Moore told his congregation that they were fighting for Protestantism in the whole of the United Kingdom; he then went on to warn them of the political power exerted by the Roman Catholic church and how this was so dangerous to them.[100] However, the religious message provided throughout the organisation was not simply one of anti-Catholicism. A special UVF form, of which, unfortunately no complete copy exists, was designed to enable persons who were 'not eligible' to sign the Covenant to enrol in the UVF, which raises the possibility of some Catholic membership.[101] In Lisburn four Catholics from one family joined the UVF, although three of them subsequently converted to Anglicanism.[102] It also seems likely that the YCV retained some middle-class Catholic membership after it became incorporated into the UVF.

Popular militarism was an obvious draw for many of those joining the UVF. One UVF veteran interviewed by Michael Foy stated that he had joined the force as, 'I wanted to march and I wanted to drill. It's as simple as that'.[103] The Rifle Volunteer movement had never been extended to Ireland and the Haldane reforms of 1908 had similarly failed to establish TF units in Ireland. This was at a time when the militarised youth movements, the Boys' Brigade, Church Lads' Brigade and Boy Scouts, were popular in Ulster. Thus it seems likely that a number of men joined the UVF because there were very limited outlets for popular adult militarism in Edwardian Ireland: the SR battalions of the Royal Inniskilling Fusiliers, Royal Irish Rifles and Royal Irish Fusiliers and the North Irish Horse required a substantial time commitment in terms of lengthy annual camps, which most men could not afford to attend. Indeed, the age groups most drawn to the UVF were exactly those which comprised the bulk of the TF.[104] Some UVF leaders hoped that the force could be incorporated into the TF. In a detailed letter to the Secretary of State for War in August 1913, W. C. Trimble asked for free ammunition for the use of the Enniskillen Horse and went on to state:

> I do not know that you have yet decided on Territorials for Ireland, but if you should think well of a Third Irish Yeomanry Corps here ... In England great efforts are being made to recruit the Territorials, which are notoriously far short of requirements. Here, in the Enniskillen Horse, you have a regiment ready made, with only a few appointments to add, with men having the finest physique, and seven-eights of the horses suitable 'troopers'.[105]

James Craig felt that the UVF, as a whole, should be incorporated in the TF to make up for the recruiting deficiencies in this force. Meanwhile Major Viscount Crichton claimed that the Enniskillen Horse had answered the call of Field Marshal Lord Roberts and the National Service League to undergo military training.[106] It seems that these desires were not entirely fanciful. Horace Plunkett, a moderate and influential Southern Unionist who had charged himself with bringing peace between the Ulster Unionists and the Liberal government noted, 'prospects [of peace] would be enormously improved if it were not necessary for Generalissimo Carson to disband his army. Through confidential enquiries of some friends at the War Office I ascertained that if things went well politically, the Authorities would be very glad to embody out of these forces a new Special Reserve'.[107]

However, we should not over-estimate the attraction of popular militarism; there was no great rush to the colours when the UVF was formed in early 1913, it was not until July 1913 that Carson risked reviewing any units and the force did receive something of a relaunch in September 1913 when the HQ staff was appointed and Orangemen and Unionist Club members were called on to join. Ulster Unionist speakers showed a marked tendency to adopt an approach which favoured the revision list over the Mauser. For example, A. L. Horner MP addressing the AGM of the South Tyrone Unionist Association, congratulated those who had drilled, but spent most of his speech commenting on Unionist success at revision work.[108] Similarly in early 1913, Colonel Pakenham, rather than raising a UVF battalion was standing as a Unionist candidate in the parliamentary by-election in Derry City, receiving public support from, among others, the drill instructor of Knock, Ballyhackamore and Bloomfield Unionist Club.[109] The leadership of the UVF was also remarkably pacific for the leaders of a paramilitary movement, conscious that sectarian fighting would both provide the Liberal government with an excuse to suppress the movement and see a rapid haemorrhaging of British Unionist support for the UVF. A number of Unionist propaganda works also suggested that British troops could never fire on the UVF.[110]

Imperial rhetoric was an important element of speeches made to the UVF in this period. For example in June 1913 the Bishop of Derry preached a sermon in which he stated, 'In this vast partnership of Empire Irish Protestants had a share which they purchased with their blood, and they only claimed to retain their place'.[111] Major Viscount Crichton, addressing a review of the regiment, stated, 'If there were more bodies like the Enniskillen Horse throughout the Empire it would be a very good thing for it'.[112] As Donal Lowry puts it, the UVF of 1913–14 claimed, 'to uphold the true interests of the Empire in the face of apparent metropolitan abdication'.[113] By raising the issue of Empire, Unionists were again raising the issue of contractual loyalty but also raising the wider issue of where, why and on what terms self-government should be granted throughout the Empire.[114]

A number of attempts were made to provide the UVF with some sort of historical lineage. The great Orange events of the Battle of the Boyne and sieges of Enniskillen and Derry were of course used, notably when the Castlecaulfield company of the UVF attended a special church service in their parish church which held the remains of the Rev. George Walker, the Governor of Derry during the siege.[115] Not surprisingly, the fact that UVF members had signed the Covenant, along with their generally militant Protestantism, brought to many minds a seventeenth-century comparison. *The Times* military correspondent noted, 'Ulster, like

Cromwell, has men "who upon matter of conscience engage in the quarrel, and thus being well armed within by the satisfaction of their own consciences, and without by good iron arms, will as one man stand firmly and charge desperately." The Ulster Protestants come of a fighting stock'. While the *Northern Whig* referred to the UVF as 'a Cromwellian army'.[116] Other historical connections claimed for the UVF were more surprising. One author stressed the similarities of the movement to that of the revolutionaries in the American War of Independence whom he referred to as 'our forefathers'.[117] There was also an attempt to link the activities of the UVF in 1913–14 with the earlier volunteers of the 1777–92 period. As early as 1912 the Unionist Club in Dungannon was styling itself Dungannon (Volunteer) Unionist Club and one author noted how the Irish Volunteers had been formed in the 1770s loyally to defend Ireland from French and Spanish invasion threats.[118] Introducing an interesting American Civil War comparison, Field Marshal Sir Henry Wilson said that the UVF closely resembled the 'New England Regiments who obeyed Abraham Lincoln's summons'.[119]

In economic terms, the widespread support for the UVF among Belfast shipyard workers suggests two things. Firstly, industrial workers in Ulster did have genuine concerns about what the effect of Home Rule would be on the Ulster economy. The issue of Tariff Reform was much debated in the Belfast press in the 1911–14 period and many must have realised that if an Irish parliament in Dublin introduced tariffs to protect Irish industries then the export-driven Belfast industrial economy would suffer through retaliation by Britain and other countries. Secondly, the support of industrial workers for the UVF shows that there was nothing incompatible between men being staunch trade unionists and members of the UVF, a point entirely neglected by historians of the Irish trade union movement.[120] Demonstrating this, there was a meeting of trade unionists of Belfast against Home Rule held in the Ulster Hall in April 1914.[121] Graham Brownlow has convincingly argued that Ulster Unionists did not adopt an extreme pro-capitalist position in this period. He notes that redistributive schemes such as land purchase, government subsidies towards labourers' cottages and old age pensions were all seen as economic benefits of the Union that a Home Rule parliament would find difficult to continue.[122]

Reaching firm conclusions on both the social composition and political motivation of the UVF is extremely difficult. However, it appears that in terms of the social groups involved, the UVF was rather more plebeian than the IRA of 1916–23 and had much more in common with the Rifle Volunteer movement in Britain and its successor from 1908, the TF. A number of units had a clear feudal basis, which meant that the employees, tenants or estate workers involved presumably had little choice about whether they would join the UVF or not. But most UVF members joined voluntarily and the social mix was significantly varied. This should not disguise the fact that the average UVF member would appear to have been a male skilled or unskilled urban worker in his twenties. The ideology behind the UVF was complex, although for individual members the choice to join may have been simply a result of family or friendship connections. UVF members in the outlying Ulster counties seem to have been concerned about partition from an early date but crucially failed to use the UVF to improve their political position within Ulster Unionism.

Notes

1 *The Times*, 18/03/1914.
2 *The Times*, 18/03/1914.
3 Morrison, *Modern Ulster*, p. 100.
4 PRONI, D.3054/4/2, enrolment book of Derry City UVF and PRONI, D.1263/3, roll book for Seaford Company.
5 TNA, CO904/27, RIC report on the Enniskillen Horse.
6 For a useful discussion of this see Patrick Maume, 'The Irish Independent and the Ulster Crisis, 1912–21' in D. G. Boyce and Alan O'Day (eds), *The Ulster Crisis 1885–1921* (Palgrave Macmillan, Basingstoke, 2006)
7 See, for example, *Wiltshire Gazette*, 11/11/1913 and *Devon and Exeter Gazette*, 02/05/1914.
8 A. T. Q. Stewart, *The Narrow Ground: The Roots of Conflict in Ulster* (Faber and Faber, London, 1967), p. 168.
9 Michael Farrell, *Northern Ireland: The Orange State* (Pluto Press, London, 1980), p. 19 and Belinda Probert, *Beyond Orange and Green: The Political Economy of the Northern Ireland Crisis* (Zed Press, London, 1978) p. 44.
10 PRONI, D.1238/120, O'Neill papers, undated memorandum [December 1912?] entitled, 'Appointments and Duties of Locality Leaders' and Morrison, *Modern Ulster*, p. 155.
11 PRONI, D.1327/4/1, Co. Down committee minute book, 20/12/1912.
12 PRONI, D/1132/6/17, R. T. G. Lowry papers, circular letter from Lord Northland to members of 4th Tyrone Regiment.
13 PRONI, D.1414/30, battalion orders for 1st (North) Tyrone Regiment.
14 PRONI, D.1414/20, printed Handbill re. 1st (North) Tyrone Regiment.
15 PRONI, D.1238/198, O'Neill papers, memorandum by Adair, 01/08/1914.

16 French, *Military Identities*, p. 211.
17 Beckett, *Riflemen Form*, p. 52. See also, S. P. Mackenzie, *The Home Guard: The Real Story of 'Dad's Army'* (Oxford University Press, 1995), p. 36.
18 Terence Dooley, *The Decline of the Big House in Ireland: A Study of Irish Landed Families, 1860–1960* (Wolfhound Press, Dublin, 2001), p. 225.
19 Neil Fleming demonstrates understandable confusion about Castlereagh's commands in the UVF in N. C. Fleming, *The Marquess of Londonderry: Aristocracy, Power and Politics in Britain and Ireland* (Tauris Academic Studies, London, 2005), pp. 35–6.
20 Terence Dooley, *The Plight of Monaghan Protestants, 1912–1926* (Irish Academic Press, Dublin, 2000), p. 22.
21 PRONI, D.3465/J/37/55, Madden papers, letter, Gerald Madden to Jack Madden, 26/12/1913.
22 Dooley, *The Decline of the Big House in Ireland*, pp. 223–4.
23 All details taken from PRONI, D.1263/3, enrolment register for Seaforde Company.
24 PRONI, D.1390/19/1, Charles Falls papers, notebook of John Sears, entry for 13/01/1914.
25 PRONI, D.1390/19/1, Charles Falls papers, notebook of John Sears, entry for 06/09/1913.
26 TNA, CO904/27/3, '1913–14 Unionist Movement v. Home Rule, Weekly Reports', 25/08/1913.
27 PRONI, D.1390/19/1, Charles Falls papers, notebook of John Sears, entry for 06/03/1914.
28 PRONI, D/1855/1, Leslie papers, note by Shane Leslie.
29 Desmond Murphy, *Derry, Donegal and Modern Ulster 1790–1921* (Aileach Press, Londonderry, 1981), pp. 196–7.
30 PRONI, D.1414/30, battalion orders for 1st (North) Tyrone Regiment. On the establishment of Sion Mills and Comber as industrial villages, see D. S. Macneice, 'Industrial Villages of Ulster, 1800–1900' in Peter Roebuck (ed.), *Plantation to Partition: Essays in Ulster History in honour of J. L. McCracken* (Blackstaff Press, Belfast, 1981), pp. 174–5.
31 PRONI, D.3743/3, enrolment register for Comber West Company.
32 PRONI, D.1327/4/2B, UUC papers, letter, J. Milne Barbour to G. S. Clark, 26/03/1914.
33 PRONI, D.1263/3, enrolment register of Seaforde Company.
34 TNA, CO904/27, RIC report on the Enniskillen Horse.
35 W. C. Trimble, *The History of Enniskillen with References to Some Manors in Co. Fermanagh and Other Local Subjects* (William Trimble, Enniskillen, 1921), vol. II, pp. 1070–2.
36 *Census of Ireland, 1911*. Province of Ulster, Summary Tables, 1912/13, XCV, Cd 6051, p. 13.

37 PRONI, D.1390/19/1, Charles Falls papers, notebook of John Sears, entries for 26/01/1914, 12/02/1914 and 23/02/1914.
38 *The Times*, 16/04/1914.
39 PRONI, D.1633/2/19, Lilian Spender diary, entry for 06/05/1914.
40 Colles, *The History of Ulster from the Earliest Times to the Present Day*, p. 249.
41 PRONI, D.3054/4/2, J. M. Harvey papers, enrolment book of Derry City Regiment.
42 Augusteijn, *From Public Defiance to Guerrilla Warfare*, pp. 354–9 and Peter Hart, *The I.R.A. at War 1916–1923*, pp. 110–40.
43 *Census of Ireland, 1911*. Province of Ulster, Summary Tables, 1912/13, XCV, Cd 6051, p. 63.
44 Beckett, *Riflemen Form*, p. 83.
45 *The Times*, 18/03/1914.
46 *The Times*, 16/04/1914.
47 PRONI, D.1390/19/1, Charles Falls papers, notebook of John Sears, entries for 26/01/1914, 12/02/1914 and 18/03/1914.
48 PRONI, D.3054/4/2, J. M. Harvey papers, enrolment register for Derry City Regiment.
49 PRONI, D/1855/1, Leslie papers, annotated photograph of Lionel Leslie in UVF uniform.
50 Peter Hart, 'Youth Culture and the Cork I.R.A.' in David Fitzpatrick (ed.), *Revolution? Ireland 1917–1923* (Trinity History Workshop, Dublin, 1990).
51 TNA, WO141/4, which contains various reports and correspondence on officers believed to be drilling UVF units.
52 On Nugent see Nicholas Perry's forthcoming publication for the Army Records Society and Nugent's obituary in *The King's Royal Rifle Corps Chronicle*, 1926, pp. 241–4. I am grateful to Dr Michael Foy for details on Ricardo's background, based on conversations with his daughter in the early 1980s.
53 PRONI, D.1498/7, Richardson papers, 'Nominal Roll of Officers Recently Serving with UVF. Who Have Been Recalled to Army Service'.
54 French, *Military Identities*, p. 150.
55 Report of Brooke drilling men at Colebrooke in TNA, WO141/26 and report on Scriven in TNA, CO904/27/3, 'Unionist Movement v. Home Rule, Weekly Reports', 28/03/1914.
56 See the personal file of Lieutenant Colonel T. V. P. McCammon, TNA, WO339/46427 and PRONI, D.1327/4/12, UUC papers, 'Headquarters Staff Enrolment Forms'.
57 PRONI, D.1498/7, Richardson papers, 'Nominal Roll of Officers Recently Serving with UVF. Who Have Been Recalled to Army Service' and War Office, *Army List* (HMSO, August 1914), c. 441.
58 On Craig's and Wallace's careers in the 5th Royal Irish Rifles see PRONI, D.1889/4/1/1, Wallace papers, out letter book.

59 On Orr see a report in TNA, WO141/26. On Penny see PRONI, D.1498/7, Richardson papers, 'Nominal Roll of Officers Recently Serving with UVF Who Have Been Recalled to Army Service' and Penny's personal file in TNA, WO339/11239.
60 Crozier, *Impressions and Recollections*, p. 143.
61 Crozier, *Impressions and Recollections*, Philip Orr's introduction to F. P. Crozier, *A Brass Hat in No Man's Land* (Gliddon Books, Norwich, 1989) and TNA, WO374/16997, personal file of Brigadier General F. P. Crozier.
62 Obituary in *The Times*, 09/12/1938 and TNA, WO339/14219, personal record of Major C. St. A. Wake.
63 PRONI, D.1633/2/19, Lilian Spender diary, entry for 10/06/1914. See also J. H. Patterson, *The Man-Eaters of Tsavo* (Macmillan, London, 1907).
64 Patrick Streeter, *Mad for Zion: A Biography of Colonel J. H. Patterson* (The Matching Press, Harlow, 2004), J. H. Patterson, *With the Zionists in Gallipoli* (Hutchinson, London, 1916), J. H. Patterson, *With the Judians in the Palestine Campaign* (Hutchinson, London, 1922) and Martin Watts, *The Jewish Legion and the First World War* (Palgrave, Basingstoke, 2004).
65 PRONI, D.1633/2/19, Lilian Spender diary, entry for 20/02/1914.
66 On the role of women in the British army in this period see Janet Lee, *War Girls: The First Aid Nursing Yeomanry in the First World War* (Manchester University Press, 2005).
67 Viviana Marsano, '"Those Who Wish for Peace Must Prepare for War." The Ulster Volunteer Force and the Home Rule Crisis of 1912–14', unpublished Ph.D. thesis, University of California, Santa Barbara, 1997, p. 7.
68 On the UWUC see, Diane Urquhart, *Women in Ulster Politics 1890–1940* (Irish Academic Press, Dublin, 2000), pp. 46–84 and Diane Urquhart (ed.), *The Minutes of the Ulster Women's Unionist Council and Executive Committee 1911–40* (The Women's History Project in association with Irish Manuscripts Commission, Dublin, 2001).
69 PRONI, D.1633/2/19, Lilian Spender diary, entry for 04/93/1914.
70 PRONI, D.1633/2/19, Lilian Spender diary, entries for 26/02/1914 and 30/03/1914.
71 Nuffield College, Oxford, MSS Mottistone 22/f. 176, HQ Irish Command report on Ulster Volunteer Force, c. September 1913 and George Peel, *The Reign of Sir Edward Carson* (P. S. King & Son, London, 1914), pp. 7–8.
72 Michael Wheatley, *Nationalism and the Irish Party: Provincial Ireland 1910–1916* (Oxford University Press, 2005), p. 183.
73 NAS, GD391/22/4, letter Hugh B. Ridgway, Assistant Secretary, British League for the Support of Ulster and the Union to John Stewart Peter, 29/05/1913. On the activities of the League see, G. Phillips, 'Lord Willoughby de Broke and the Politics of Radical Toryism', *Journal of British Studies*, 20, 1980 and Rodner, 'Leaguers, Covenanters, Moderates'.

74 PRONI, D.1327/4/2C, UUC papers, letter, T. Comyn Platt to Dawson Bates, 06/04/1914.
75 *Morning Post*, 28/09/1913
76 Dan Jackson, ' "Friends of the Union": Liverpool, Ulster and Home Rule, 1910–1914', *Transactions of the Historic Society of Lancashire and Cheshire*, 152, 2004 and D. M. Jackson and D. M. MacRaild, 'The Conserving Crowd: Mass Unionist Demonstrations in Liverpool and Tyneside, 1912–13' in Boyce and O'Day, *The Ulster Crisis 1885–1921*.
77 *Northern Whig*, 11/07/1914 and Steven Bruce, 'The Ulster Connection' in Graham Walker and Thomas Gallagher (eds), *Sermons and Battle Hymns: Protestant Popular Culture in Modern Scotland* (Edinburgh University Press, 1990), p. 236.
78 Personal records of Lieutenant Eric Crawley (TNA, WO339/20586), Second Lieutenant Frank Quicke (TNA, WO339/20583) and Second Lieutenant H. M. Allom (TNA, WO339/20579).
79 PRONI, D.3465/J/37/48, Madden papers, letter, Gerald Madden to Jack Madden, 25/06/1913.
80 PRONI, D.3465/J/37/48, Madden papers, letter, A. A. Somerville to J. C. Madden, 19/07/1914.
81 David Fitzpatrick, 'Militarism in Ireland 1900–1922' in Bartlett and Jeffery (eds), *A Military History of Ireland*, pp. 389–91
82 Neal Garnham's statement that there were plans to form a sporting battalion in the UVF is based on a misreading of the evidence. There were still-born plans to raise a sporting battalion in the 36th (Ulster) Division. Neal Garnham, *Association Football and Society in Pre-Partition Ireland* (Ulster Historical Foundation, Belfast, 2004), p. 188 and PRONI, D.3867/A/5, IRFU minute book, 12/09/1914 and 20/09/1914.
83 *Northern Whig*, 11/02/1914.
84 Notebook of John Sears, entry for 02/02/1914, Charles Falls papers, PRONI, D.1390/19/1. I am grateful to Dr David Hume, the Executive Officer of the Orange Order, for details on their archival holdings, which are mostly post-1920. For studies of the Orange Order see, Ruth Dudley Edwards, *The Faithful Tribe: An Intimate Portrait of the Loyal Institutions* (Harper Collins, London, 2000), David Fitzpatrick, 'The Orange Order and the Border', *Irish Historical Studies*, 33, 129, 2002, T. G. Fraser, *The Irish Parading Tradition: Following the Drum* (Macmillan Press, Basingstoke, 2000), Aiken McClelland, 'The Later Orange Order' in T. Desmond Williams, *Secret Societies in Ireland* (Gill and Macmillan, Dublin, 1973) and Elaine McFarland, *Protestants First: Orangeism in 19th Century Scotland* (Edinburgh University Press, 1990).
85 Nuffield College, Oxford, MSS Mottistone 22/f. 174, HQ Irish Command report on Ulster Volunteer Force, c. September 1913.
86 PRONI, D.1263/3, enrolment register of Seaforde Company.

87 *The Red Hand*, June 1914, cutting in PRONI, T.2891/1.
88 On these officers' UVF roles see PRONI, D.1507/A/10/10, Carson papers, 'Return of Officers on Reserve or Special Reserve Serving as Commanders + Staff Officers with the Ulster Volunteers Force', c. August 1914. On their roles in the Egyptian army, see Henry Keown-Boyd, *Soldiers of the Nile: A Biographical History of the British Officers of the Egyptian Army 1882–1925* (Thornbury Publications, Thornbury, 1996), pp. 89, 99–100, 140–1.
89 Nuffield College, Oxford, MSS Mottistone 22/f. 176, HQ Irish Command report on Ulster Volunteer Force, c. September 1913.
90 For a particularly unflattering view of Ulster Unionist ideology see J. J. Lee, *Ireland 1912–1985* (Cambridge University Press, 1989), pp. 1–18.
91 D. W. Miller, *Queen's Rebels: Ulster Loyalism in Historical Perspective* (Gill and Macmillan, Dublin, 1978), especially pp. 87–149.
92 PRONI, D.1238/141, O'Neill papers, confidential memorandum by W. T. Adair, 16/05/1914.
93 PRONI, D.1238/152, O'Neill papers, letter, R. O. Morrison to Adair, 23/05/1914.
94 Linda Colley, *Britons: Forging the Nation, 1707–1837* (Yale University Press, 1992).
95 John Harrison, The *Scot in Ulster: Sketch of the History of the Scottish Population of Ulster* (William Blackwood, Edinburgh, 1888), pp. 97–115, J. B. Woodburn, *The Ulster Scot: His History and Religion* (H. R. Allenson, London, n.d. but 1913), pp. 396–400 and Hansard, Fifth Series, 07/07/1913, LV, c. 71.
96 PRONI, MIC/571/9, Farren Connell papers, 'Cavan Volunteer Force scheme, Copy No. VI'.
97 PRONI, D.3465/J/37/51, Madden papers, letter, Gerald Madden to Jack Madden, 09/10/1913.
98 PRONI, D.1633/2/19, Lilian Spender diary, entry for 11/03/1914.
99 NAS, GD391/22/4, letter, Hugh B. Ridgway, Assistant Secretary, British League for the Support of Ulster and the Union to John Stewart Peter, 29/05/1913.
100 Morrison, *Modern Ulster*, pp. 93–9.
101 PRONI, D.1238/178, O'Neill papers, UVF Order 74, 18/07/1914.
102 *Fermanagh Times*, 04/09/1913.
103 Hugh Neilly, interviewed 25/05/1981, cited in Foy, 'The Ulster Volunteer Force', p. 56.
104 Ian F. W. Beckett, *The Amateur Military Tradition, 1558–1945* (Manchester University Press, 1991), pp. 218–22.
105 TNA, CO904/27/1, 'Enniskillen Horse', letter, W. C. Trimble to J. E. B. Seeley, 01/08/1913.
106 *Irish Times*, 18/10/1913.

107 Bodleian Library, Oxford, Asquith, 39, f. 103, letter, Horace Plunkett to M. Bonham Carter, 30/01/1914.
108 *Fermanagh Times*, 29/05/1913.
109 *Belfast Evening Telegraph*, 23/01/1913 and 31/01/1913.
110 See, for example, Pembroke Wicks, *The Truth About Home Rule* (Pitman & Sons, London, 1913), p. 93 and Esme Wingfield-Stratford, *Home Rule and Civil War: An Appeal to the British People* (Bell & Sons, London, 1914), pp. 15 and 107–8.
111 *Fermanagh Times*, 12/06/1913.
112 *Irish Times*, 18/10/1913.
113 Donal Lowry, 'Ulster Resistance and Loyalist Rebellion in the Empire' in Keith Jeffery (ed.), *'An Irish Empire'? Aspects of Ireland and the British Empire* (Manchester University Press, 1996), p. 191.
114 See for example 'An Irishman', *Is Ulster Right? A Statement of the Question at Issue Between Ulster and the Nationalist Party and of the Reasons – Historical, Political and Financial – Why Ulster Is Justified in Opposing Home Rule* (John Murray, London, 1913), pp. 232–58.
115 *Belfast Evening Telegraph*, 20/04/1914.
116 *The Times*, 18/03/1914 and *Northern Whig*, 05/02/1914.
117 Morrison, *Modern Ulster*, p. 155.
118 PRONI, D.1327/1/12, UUC papers, 'Report for 1912' in printed booklet, 'List of the Unionist Clubs of Ireland (Established January, 1893) (Revived January, 1911) and List of the Executive Committee of the Council for 1913', *Belfast News Letter*, 15/02/1911, *Belfast Evening Telegraph*, 02/10/1913 and Wingfield-Stratford, *Home Rule and Civil War*, pp. 50–1.
119 *Northern Whig*, 21/11/1921.
120 See, for example, John Lynch, *A Tale of Three Cities* (Macmillan, Basingstoke, 1998) which makes no reference whatsoever to the UVF in a comparative study of the labour movements in Belfast, Dublin and Bristol.
121 *Belfast Evening Telegraph*, 28/04/1914 and Jennifer Todd, 'Unionist Political Thought, 1920–72' in D. G. Boyce, Robert Eccleshall and Vincent Geoghegan (eds), *Political Thought in Ireland since the Seventeenth Century* (Routledge, London, 1993), p. 193.
122 Graham Brownlow, 'The Political Economy of the Ulster Crisis: Historiography, Social Capability and Globalisation' in Boyce and O'Day (eds), *The Ulster Crisis 1885–1921*, pp. 31–6.

3

Command, control and military efficiency

This chapter considers a number of diverse but related topics. The command of the UVF, while theoretically a standard military hierarchy, was in reality anything but. Command of UVF units was actually in the hands of local divisional, regimental, battalion and company officers, some of whom had little respect for and, indeed, openly disobeyed instructions from UVF HQ housed in the Old Town Hall in Belfast. The UVF was often called Carson's army by contemporaries and this practice has been followed in the title of this book. This reflects the fact that while there was a UVF HQ staff and a GOC, Lieutenant General Sir George Richardson, the crucial decisions about the formation, arming and possible deployment of the UVF were all being made at the political level with Sir Edward Carson ultimately having the final say, despite his protestations that he was leaving the command of the UVF to a professional soldier. The military efficiency of UVF units differed significantly over time and region. Many UVF units had serious problems with absenteeism; in fact some units seem to have had a large number of members who were nothing more than members on paper; having enrolled for the force (enrolment in some areas was certainly carried out by a door to door canvass) they refused to attend any training sessions. As noted further in chapter 5 there was also a lack of rifles for training purposes, at least until the Larne gunrunning of April 1914 and possibly for some time after this. This chapter will examine issues such as the command structures of the UVF, the contingencies prepared for, the disciplinary problems involved, the amount of training conducted by weekly drill sessions, the utility of the camps of instruction and larger regimental camps held by certain UVF units and the military credentials of the officers secured for the UVF.

As historians of the Unionist high politics of the UVF have noted, the Unionist and Conservative leadership were well aware of the difficulties

Command, control and military efficiency   77

which the militarisation of their political campaign entailed. If Carson and other Unionists effectively preached treason in front of their assembled regiments, they appear to have been much more circumspect in private.[1] Unionists never abandoned the parliamentary arena, even when reviewing paramilitary forces. However, the Irish Unionist political leadership was, initially, enthusiastic about forming the UVF and this was for a number of reasons. Firstly, paramilitary forces were already in existence and the leadership must have felt that it was better that these were under political control than left as fringe movements. Indeed, the Ulster Unionist leadership, having recently overcome the Russellite and Sloanite challenges from disgruntled tenant farmers and Belfast industrial workers respectively, was all too aware of the dangers inherent in a divided Unionism.[2] Secondly, as Paul Bew has argued, Carson was all too aware of the damage that would be caused to the Unionist case if the campaign against Home Rule degenerated as it had, in previous years, into rioting.[3] Thirdly, the formation of the UVF would enable Ulster Unionism to be presented as something of a solid block; an important issue in the parliamentary debates on partition.

While most Ulster Unionists were initially supportive of the formation of the UVF problems soon became apparent. By seeking to consolidate Ulster Unionism there was the danger that wider British Unionism would be fractured. Bonar Law was probably the most enthusiastic supporter that Ulster Unionists could have hoped for but it is clear that he spoke for a small minority of his party and was embarrassed by the militancy of the British League for the Support of Ulster and the Union, formed by the maverick Lord Willoughby de Broke.[4] Equally, Walter Long and other senior Conservatives pledged their support to Southern Irish as well as Ulster Unionists, and Ulster Unionists in Cavan and Monaghan, much less Southern Irish Unionists as a whole, saw considerable problems inherent in a Unionist military strategy.

Within Ulster Unionism, the existence of the UVF soon proved problematic. Initially formed to solve a leadership problem (how to maintain Ulster Unionist cohesion and discipline during the Home Rule crisis) the UVF soon provided a forum for those critical of the Ulster Unionist leadership to air their opinions. It was through the UVF that Co. Antrim Unionists expressed their view that the Unionist campaign was loosing its momentum, Cavan Unionists expressed their concerns about where a military strategy would leave them in the event of civil war and Fermanagh Unionists demonstrated that their county's membership of a partitioned Ulster state was not open for negotiation.[5]

As will be discussed further in chapter 5, the conflict between the 'hawks' and 'doves' in Ulster Unionism became particularly marked over the issue of arming the UVF.

The relationship between the Ulster (and indeed, British) Unionist leadership and the UVF is a confusing one. Technically, the UVF was formed as the military force which would ensure that the writ of the Ulster Provisional Government would run throughout the nine counties of Ulster. However, the Ulster Provisional Government, or rather the bewildering array of separate boards (Military Council, Supply Board, Transport Board, Railway Board, Medical Board, Volunteer Advisory Board and Personnel Board) that comprised it, met irregularly and do not seem to have been policy-making bodies.[6] Carson, unlike many of his detractors, never saw himself as a 'General' much less a 'King'.[7] Unlike many senior Ulster Unionists Carson had no military background whatsoever, whereas his predecessors, Edward Saunderson and Walter Long had both been Colonels in the auxiliary forces (of the 4th Royal Irish Fusiliers and Wiltshire Yeomanry respectively). Indeed, Carson made it clear to his followers in his whirlwind tour of provincial Ulster in September 1913 that Lieutenant General Sir George Richardson was the professional soldier who would command the UVF and he made much of the role of his 'friends in Ulster' in the various committees of the Ulster Provisional Government set up to administer the UVF.[8] This, in itself, throws up the obvious and, it seems, insoluble question of who was supposed to be in command of the UVF between its formation in January 1913 and Richardson's arrival in Ulster in September of that year.

In this power vacuum and well into 1914 the Unionist Clubs and Orange Order continued to perform a number of military roles in many areas. In Newry the Unionist Club saw the UVF as simply a section of the club itself and wanted to appoint its own officers, rather than accept those appointed by UVF HQ.[9] As late as January 1914 clubs rather than companies were noted as holding shooting competitions in Fermanagh.[10] In August 1913 Colonel Wallace, Secretary of the Ulster Provincial Grand Lodge of the Orange Order, wrote to the masters of Orange Lodges asking them to ensure that all members of the Order joined the UVF. He continued, 'In some places the Orange lodges have organised the drilling, and members of Unionist clubs have drilled along with them, in which case it is commonly stated that the Orangemen are drilling. In other places it is the other way round, and it is said that the Unionist Club is drilling. From the present time on Sir Edward wants it to be that "the Ulster Volunteers" are drilling and all loyal Ulstermen are members of the Ulster Volunteers'.[11] In Belfast itself it appears that the Orange Order was the basis for popular opposition to Home Rule, independent of the UVF, until this message from Wallace. In April 1913 Sergeant Joseph Edwards of the Belfast Detective Branch of the RIC reported both that the Orange Order planned to arm its members in the city and that Orangemen had responded favourably to a request that they pay 6d each per month towards the cost of their arms.[12]

However, while the Orange Order retained its traditional functions during the marching seasons of 1913 and 1914, it appears that after March 1914 the Unionist Clubs went into something of a decline; certainly the meetings of the central council ceased, the next one not occurring until September 1919.[13] As early as October 1913 it was noted that, 'The work of the Clubs is still progressing, although those in Ulster have, during the Summer, been devoting their attention principally to home defence'. In February 1914 it was recognised that, 'The work of the Clubs in Ulster has been largely taken over by the UVF and the energies of their members have been devoted to "home defence". Many Clubs are, however, still keeping up correspondence with constituencies and individuals across the water'.[14] It seems likely that the Unionist leadership preferred military activity to continue through the UVF rather than the Unionist Clubs and one suspects that in many areas there had been an overlap of membership for some time. Nevertheless, at least in Fermanagh, the Unionist Clubs remained an important element of grassroots Unionist militancy and it appears that some clubs were reluctant to give up their independence and join the UVF. The different attitudes of Unionist Clubs is evident in Co. Tyrone: while in Cookstown men were being enrolled directly into the UVF from January 1913, in Omagh as late as August 1913 the Unionist Club was discussing how it could transform itself into a UVF battalion and suggesting that this would take some time.[15] These local variations mean that while in some areas (the minority) the UVF was forming from January 1913, in other areas it was not in being until mid-1913 (when Carson held his first inspections of UVF units in North Down) and in others, the UVF was only reluctantly formed in September 1913 when Carson and Colonel R. W. Wallace urged all Orange Lodges and Unionist Clubs to amalgamate in the UVF.

Even at its highest levels the UVF comprised a strange combination of the very experienced and utterly amateur. If we consider the HQ staff, it is worth making the observation that this contained more civilians than soldiers, with 10 former or serving soldiers and 12 civilians.[16] Of these soldiers it is also worth noting that some were members of the HQ staff for political rather than military expertise. James Craig MP, although a former captain in the 13th Battalion, Imperial Yeomanry in the South African War and 3rd Royal Irish Rifles from 1900–8, was described as 'Political Staff Officer, UVF.'[17] Similarly T. V. P. McCammon, though a major (and shortly after a lieutenant colonel) in the 5th Royal Irish Rifles, was given his headquarters post of 'I[n] C[harge] Administration' as much due to his position as Deputy Grand Secretary of the Provincial Grand [Orange] Lodge of Ulster as due to his military experience. Similarly, the appointment of Colonel T. E. Hickman, MP for Wolverhampton, as Inspector General appears to have been an attempt to emphasise British Unionist support for Ulster as Hickman's visits to Ulster were infrequent, although he may have played a role in recruiting officers, including Richardson, for the UVF.

What then are we to make of Michael Foy's claim that, 'The Headquarters Staff of the UVF therefore had entirely adequate military credentials'?[18] Certainly, on the technical side, Lieutenant Colonel Robert Davis, a 57-year-old-retired officer of the Indian Medical Service was well qualified to be the secretary of the UVF Medical Board and Major F. H. Crawford, a 52-year-old retired Royal Artillery officer was well qualified to be the Director of Ordnance. Similarly, Lieutenant General Sir George Richardson, the GOC, Colonel G. W. Hacket Pain, the Chief Staff Officer, and Captain Wilfrid Spender, the Assistant Quartermaster General, brought appropriate command and staff experience with them. Richardson was eminently qualified to hold the position of GOC having gained considerable combat experience on the North West Frontier of India and in China; between 1904 and 1908 he had commanded the Poona Division and thus had experience of commanding a large military formation. Indeed, it seems that he was recommended for this position by Field Marshal Lord Roberts, a keen supporter of Ulster.[19] Colonel G. W. Hacket Pain, the Chief Staff Officer, was certainly well qualified to hold his position having considerable combat experience in both the Sudan and South Africa and having held the post of assistant adjutant general in the Egyptian Army in 1897.[20] Spender, was one of the relatively few officers of the British army to hold the coveted 'psc' distinction after his name in the *Army List*, denoting that he had been selected for and passed through the Staff College course. This was no mean feat, especially given the tough competition among Royal Artillery officers for the small number of Staff College places allocated to this corps. However, Spender did not really live up to these high expectations; entering the Great War as a captain he ended it as a lieutenant colonel, slow progress in a war where promotion was unusually fast. This should not distract us from the fact that Spender was perfectly competent to carry out the duties entrusted to him at UVF HQ, though as effectively Quartermaster General (QMG) and secretary to the Provisional Government and three of its subcommittees these duties were, if not onerous, certainly diverse and complicated.[21]

However, beyond this the picture is more confusing. McCammon was a brave man and good CO; he achieved the lieutenant colonelcy of the 5th Royal Irish Rifles at the age of 38, young for an SR unit, and was killed in action in April 1917 while commanding the 2nd Hampshire Regiment; the fact that he had been cross posted to a regular battalion demonstrated his sound military credentials.[22] But McCammon was not viewed as a satisfactory staff officer, when temporarily holding the position of Assistant Adjutant and Quartermaster General (AAQMG) in the 36th (Ulster) Division.[23] H. O. Davis, who had retired from the army as a mere lieutenant, seems to have been poorly qualified to hold the post of 'S[enior] O[fficer] for Instructors'; however he was praised for his work at the Fermanagh Regiment Camp of Instruction held from 2 to 8 November 1913 on the Earl of Erne's estate.[24] What skills Lloyd Campbell, who had never held any military rank, had to be appointed 'Director of Intelligence' are completely unclear and there is certainly no paper trail to suggest that he discharged these functions to any degree.[25] Indeed, the intelligence gained by the UVF seems to have been gained through local initiatives or happy coincidence rather than through anything organised at UVF HQ. Certainly in Co. Antrim detailed lists had been compiled providing information on the perceived political views and religions of police and postal officials.[26] However, given that senior military officers, including Brigadier General Count Gleichen, were friendly with leading Ulster Unionists, perhaps intelligence was very easy for the UVF to obtain.

UVF HQ was far from hard working. Despite the large number of written orders issued (the main role of which was to record UVF parades), many of these were issued on one day, as on 23 May 1914 when no less than five separate orders were issued. One of these orders noted that members of the HQ staff were most likely to be available from 11am to 1pm; presumably between a leisurely breakfast and lengthy luncheon.[27] The role of UVF HQ in appointing local officers remains unclear. Captain Hon. Arthur O'Neill MP had clearly been leading a unit in the Co. Antrim UVF long before 10 October 1913 when Lieutenant General Sir George Richardson approved his appointment. Indeed, the Co. Antrim committee had elected him as commander of the North Antrim Regiment in early September 1913.[28] This was also the case for A. P. Jenkins, the owner of a linen mill, who had formed a UVF battalion in Lisburn in early 1913 and who was confirmed in command of the 1st South Antrim Regiment on 17 October 1913.[29] Thus it seems that UVF HQ merely confirmed in office those who had already established themselves as local Unionist leaders.

Clearly there was an obvious conflict between the establishment of an HQ, whose staff were effectively appointed by Sir Edward Carson, and the desire to have a 'democratic' element to officer and NCO selection in the UVF. In theory, if not always in practice, men were to be enrolled in squads of 12, which would each elect their squad leader; two squads were to form a section with the men again electing their section leader, two sections were to form a half company, again electing a half company commander.[30] Repington suggested that the system extended to the higher ranks of the UVF. He noted that company commanders were elected by the section leaders and they would then elect the CO of their battalion, who would be appointed subject to the approval of UVF HQ. Commanding officers might, or might not, be given the power to appoint their own second in commands and adjutants.[31] This system of election was reminiscent of the manner in which Rifle Volunteer units in Great Britain had initially elected their officers, although Ian Beckett and Hugh Cunningham note that this practice largely faded away in the 1860s and early 1870s and had ceased entirely by the mid-1880s.[32] It was also a forerunner of the practice in the Local Defence Volunteers of 1940 when some early units did elect their own officers.[33]

It is unclear why the UVF adopted their own system of ranks, rather than using British army practice. It may have been to provide flexibility over the employment of retired officers. However, this rank system was not uniformly popular and in February 1914 Colonel Hacket Pain reprimanded some units, 'It having come to the notice of Headquarters that in certain cases Army titles are being used in units of the Volunteer Force, it is notified for the information of all concerned that the following designations of Rank shall be strictly adhered to:- Divisional, Regimental, Battalion, Company, Half-Company, and Section Commanders and Squad Leader, Second in Command, Adjutant, Quarter-master, Sergeant-Major and Quarter-Master Sergeant'.[34] To add further confusion to UVF ranks and structures, the commander of

Co. Antrim suggested that, ideally, companies were to consist of a commander and two subcommanders (officers), four section leaders (NCOs) and 96 men and squad leaders. However, the company structure and numbers could be altered to meet local circumstances.[35]

In one of the earliest Loyalist units, the Enniskillen Horse, William Copeland Trimble suggested that democracy was sometimes taken to extreme lengths, recording pompously but apparently truthfully, 'No local military gentleman would undertake the command; and sitting in the saddle at Castlecoole gate, troop by troop the men themselves elected Mr. Trimble as Commander'.[36] However, not all battalion COs implemented the democratic system outlined by UVF HQ. E. C. Herdman, who seems to have assumed command of the Sion Mills volunteers on the basis that he was part-owner of the extensive linen mills in the town, an officer in the North Irish Horse and chairman of the North Tyrone Unionist Association, wrote to his sectional leaders stating that they should simply appoint 'smart young men' as their squad leaders.[37] In the Tyrone Regiment, UVF personnel were informed that instructors (i.e. men with some military experience) should not be elected as section commanders. They could be elected as company commanders but it was felt that they would be most valuable as colour sergeants. This attitude may also have reflected a certain degree of snobbery in the UVF as most former soldiers were employed in low-status jobs, whereas there seems to have been a sense that UVF officers, if not gentlemen, should at least be middle class.[38]

If unwilling to replace local officers, UVF HQ does seem to have been quite happy to replace local structures. Early UVF units appear to have been formed from Unionist Clubs, Orange Lodges or within workplaces. However, soon after his appointment, Lieutenant General Sir George Richardson instituted a British regimental-style organisation. This certainly seems to have led to problems in the Belfast shipyards as units were initially recruited from the areas where the men worked rather than lived.[39] The difficulties inherent in this system are clear in the case of Derry City, for which the membership lists survive: if men moved to another part of the city they also moved battalion, as in the case of William Allison who was originally in 'E' Company, 2nd Battalion when living at 16 Belview Avenue but transferred to 'D' Company, 3rd Battalion when he moved to 55 Argyle Street.[40] This did little to maintain either unit cohesion or *esprit de corps*. From quite an early stage reserve units were set up, further undermining the regimental system, for example in the 1st (North) Tyrone Regiment it was stated, 'A Reserve

Force will be formed for those who, from age or similar disability, cannot join the Regular Force; but it is most advisable that, if possible, all should have a course of Drill and Musketry, without which no Volunteer is efficient'.[41] Ultimately UVF members were able to qualify their own service by joining Special Service Force units, which were to be mobilised rapidly; ordinary battalions, which would be mobilised in the event of serious trouble for use in their own districts or further afield at their COs insistence; or in a reserve force, used only for home defence.

UVF HQ, hampered by a lack of finance, which will be discussed in chapter 5, was unable to rectify some of the glaring inadequacies within the force. While cavalry remained vital for reconnaissance, if not shock action, the UVF had pitifully few cavalry units to call on. The Enniskillen Horse was the only full cavalry regiment in the UVF and there appear to have been plans to move it to Belfast in the event of hostilities. Otherwise there were only a few cavalry detachments available in Aghadowey, Newtowncunningham, South Down and Ballymena.[42] Brigadier General Count Gleichen, the GOC of British troops in Belfast district did believe that, in the event of civil war, this would be rectified to some degree as the North Irish Horse, an SR unit, would go over to the UVF. He also believed that the UVF would have access to a few aeroplanes for reconnaissance purposes.[43] Perhaps conscious of the cavalry deficiency, Major General Adair, belatedly in May 1914, tried to organise cyclist units in the Antrim UVF Regiments.[44] It is strange that cyclist units were not proposed by UVF HQ, especially given their prominence in the TF.

There is little evidence that the UVF possessed any artillery pieces, although Brigadier General Count Gleichen, the commander of British troops in Ulster, believed that there were, 'a few isolated field guns, but no organised field artillery'.[45] It seems likely that, in the event of trouble, attempts would have been made to seize artillery from Royal Artillery units based in Ulster.[46] Other aspects of UVF HQ organisation received more praise. The communications section was seen to be well organised, especially the Signalling and Dispatch Corps, as was the medical establishment. The latter was, of course, seen largely as the domain of women, Gleichen stating, 'Very large numbers of ladies + women of all sorts have been trained, ambulance classes forming the chief amusement + occupation of the feminine population for the last six months'.[47]

Central HQ was content to leave the key issue of logistics to local units. The UVF Transport Board merely suggested that each UVF company should equip itself with two first line transport carts – one for ammunition, the other for tools – with two heavier wagons as second line transport, and conscientious company commanders appear to have followed this advice.[48] While Ian Maxwell, in his unfortunately unpublished Ph.D. thesis, accepted Wilfrid Spender's account that the UVF motor car corps was very well organised, this was far from the case. Shortly before the Larne gunrunning General Adair wrote to one of his regimental commanders, 'You must try and get enough transport for the 1000 rifles I have allocated to the N[orth]. Ant[rim]. Reg[imen]t. ... We are lamentable [sic] short in Co. Antrim + have not half the transport we want'.[49]

Thus the extent to which UVF HQ exercised centralised control over the UVF as a whole is debatable. Indeed, David Harrell, a former Under Secretary at Dublin Castle, was convinced in January 1914 that, 'things have now gone too far for the Covenanters to sit quiet, even if Carson and other leaders were to advise them to lay down their arms. The rank and file would not tamely fling their bandoliers into the cupboard'.[50] The major problem for the UVF was that it was responsible to the Ulster Provisional Government, a body which met infrequently and briefly. It seems likely that this raised questions about the legitimacy of UVF HQ and that, in the event of trouble erupting, UVF members would have looked to established local Unionist leaders, rather than Belfast, for orders.

There was a large degree of local autonomy given to UVF units. Each county was to be in charge of a committee which was to elect five representatives to HQ. Counties were to be subdivided into divisions, districts and localities by their county committee.[51] Michael Foy has noted, 'The scheme of organisation which the county committees were to implement was one that was more congenial to a party political agent than to a professional soldier. It was based on the existing electoral system ... When later in 1913 a professional Headquarters staff of the UVF was recruited the original scheme was to be scrapped and replaced by one familiar to a British army officer'.[52] Foy's analysis reflects the curious situation, outlined above, that while the UVF was supposedly established in January 1913, it did not have a commander in chief or headquarters staff until September 1913. Indeed, it seems that for much of the 1913 period and, in certain cases, well into 1914, the UVF in some rural areas was little more than the Unionist Clubs by any other name. This was reflected by Carson in August 1913 when in a printed circular letter to 'Fellow Covenanters' he praised the members of the Unionist Clubs who had already joined the UVF but then went on:

Because I know that the nearer the crisis approaches the more men will desire to combine together for mutual encouragement and help, I sincerely trust and expect that those who are now eligible and have not enrolled will without loss of time join the unit most convenient for administrative purposes.

As leader, my responsibility compels me to point to the danger of ANYONE holding aloof at this juncture, when it is necessary to perfect final arrangements.

My request is that ALL our men should join the Ulster Volunteers. Even old men can help to guard their property, their hearths, and homes, and thus release the younger and more active for whatever work may be necessary.'[53]

Carson's demand did not have the desired effect in many areas. In January 1914 it was noted that the UVF unit in Aughnacloy had only been formed for five weeks.[54]

However, Foy neglects to mention that the county committee system, established by the UVF, was not entirely alien to British army officers. In its essentials the UVF county committees were not dissimilar to the TF's county associations, a point not lost on *The Times* military correspondent.[55] As Ian Beckett notes, of the TF's county associations, these were designed to, 'forge links between the army and society through a distinctive elective element provided by borough and county councils although they would also incorporate traditional county military elites with lords lieutenant, who would retain the right of nomination to first territorial commissions, normally becoming association presidents'.[56] Certainly, in the case of the Co. Down UVF committee one sees a similar composition, with its membership of two deputy lieutenants of the county, Captain Holt Waring and Captain Roger Hall, two peers, Lord Dunleath and Viscount Bangor (who both, incidentally, had military experience) and seven other members there as political representatives, either in the form of local councillors, like S. H. Hall-Thompson, or as representatives of the Orange Order or Unionist Clubs, as in the case of Dr Knight.[57] The incorporation of existing county military elites was even more marked in Co. Londonderry, where seven of the 12 members of the county committee were former army officers.[58]

Why exactly the UVF was formed around these county associations is unclear. As suggested above, it may have been the case that the Ulster Unionist leadership wanted to imitate existing British practice in their amateur military formations. Repington suggested that the establishment of county committees both emphasised the democratic nature of the UVF and meant that if UVF HQ in Belfast was broken up by the government nothing would be found, 'except a few men and unimportant papers'.[59] Interestingly, critics of the TF in Great Britain saw the establishment of the county associations as a centralising, not decentralising influence, which removed power from individual unit commanders.[60] That the converse seems to have been the case in the UVF is another reflection of the weak authority exercised by UVF HQ over the force.

Other reasons, for the formation of these county committees, can be meaningfully posited. The county structure meant that the UVF, at least on paper, existed throughout Ulster; an issue surely of some concern when emphasising the involvement of the widely dispersed Unionists of Cavan, Donegal and Monaghan in Unionist opposition to Home Rule. The county committees also provided suitable posts for civilian political leaders who, in many cases, did not command UVF units. In other words it enabled UVF HQ, at least to some degree, to place experienced officers in command of units without upsetting local political sensitivities. Practically, county committees were given limited roles in raising funds and procuring arms for the UVF.

Only the minute book of the Co. Down committee survives demonstrating the relatively minor roles which these bodies actually fulfilled and the infrequency of their meetings. By October 1914 the committee had raised a mere £172 19s 5d and the only appointment which it had made was that of former Regimental Sergeant Major Fridlington as the county drill instructor and even this had been indirect as a military subcommittee actually interviewed Fridlington. Indeed, one gets the distinct impression that the county committees spent most of their time demanding more arms, equipment and finance from HQ. The extent to which the county committees were left out of the decision-making process is shown by the fact that the Co. Down committee apparently had no function in appointing UVF unit commanders and in April 1914 its secretary was writing to HQ to enquire about pay for volunteers when they were mobilised, separation allowances and rations.[61] Only in June 1914 was it made clear that counties, rather than HQ, would be responsible for feeding UVF members if mobilised and serving in their own county. This was a heavy burden for shaky county finances as it was estimated that emergency rations of tinned meat, biscuit and tea for 1,000 men would cost about £53 per day.[62]

However, this strict county organisation of the UVF could lead to problems. Rev. C. Mannerstack from Kells in Co. Monaghan wrote to

Colonel Madden in May 1914 demonstrating some of these. He noted that he had been drilling 23 men for some time and that Captain Audley Pratt of Cabra in Co. Cavan had offered to help them but only if Madden gave his permission. Mannerstack also complained that the UVF county instructor for Monaghan had never visited his unit and clearly wanted his men to be taken into the Ballyboy Company of the Cavan Regiment.[63] Thus cumbersome county structures could stand in the way of local initiative and could also serve to act against existing inter-county co-operation.

Discipline was a difficult issue for UVF HQ or battalion commanders to enforce. The UVF was, after all, an unpaid, part-time force, so the sanctions used in the regular army were of little use. The threat of extra duty or drills was hardly effective in a force where a man could resign simply by informing his CO in writing.[64] It is also unclear how this situation would have changed in the event of hostilities as no one had been designated as adjutant general to the UVF and no disciplinary code appears to have been devised.

Surprisingly, given the political tensions in Ulster during the 1912–14 period, especially after the formation of INV units in late 1913, there are very few examples of UVF discipline threatening to break down in the sense that UVF members would attack Catholics in Ulster. Rival Unionist and Nationalist crowds were involved in a stand off in Kilrea on 11 July 1914 during which revolver shots were fired and Unionists cried 'Bring out the rifles'. However, the local RIC, aided by some prominent local Unionists, succeeded in defusing the situation.[65] UVF members in Ballycastle refused to retaliate when one of their members, Samuel Hutchinson, was attacked by a group of Nationalist Volunteers on 13 July 1914.[66]

UVF officers did have some disciplinary measures at their disposal. Obviously in situations where a UVF officer and other rank were also employer and employee, financial penalties were possible, though no direct evidence of these being used has been found. Officers could dismiss men from the UVF, although given the high levels of absenteeism, this was probably not a very effective way of maintaining discipline.[67] At least in Co. Antrim the decision to dismiss a UVF member rested with the divisional commander.[68] In 'J' Company of the 4th (Dungannon) Battalion, Tyrone Regiment, it is clear that at least 30 members of this unit received what the Battalion's CO Lord Northland termed 'stinker letters'. These predicted a bleak prospect for those who were not regularly attending drill, threatening:

On 31st March, 1914, any enrolled man who is not an efficient Volunteer in either the Active or Reserve Branches of the UVF will be struck off the strength of the Battalion.

It must be borne in mind that, should times of hardship and distress arrive, those who do not take the trouble to make themselves efficient will be left to shift for themselves.

Except under special circumstances there will be no Recruits' Classes after the month of January, 1914, so that those who do not start now will not have a chance of doing so again.[69]

Northland's letters seem to have produced some response. While some members of the battalion clearly stated that business or family commitments or ill-health meant that they could not continue as members of the UVF at least 14 of these 30 undertook to resume drill.[70] Dismissal was similarly threatened to members of the Co. Antrim Regiments who had not attended a sufficient number of drills by 1 June 1914. A pencilled note on a circular letter suggests that up to 1,100 men in the 1st North Antrim Regiment and 400 in the 2nd North Antrim Regiment were threatened with dismissal for this reason.[71] Certainly in 'A' Company, 2nd North Antrim Regiment, one man was dismissed 'owing to bad conduct' and 19 other men struck off for not attending any drills.[72] Perhaps the most effective disciplinary measure available was the threat of 'community sanction', which David French believes was effective in TF units. Certainly Percy Crozier attempted to mobilise this: when he dismissed a man from his Special Service Force in the West Belfast Regiment he made a point of calling at the man's house to retrieve his uniform; this led to men being ridiculed by their wives and children.[73]

There were also a number of incentives available for UVF personnel. A variety of certificates in drill, musketry and machine gun use were distributed, often at impressive ceremonies attended by senior UVF officers. Originally these seem to have been produced as local initiatives but proficiency certificates were introduced for all UVF units in November 1913.[74] UVF badges were only issued to men who were thought trustworthy, if not well drilled, thus there was some concern when eight badges were stolen from the office of a battalion in Co. Down.[75] Certainly officers could refuse to issue badges to men who they felt did not deserve them.[76] In November 1913 HQ stated, 'It has been decided that the Badge, in addition to being worn on Parade, should be worn on all occasions, it should therefore be thoroughly impressed on all members of the Volunteer Force, that are in a position to do so, that the Badge should be worn always'.[77]

One of the major incentives at the disposal of UVF officers related to the issuing of rifles and it was emphasised, even after the Larne gunrunning, that these should only be given out, 'to men who, in the opinion of their Battalion Commanders, are fitted in all ways to be entrusted with them'.[78] These seem to have been regarded as prized possessions in many UVF units, as of course they were later to be in the Home Guard. Certainly it was made clear that one of the major punishments which could be inflicted on a volunteer was the confiscation of his rifle.[79]

In the absence of a proper higher command structure, pitifully few contingency plans were put together for the UVF. Lieutenant Colonel T. V. P. McCammon and Colonel G. H. Hacket Pain did provide some concrete planning. Perhaps the most realistic contingency planning was provided by McCammon in March 1914 when he sent a circular to all UVF senior officers stating, 'Information has been received that the early arrest of the Leaders is probable. As this may effect yourself, please take immediate steps to warn your Second-in-Command, Adjutant, or other Officer, whom you desire should act for you in such an unfortunate event, to do so, and you must arrange means whereby any communications from Headquarters delivered at your address, are at once taken to him'.[80] There were fears at HQ that during the mass Orange Order parades being held on 13 July 1914, Nationalists would attempt to seize UVF arms.[81] Similarly, on the passing of the third reading of the Home Rule Bill in the House of Commons, McCammon authorised UVF divisional and regimental commanders to take whatever measures they felt necessary to deal with 'Nationalist rowdyism', which might manifest itself through disloyal processions, bonfires or other provocative actions.[82]

Hacket Pain brought in some emergency planning in May 1914 stating, 'It appears that the formation in each Regiment of "marching Battalions" (*bataillon de marche* [sic]) should now be undertaken, and Divisional, Regimental, and Battalion Commanders are requested to consider this proposal with the object of organising the collecting of armed men in their Commands into as many marching Battalions as can be formed, prepared to move, in a great emergency, where required'.[83] However, the formation of these marching battalions was no easy matter and the rapid unravelling of this piece of contingency planning serves to show the problems that UVF HQ had in enforcing their wishes. Captain Hon. Arthur O'Neill, commanding the North Antrim Regiment, utterly rejected this scheme stating:

Command, control and military efficiency 91

In accordance with your desire that the North Antrim Regiment should furnish some 1100 men for service away from their own districts (*Batallion de marche*). I have the honour to draw your attention to the following facts which make it impossible for this regiment to supply anything approaching this number:-

(1) The Regimental District is situated at a very much greater distance from Belfast (the probable centre of any operations) than either of the other [Co. Antrim] Regiments.

(2) There are more nationalists – and proportionately less unionists and Ulster Volunteers than in any other part of the County.

(3) The Regimental area is about twice as large as either the central or South [Antrim Regiments] and contains only two Battalions as against three in each of the other [Co. Antrim] Regiments.

I informed the commander of 2nd Batt[alio]n. [North Antrim Regiment] that he should endeavour to furnish 100 men, but he is evidently not of this opinion.[84]

The nature of the force did, of course, lead to other problems over contingency planning. This was rather belatedly recognised in May 1914 when HQ recommended, 'In selecting the required number of Volunteers to be assembled for any Particular Service, it is considered specially desirable that if any Operation is about to be undertaken, which is likely to extend into the following day, men employed in Mills, Factories, etc., in which a large number of female hands are working, should not be warned for such Assembly. The object of this is to prevent the withdrawal of men by whose absence a large number of women might be temporarily stopped working, and consequently crowd the Streets, and thereby might be the cause of disturbances under certain conditions'.[85]

More secretive contingency planning did take place. At a meeting in London in December 1913, between the Ulster Unionist leadership and UVF staff, there was a curious mix of indecision and prevarication. If arms were to be seized by the government the view was taken that organised resistance should take place but with 'No shooting'. Action was to be considered later if it became clear that large numbers of troops or police were to be drafted into Ulster.[86] As late as April 1914 it was still unclear what local UVF units could expect to receive from UVF HQ in Belfast in the event of civil war.[87] It seems that a series of more detailed contingency plans were drawn up by Captain Wilfrid Spender in early 1914, although it is unclear the extent to which these were discussed, much less approved.[88] The 'Headquarters Defence Scheme' put its emphasis on maintaining communications and rapidly concentrating

UVF units in an emergency. In the scenario which it suggested, the role of the UVF was to be as a police rather than a military force:

> The Leaders have decided to establish the Provisional Government, no Military opposition has been met with, and no additional Forces, Military or Constabulary have been drafted in. It will be necessary for the Provisional Government to assert its authority from the first, and its authority will depend on the Ulster Volunteer Force behind it. The first essential will be to maintain order throughout Ulster, as far as this is possible, and to give no excuse for the introduction of outside Forces. The Provisional Government will probably have to assert itself, by showing that it is able to take over control of various Government, Local Government, and Civil Departments, it may also have to impose its will on private companies and individuals, who will be prepared to recognise *Force Majeure*, but who will not recognize its authority otherwise.[89]

In this event it was hoped that local forces would be able to maintain order in their districts. However, it was hoped that in 'certain counties', and certainly in Belfast, a general reserve of the UVF could be formed which could, 'put down at once any serious disturbance in any part of Ulster which the Local Forces are unable to deal with themselves'.[90]

Another plan, 'Contingency No.1', suggests that by early 1914 some key issues had not been (and perhaps never were) settled. For example, this document raised the issue over what should be done with the RIC in the event of the Provisional Government being declared. Should they be disarmed throughout Ulster, disarmed only in districts where this could easily be accomplished or permitted to carry on their duties as long as they did not act against the Provisional Government?[91] Further contingency plans were prepared to deal with railway policy, police reinforcements and the attempted seizure of UVF arms. Strangely these read as discussion documents and there is no evidence to suggest that UVF HQ had definitively decided many key issues by mid-1914. As an example, one plan stated, 'It might be advisable to issue instructions now (? Secret instructions to the Railway UVF, or instructions to Officers Commanding Counties bordering the Southern Railways of Ulster, that they are authorized to hold up trains bringing in "police in Force" from the South?)'.[92]

Indeed, these various plans show that UVF HQ was somewhat unwilling to contemplate where its actions might lead. Local commanders must have been terribly confused by advice such as, 'If a search for Arms is instituted, our policy is quite clear. Should it be merely a search of one or two houses, those who are living in those Houses, should offer as much resistance as possible, short of taking life, before parting with their weapons. If such a house to house search is instituted on a general scale, Headquarters will certainly order the whole of the UVF to mobilise, preparatory to offering forcible and combined resistance'.[93] There was also a suggestion that unarmed UVF members would be able to overpower the RIC and that armed UVF members should only be used in this role if the police produced arms first.[94] It was not until July 1914 that the refugee question was being properly addressed, with priority given to the wives and families of UVF members, 'whose protection would set free the men to fight where required'.[95] In this planned evacuation there seems to have been particular concern about Unionists in South Down.[96] Interestingly the contingency which was not planned for was the one that was becoming increasingly likely by early 1914, namely how would the UVF react to an advance of British troops from Southern Ireland into Ulster combined with the landing of a Royal Marine Brigade on the shores of Belfast Lough? This was probably an attempt to disguise the divisions within the UVF leadership over how they should react to firm action by Crown forces. James Craig thought that the UVF should risk all in one 'stand up fight' with crown forces, while Fred Crawford felt that guerrilla warfare was the obvious response.[97]

It seems that some local units rose to the challenges of contingency planning much better than UVF HQ. The Central Antrim Regiment, for example, had noted that UVF members were over-awed by Nationalists in Cushendun and Cushendall and plans were made to send two companies from Ballymena to these areas in the event of the Provisional Government being established.[98] As the crisis worsened efforts were also being made by the North Antrim Regiment to estimate how many INV members there were in their area and how many UVF personnel would be required to keep them in check in the event of trouble.[99] However, by July 1914 a major concern was how the North and South Antrim Regiments would prevent Nationalists crossing the River Bann into Co. Londonderry.[100] Other units made it clear that they could do little more than garrison their own areas in the event of hostilities. Colonel H. T. Lyle in Co. Londonderry stated, 'I would like you to clearly understand that I doubt whether we could spare any men from here to go elsewhere'.[101] By contrast the leaders of the tiny Co. Monaghan Regiment took a highly optimistic view of what they would be able to achieve in the event of civil war and seem to have been considering sending some of their men into Southern Ireland, to protect Protestants there.[102]

How the UVF would have responded had Home Rule been introduced must be left open to some conjecture. One RIC District Inspector who served in Lisnaskea reflected the confusion of contemporaries, 'I had heard of the Ulster Volunteers in the North, but before going there knew nothing about them. Indeed I knew little about them when I left, as I could not have told whether they meant business or not'.[103] Sharing this confusion, Lilian Spender noted in late June 1914 that her husband, 'had a very long talk with Capt.[ain] Craig the other day, so now he knows as much as the Unionist party knows (and a good deal more than some of them) but that is not saying very much, except that next month will probably see decisive action of some sort'.[104]

Gerald Madden, a leading figure in the Co. Monaghan Regiment, made his views quite clear, stating, 'I hope everything is being done to make the Monaghan Volunteers efficient, remember our whole credit and honour is at stake in this Movement, we said we would fight and I do hope that there will be no climb down in Belfast or by the English Unionist Party'.[105] By contrast, Lord Dunleath, a senior figure in the Co. Down UVF stated:

> Many of us are undoubtedly willing, if necessary to risk our lives in defence of what we believe to be our rights and liberties, but I venture to think that an encounter with the armed forces of the Crown would inflict a serious injury upon our cause, and that every possible effort should be made to avoid the possibility of any calamity of this character. Moreover I do not believe that our men are prepared to go into action against any part of His Majesty's Forces, and we (their leaders) should not consider ourselves justified in calling upon them to do so.
>
> As I said just now, many of us are prepared to risk a great deal for our cause, but even our Covenant does not compel us to run our heads against a wall.[106]

However, it does seem likely that if Home Rule had been declared, the Unionist leadership would have been firmly committed to a military response. The shape that this would have taken would have depended on the actions of local leaders and would have been subject to regional variations in training, equipment and arms.[107]

Hew Strachan, reflecting on the officers available to the UVF, has stated that, 'The army's close link with the Ulster Volunteers was confirmed by the fact that 62 per cent of the latter's divisional, regimental, and battalion commands were held by former officers'.[108] However, this figure is rather misleading regarding the professional officer corps available to the UVF as it disguises problems of elderly and incompetent officers, the widespread problem of dual command which existed in the force and the fact that many officers, especially those of amateur units, saw no contradiction between retaining their commissions in their own units (often based in Great Britain) and offering their services to the UVF.

Overall, 132 serving or former officers, including cadet members of OTC units, have been positively identified as being involved as officers in the UVF (see Table 3.1). The composition of the officer corps of the UVF is discussed in more detail in chapter 2 and the HQ staff above. However, in terms of command and control it is worth making a few points regarding officers at the local level in terms of the type of experience these officers had gained, their distribution throughout the UVF and the practice of dual appointments which was prevalent in the UVF.

Table 3.1 The former or current rank of British army officers involved in the UVF

Current or retired rank	Number
Lieutenant General	1
Major General	3
Colonel	15
Lieutenant Colonel	7
Major	29
Captain	48
Lieutenant	19
Second Lieutenant	2
OTC cadet	8
TOTAL	132

Source: This table has been compiled using a wide variety of source material, principally, PRONI, D.1498/7, Richardson papers, 'Nominal Roll of Officers recently serving with UVF who have been recalled to Army Service', MSS Mottistone 22/f.171, Mottistone papers, Nuffield College, Oxford, HQ Irish Command report on Ulster Volunteer Force, c. September 1913, PRONI, D.1507/A/10/10, Carson papers, 'Return of Officers on Reserve or Special Reserve serving as Commanders + Staff officers with the Ulster Volunteer Force', c. June 1914, TNA, CO904/27/2/II, printed pamphlet, `Ulster Volunteer Force, Belfast Division, Inspection by Sir Edward Carson and the General Officer Commanding UVF in the Agricultural Showgrounds, Balmoral, 27/9/13, PRONI, D.1327/4/12, UUC papers, 'Headquarters Staff Enrolment Forms', TNA, WO141/26, returns of officers involved in drilling civilians in Ulster, 1912—14, Crozier, *Impressions and Recollections*, pp. 142—58 and Trimble, *History of Enniskillen*, pp. 1070-2.

The experience of officers at the local level ranged widely. One major problem was that many of the gentry who assumed command of battalions in a feudal manner had little military experience. For example, Viscounts Acheson and Northland, who each commanded battalions of the Tyrone Regiment, had retired from the army as mere lieutenants.[109] Similarly, of these officers at least 14 had gained experience only in the SR and nine in the TF. Both of these forces were part-time in nature and thus the officer training provided in them was minimal, with promotion based on little more than seniority. It is noticeable how few OTC cadets were involved in the UVF, given that The Queen's University of Belfast contingent had something over 200 members in 1914. It may be that these cadets simply enlisted in the ranks of the 6th South Belfast Regiment which recruited in the university area of the city.[110]

The distribution of experienced officers throughout the UVF was also problematic. A good example of this is in the roles taken by the three major generals who served in the force. Major General Sir William Adair was the divisional commander of all UVF units in Co. Antrim and the county secretary for Antrim, while Major General C. H. Powell held the divisional command of Co. Down.[111] By contrast Major General W. E. Montgomery was unwilling or unable to do anything more than command the Greyabbey Company of the UVF.[112] This disparity is particularly clear in Derry City where the senior military officer available to the three battalion strong force was Thomas Ernest Hastings, a 19-year-old cadet in the Edinburgh University OTC.[113] In Belfast, the situation was little better with a heavy reliance on the small number of officers secured by the British League for the Support of Ulster and the Union, obtained to command units there. In rural regiments there was a wide range of experience within regimental and battalion commands. This is clear in the case of Co. Londonderry. In the North Derry Regiment, the 1st (Faughan Valley) Battalion was commanded by Major Ross Smyth, the 2nd (Roe Valley) by J. C. B. Proctor and the 3rd (Bann) by Captain Gausson. In the South Derry Regiment the 1st (Aghadowey, Garvagh and Kilrea) Battalion was commanded by C. E. Stronge, D.L. and the 2nd (Moneymore, Magherafelt, Maghera and Bellaghy) by Major Lennox Cunningham.[114]

The example of T. E. Hastings, who as an undergraduate at the University of Edinburgh could only have served in the UVF during university vacations, raises another problem which the UVF suffered from, namely the distinctly temporary commitment which some officers showed to it. W. C. Trimble seems to have secured the services of three

English Yeomanry officers to command elements of the Enniskillen Horse but as these officers retained their commissions in the Leicester, York [sic] and East Kent Yeomanry Regiments and their presence at parades was not reported by the RIC we have to question how frequently they were actually involved in training this UVF unit.[115]

It is also worth considering the dual appointments which seem to have been widespread in the UVF. The most outrageous example of this is Lord Castlereagh, who seems to have seen no contradiction between commanding the Mountstewart estate contingent, Newtownards Battalion and entire North Belfast Regiment, all while a Member of Parliament who rarely seems to have been in Ulster.[116] Indeed, even when the 2nd North Down Regiment attended a Camp of Instruction at Mountstewart in July 1914, Castlereagh does not seem to have been present.[117] However, other examples abounded and one wonders how Major Lennox Cunningham would have reconciled his roles as chairman of the Co. Londonderry committee, commander of the South Derry Regiment and commander of the 2nd South Derry Regiment had hostilities broken out.[118]

Some of those instructing UVF units faced intimidation in this role. In January 1914 Major Lord Farnham, commander of a battalion in the Cavan Regiment, narrowly avoided being decapitated by wire stretched across the road when returning in an open- topped car from a UVF drill.[119] In Dungannon William McMenemy was assaulted by two men in April 1914, the local press assuming that this was due to his role as a drill instructor in the local UVF.[120] UVF members in other areas, where Unionists were a minority of the population, were obviously concerned about similar action as Gerald Madden advised his brother to take care when returning home from drills in Co. Monaghan, suggesting that he should always be accompanied by some trusted men.[121]

Of course many UVF battalions were commanded by men with no military experience whatsoever. This is most noticeable in Belfast where at a parade of all 14 battalions of Belfast City UVF at the Balmoral Show grounds in September 1913, nine were commanded by men with no military rank.[122] Some of these men seem to have held their rank on the basis of their position as prominent businessmen, this certainly seems to be the case with George Clark Junior, heir to a part share of Workman and Clark's shipyard, and H. V. Coates, owner of a large engineering firm in the city. Elsewhere in Ulster, the role of prominent businessmen was similarly obvious, for example in the case of A. P. Jenkins who commanded the Lisburn battalion and was a linen manufacturer in the town.[123] Elsewhere Ulster's small professional class was tapped, as in the case of Dr William Gibson, a medical doctor, who commanded the 3rd East Belfast Regiment and Charles Faussett Falls, a solicitor, who commanded the 1st Fermanagh Regiment.[124] Of course many of these civilians were to prove to be excellent COs in the UVF and a number, as examined in chapter 6, went on to gain commissions and serve with distinction in the 36th (Ulster) Division. However, some civilians sought UVF commands for purely political reasons as in the case of Stewart Blacker Quinn, an accountant, who seems to have taken command of the 2nd West Belfast Regiment on the basis that this would aid his parliamentary ambitions for this seat, despite earlier having confessed his lack of both military experience and sufficient free time to command a UVF unit.[125]

Indeed, the problems of officering the West Belfast Regiment, a unit formed in an area where few retired army officers or middle-class professionals lived, were manifest. A UVF internal memorandum noted, 'Graham ... has the makings of a very good commander and stands no nonsense with the men and knows them well. S. E. Thompson we tried as Adjutant 2nd Batt.[alion] but he didn't do at all. They kicked up an awful dust over it, and although he runs the Unionist Club he never goes down with the UVF There is a man called Speirs in the 2nd Batt.[alion] who was very anxious to get command of a Batt.[alion] but he was most injuditions [sic], among other things he deliberately put a damper on recruiting at the start'.[126]

As the UVF took shape, more professional officers, many obtained through the British League for the Support of Ulster and the Union, were sent to command UVF units, especially in Belfast. The most famous example of this is probably in the case of F. P. Crozier, the author of a number of books detailing his wide military experiences, who rose to be a brigadier general during the Great War. Crozier was given the post of commander of the Special Service Force of the West Belfast Regiment. In his memoirs Crozier, not surprisingly, suggests that this was a key appointment, commanding the formation which often acted as guards to Sir Edward Carson and James Craig.[127] However, it is noticeable that Crozier's importance within the UVF seems to have been rather less important than he suggested. His command of a mere company when he was a former captain looks far from impressive, though this may be explained by the necessity to appease political interests within West Belfast Unionism by enabling civilians to continue as battalion commanders, rather than any slight against Crozier's professionalism.

Conversely, Lilian Spender noticed him in little more than passing when viewing a West Belfast Regiment parade.[128] Similarly, Crozier appears to have been recommissioned into the British army on the basis of service in the Canadian Militia, with Lieutenant General Sir George Richardson omitting him from a list of officers he specifically wanted for the 36th (Ulster) Division.[129] Other professional soldiers obtained for the UVF were given more important commands, for example Major Tempest Stone was appointed CO of the South Belfast Regiment in April 1914.[130] However, Crozier was scathing in his criticisms of other officers secured by the British League for the Support of Ulster and the Union stating:

> I was offered a room in an office, where a Colonel [J. H.] Patterson was at work with Captain C. St. A. Wake, who acted as his adjutant, but declined to mix myself up with red tape and paper transactions, as I had been told my men were required for active work, and might be called upon to do things.
>
> Similarly, I declined to mix myself up with Major Stone and Captain Malone of the Royal Fusiliers, who were working out problems on paper in Colonel Couchman's office. I was my own clerk, sergeant-major, adjutant, quartermaster and commanding officer, all rolled into one.[131]

The competence of some of the former British army officers involved in the UVF can also be questioned on the basis of their Great War experience.[132] Many of those involved, Lieutenant General Richardson and Major General Adair for example, were simply seen as too old to rejoin the army. Major General C. H. Powell was considered perfectly competent to train the 36th (Ulster) Division when it was based in the UK but was considered too old to command it in action. Some proved to be utterly incompetent; the worst example being Brigadier General Couchman removed from his command of the 107th Brigade, 36th (Ulster) Division soon after it arrived in France as the GOC believed that it had been very poorly trained and officered, for which he held Couchman responsible. On the basis of this one cannot imagine that Couchman would have proved a satisfactory commander of the Belfast Division of the UVF if the force had seen action.[133] Captain A. F. Penny, 7th Royal Fusiliers, who had served for a brief period in the Belfast Division of the UVF, had to relinquish his commission in October 1914 as, while with his regiment and based in England, he had suffered from a complete mental breakdown, convinced that his fellow officers were threatening to kill him.[134]

By contrast, some UVF officers proved to be excellent battlefield commanders and gained rapid promotion. Colonel Oliver Nugent having commanded the Cavan Regiment of the UVF went on to command the 36th (Ulster) Division and ended the war as a lieutenant general. Similarly, Captain Ambrose Ricardo who had commanded the Tyrone Regiment ended the war as a brigadier general as did F. P. Crozier. Other officers who had served in the UVF, Captain Hon. Arthur O'Neill and Lieutenant Colonel T. V. P. McCammon being good examples, were killed in action on the Western Front, exhibiting the heroism and leadership skills which elements of the pre-war UVF could have relied upon.

The metric on which the training and military efficiency of the UVF can be measured is a difficult one. On an Irish basis, the Unionist press were keen to report UVF parades and training camps as highly successful affairs and often made flattering comparisons between the UVF and British army units. This highlights a fundamental problem in training UVF units, in that while their performance on parade was important for political reasons, learning complicated drill movements did little to prepare them for tactical operations. General Adair initially advised his units to neglect the former for the latter.[135] Internal UVF assessments are sparse. Colonel T. E. Hickman, the force's Inspector General seems to have done little to fulfil his duties and, in any case, none of his private papers survive. UVF orders certainly mentioned parades, but normally only so that units could be praised, for example complimenting the North Londonderry Regiment, 'It was a splendid Parade. The Regiment is fit for service, the material is excellent and well drilled, reflecting the greatest credit on Major Ross Smythe, and the Officers and men under his command'.[136] There were some rare exceptions to this. In the case of the City of Derry Regiment, where one assumes the situation was poor due to the lack of both military expertise and middle-class involvement in this unit, UVF orders noted, 'This Regiment has laboured under many disadvantages the want of Officers and a Staff was much felt, but this has now been remedied'.[137] Whereas in the 1st Donegal Regiment it was noted that, 'The Battalion suffers from a dearth of Instructors. The March Past and Parade movements were good, but the work in the Field shows a want of Instruction in Field work'.[138] An account of a field day carried out by the Enniskillen Horse in June 1914 noted ominously, 'Subsequent operations, involving an attack on a position, held by dismounted men, were not of a practical nature', suggesting either that training had been utterly substandard or that there were serious doctrinal differences on the *arme blanche* controversy between UVF HQ and the CO of their only full cavalry regiment.[139] There were also some highly optimistic comments emanating from HQ, such as those regarding the presentation of colours to the 3rd East Down Regiment, 'A Battalion which can carry out successfully a ceremony which requires discipline and steadiness will have no difficulty in picking up fieldwork'.[140]

On a wider, British basis, there was much public debate over how much training amateur forces required as the National Service League was pushing for a conscription scheme, involving one year's full-time service, whereas the requirement for TF training fell considerably short of this. Following the Haldane reforms of 1908 it appears that Territorial infantry unit members carried out a maximum of 60 parades in their first year, followed by 40 in subsequent years; the average parade was a one hour drill held one evening a week but the annual camp of up to two weeks could count for up to 28 parades, though few men were able to attend all 14 days of this camp. The Haldane scheme did, however, assume that units when mobilised in wartime would have six months' full-time training before being sent into combat.[141]

It seems that most UVF units carried out one evening's drill per week, with occasional parades. Camps of instruction were set up for UVF officers and NCOs from autumn 1913 and for entire UVF regiments from Easter 1914. Again there was wide variation depending on the availability of instructors, suitability of accommodation and the number of rifles available. John Sears, the intructor for Co. Fermanagh witnessed this in the 1st Fermanagh Regiment in August and September 1913, noting that drilling ranged from poor to exemplary and that it had already ceased in some areas.[142] By December 1913 the City of Derry Regiment was deemed to be carrying out only 'very elementary' work.[143] As late as February 1914 the commander of 'A' Company 2nd North Antrim Regiment admitted that out of his 73 'effectives', 'only a small proportion of them have had any musketry practice or would know anything about a rifle'.[144] As the crisis worsened there is some evidence that training became more intensive, at Crom Castle, Co. Fermanagh by early March 1914 drill was taking place on Tuesday and Saturdays and shooting on Thursdays.[145] It seems to have been early 1914 before training changed from drill to anything more advanced. At Kilroot in Fermanagh it was noted that a company attack, the first outdoor work, was held on 24 January, 'Great interest taken in work by all'.[146] The move to activities other than drill, such as company attacks and skirmishing, seems to have been very popular among UVF members, though in Co. Fermanagh this was not happening on any large scale until March 1914.[147]

There were high absentee rates in a number of UVF units, as of course was the experience for many TF units. In No. 1 section, 'J' Company of the 4th (Dungannon) Battalion, Tyrone Regiment, of 59 members in November 1913 the average drill attendance was only 32 with nine men attending all drills and eight none at all.[148] In 'A' Company of the 2nd North Antrim Regiment the CO reported 73 'effectives' and 58 'non-effectives' in February 1914 continuing, 'A large proportion of the above [non-effectives] have never attended any drills + it is questionable whether these men intend to turn out in any capacity'.[149] John Sears was rather blasé about the poor parade attendance in the 1st Fermanagh Regiment. When inspecting the supposedly 48 strong 'B' Company on 30 July 1913, he noted, 'The attendance (19) was fairly good considering busy time of year causing many men to be late'.[150] Seasonal factors also influenced drill attendance at other times of the year; a poor turnout at Enniskillen of just 42 men out of a unit of 133 was thought to be due to the proximity of Christmas and in Co. Fermanagh as a whole, drills were poorly attended during the harvest season.[151] Absenteeism was more widespread a problem than the few detailed rolls which survive suggest. By March 1914 Mr G. Young, commanding a battalion of the Central Antrim Regiment, reported that he had 950 'effectives' but 1,100 non-effectives, 'many being unknown to him or any other commander'.[152] The following letter, which may have been similar to those circulated in other units at the same time, was sent to recalcitrant members of the 2nd North Antrim Regiment by the battalions CO, Lieutenant Colonel H. J. Lyle:

> It appears from the Attendance Rolls of your Section that you are not taking any steps to make yourself an efficient member of the 2nd (North Antrim) Battalion.
>
> Arrangements have been made at each Drill Centre to enable every man to obtain a Certificate of Proficiency in Drill and Shooting.
>
> On 31st March 1914, any enrolled man who is not an efficient Volunteer in either the Active or Reserve Branches of the UVF will be struck off the strength of the Battalion.
>
> It must be borne in mind that, should times of hardship and distress arrive, those who do not take the trouble to make themselves efficient will be left to shift for themselves.[153]

This threat was repeated by General W. T. Adair, the UVF commander for all of Co. Antrim, who issued circular letters to serial defaulters which stated:

> Take notice that, in accordance with the orders of the General Officer Commanding UVF, your name will be removed from the lists from the 1st June, 1914, unless you previously show good reason to the contrary, in consequence of your failing to attend a sufficient number of drills.[154]

It seems likely that UVF attendance at parades was better than that for drills but it is difficult to be certain in this respect as the Unionist press tended to over-estimate the numbers on parade; certainly in January 1914 the 10,000 strong East Belfast Regiment was reported as mustering just 3,000 to 4,000 on parade.[155]

It seems likely that the turn out for drills deteriorated over time as, under efficient instructors, men could have been taught the basics of company drill in three months, after this period if not instructed in field craft or provided with rifle practice it is easy to understand how enthusiasm would have waned. It also seems likely that drill was difficult to organise in rural areas, especially in winter-time when men would have had to walk long distances in cold and rain to attend drill. As discussed in chapter 4, various mock battles and field days were carried out in spring and summer 1914, which were of some training value but were also organised to provide publicity for the UVF and boost morale within the force.

While some UVF members did not attend drill at all, lateness was also a problem, especially in rural areas. In Co. Fermanagh, the county instructor noted that men often arrived late for drill. In the most extreme case, at Blaney in August 1913 he noted, 'Instructed to attend here at 4 p.m. only two men were present and until 7 p.m. no other men turned up. At 8.30 p.m. 7 men were present but it was then useless to commence'.[156]

Rifle practice was very difficult to organise as it was mid-1914 until most UVF units received a significant amount of firearms. The first mention of a Fermanagh Regiment company using rifles is in January 1914 when it was noted that the Colebrook 'club' had 18 Mauser rifles.[157] The issue of passing men as 'effective' without them having undergone rifle drill was addressed by Major General Adair who stated, 'So long as the authorities keep us short of arms men may at the discretion of Batt[alio]n. Com[man]d[an]t. be passed in drill without arms; but the use of even broomsticks when drilling, especially in extended order, is most desirable'.[158]

Finding experienced drill instructors was a great problem for many UVF units, especially as not all former or serving soldiers automatically made good instructors. In Tempo, Co. Fermanagh, the local UVF had been poorly drilled, despite the fact that their instructor was a member of the North Irish Horse.[159] In Aughnaskew the instructor was 'an old man' whose only military experience had been around 40 years previously, serving in the militia.[160] The result of this was that by November 1913 the number of men who had passed the basic drill test in Co. Fermanagh was very low with just 198 in the 1st Fermanagh Regiment, 79 in the 2nd Fermanagh Regiment and 279 in the 3rd Fermanagh Regiment.[161]

The success of UVF training was, to some degree, dependant on the premises available; this was particularly the case in autumn and winter and in areas where Unionists were a small minority of the population and did not want to drill in public. In Co. Fermanagh Jack Sears noted that at Kinowley the hall was 'very small for drill purposes' while at Crom, 'Drill is carried out in riding school where practically any movement with these men could be carried out'.[162] It seems likely that drill was easy to arrange in Belfast, where factories and warehouses were available and in various outbuildings that supportive landowners would provide, but otherwise could be impossible to perform properly in rural areas where only a small church or Orange hall would be available. How to carry out drilling in private was a constant worry for the UVF. General W. T. Adair wrote to units in Co. Antrim in March 1914 stating, 'the Police are not to be allowed to enter any private demesnes where U.V. Forces are assembled, force being used if necessary … in the event of the Police unduly interfering with any movements of the UVF, on duty, or going and coming from any such Camps or exercise, the police are to be warned that if they persist in such interference force will be used to prevent the same'.[163]

One test of the military efficiency of UVF units is how quickly they could have turned out in the event of an emergency. Curiously, such exercises were not supported by UVF HQ, an order of May 1914 noting, 'The General Officer Commanding deprecates such Mobilizations being carried out more than once, except where grave defects have been experienced the first time, as he considers it is an unnecessary hardship on the men, and in some cases a serious loss to employers'.[164] Detailed figures for the Pomeroy UVF during practice alerts were certainly not encouraging. At this trial mobilisation on 13 February 1914, the first man did not arrive until 69 minutes after the warning was sent out at 5.06 p.m., while 204 minutes after the warning had been sent out only 57 per cent of the unit had arrived.[165]

A large number of camps of instruction were organised, which were designed to teach UVF officers and NCOs their duties. Only in July 1914 were camps for whole battalions being formed, as in the case of that for the 2nd North Londonderry Regiment which was at Magilligan for three days.[166] The Tyrone Regiment camp was the earliest held from 4 to 11 October 1913 at Baronscourt demesne. These camps did vary considerably in size. The North Down Regiment camp at Clandeboye in Easter 1914 had about 300 men, whereas the North Antrim Regiment camp at Lissanoure had just 116.[167] Attempts were made to run these camps in a thoroughly soldierly manner. At the one held at Lissanoure Castle in April 1914 for the 1st and 2nd North Antrim Regiments no dogs or alcohol were allowed and it was made clear that the camp would be organised under military discipline.[168] Those attending were also requested not to interfere with the game or damage any trees or shrubs.[169]

It seems debatable how useful these camps were. They were all much shorter than the TF's recommended two-week camp but other problems were more apparent. UVF HQ made only small grants towards the running of these camps (a grant of only £75 was made towards the Baronscourt camp) and this meant that additional finance was required. Interestingly it was felt that employers would provide employees in UVF command roles with a week's leave on full pay so that they could attend the camp; in situations where this did not happen men were left in the position of both giving up their annual holiday and being considerably out of pocket themselves for the privilege of attending one of the camps of instruction.[170] When a number of camps were held over Easter 1914, this not surprisingly saw a serious shortage of both instructors and equipment.[171] Colonel Pakenham had to write to Captain Hon. Arthur O'Neill, 'I had a most imperative wire from McCammon ordering me to send all palliasses immediately to North Down and as I had these on loan from H[ea]d. Q[uarte]rs. I have had to comply with such instructions. You will I am afraid have to find these elsewhere'.[172]

It says much for the UVF's logistical arrangements that the catering at these camps of instruction seems to have been handled by commercial firms.[173] Finding experienced personnel to act as instructors at these camps was also difficult. Colonel Chichester refused to lend any NCOs from the YCV to Captain Hon. Arthur O'Neill for the North Antrim Regiment claiming that they were all required with his unit.[174] Incredibly in the wake of the Curragh Incident, some regular NCOs were prepared publicly to identify themselves with the UVF. Colour Sergeant Leatern of the Royal Irish Rifles apparently served as an instructor to the North Antrim Regiment camp in April 1914.[175]

Clearly the UVF command structures and training regime were in no way comparable to those of the British regular army. However, there are some appropriate comparisons which can be made with the TF in terms of structure and training. The command structure of the UVF was confused and confusing with, it seems, Carson having the ultimate decision-making powers over the use of the force, despite the presence of Richardson as GOC, the various committees of the Ulster Provisional Government and the county committees. Training was subject to considerable local variations, based on the availability of instructors, premises and rifles. The number of experienced officers available to the UVF was not as plentiful as has sometimes been suggested, but there were enough to ensure that some units were effectively trained and commanded. Asquith himself felt that the UVF was not a serious military force; writing in September 1913 he noted, 'The importation of rifles has, so far, been on a small scale, and the drilling and training of volunteers though it is no doubt accustoming numbers of men to act together, + obey orders, and to develop esprit de corps, is not likely to produce a body which can stand up against regular troops'.[176] This was a rather limited view of the military capacities of the UVF; although, as noted above, Lord Dunleath agreed that UVF members would not fire on British troops, though for ideological reasons rather than as a result of poor training. However, this quotation from Asquith does raise the question of what the UVF could have done. Certainly facing two British army divisions marching from Southern Ireland and possible naval landings in Belfast Lough it seems that the UVF would quickly have been defeated as a field force. Whether it would then have continued guerrilla activity in rural Ulster and bitter street to street fighting in Belfast is impossible to ascertain. Of course, early in the Third Home Rule crisis and certainly after the Curragh Incident of March 1914, the possibility of the Liberal government using a military solution against the UVF was severely limited. What does seem clear is that military decisions would probably have devolved very quickly, leaving the decision over whether or not to fire on British troops in the hands of local commanders. What is certain though is that the UVF did have the military capacity to over-awe or, if necessary, militarily defeat RIC and INV members in Ulster; this was partially demonstrated during the Larne gunrunning. In short, without the intervention of the British army, Carson's army would have been able to establish the 'Carsonia' much written about by Liberal and Nationalist commentators: a nine county Ulster governed by the Ulster Provisional Government in the event of Home Rule being passed.

Notes

1 Alvin Jackson, *Sir Edward Carson* (Historical Association of Ireland, Dublin, 1993), pp. 29–57. See also Smith, *The Tories and Ireland 1910–1914*,

Murphy, 'Faction and the Conservative Party and the Home Rule Bill', and Rodner, 'Leaguers, Covenanters, Moderates'.
2 On these movements see, J. W. Boyle, 'The Belfast Protestant Association and the Independent Orange Order 1901–1910', *Irish Historical Studies*, 13, 50, 1962 and Alvin Jackson, 'Irish Unionism and the Russellite Threat 1894–1906', *Irish Historical Studies*, 25, 100, 1987.
3 Paul Bew, *Ideology and the Irish Question: Ulster Unionism and Irish Nationalism 1912–1916* (Clarendon Press, Oxford, 1994), pp. 92–8.
4 Adams, *Bonar Law*, pp. 95–167.
5 PRONI, D.1238/108, O'Neill papers, 'Statement on the Arms Question', PRONI, MIC/571/9, Farren Connell papers, 'Cavan Volunteer Force Scheme, Copy No. VI' and PRONI, D.1507/A/6/33, Carson papers, telegram, Lord Archdale to Carson, 22/07/1914.
6 *Northern Whig*, 25/09/1913.
7 For a balanced survey of this see Andrew Gailey, 'King Carson: An Essay on the Invention of Leadership', *Irish Historical Studies*, 30, 17, 1996. Two contemporary works highly critical of Carson's status are, St. John G. Ervine, *Sir Edward Carson and the Ulster Movement* (Maunsel & Co. Ltd, London, 1915) and Peel, *The Reign of Sir Edward Carson*.
8 Bew, *Ideology and the Irish Question*, p. 92.
9 PRONI, D.1540/3/12, Hall papers, letter, J. A. Orr to Roger Hall, 01/10/1913.
10 PRONI, D.1390/19/1, Charles Falls papers, John Sears's notebook, entry for 21/01/1914.
11 Circular letter from Colonel Wallace to the Masters of Orange Lodges, *Fermanagh Times*, 21/08/1913.
12 TNA, CO904/27/2/I, report by Sergeant Joseph Edwards, 26/04/1913.
13 PRONI, D1327/1/1, UUC papers, 'Minutes re. Unionist Clubs', minutes of AGM, 20/03/1914 and special meeting, 29/09/1919.
14 PRONI, D1327/1/2, 'Minutes of the Meetings of the Executive Committee of the Unionist Clubs Council', entries for 17/10/1913 and 25/02/1914.
15 TNA, CO904/27/3, '1913–1914 Unionist Movement v. Home Rule, Weekly Reports', summary for Tyrone and report by DI, Tyrone, 03/01/1913.
16 PRONI, D.1327/4/12, UUC papers, 'Headquarters' Staff Enrolment Forms'. Curiously Lieutenant General Sir George Richardson (the GOC), Colonel G. W. Hacket Pain (the Chief Staff Officer), Colonel T. E. Hickman (Inspector General) and Captain W. B. Spender (Assistant Quartermaster General) never appear to have been formerly enrolled in the UVF.
17 For Craig's military career see his personal file, TNA, WO339/3792, obituary in the *Belfast Telegraph*, 28/11/1940 and St. John Ervine, *Craigavon: Ulsterman* (George Allen & Unwin Ltd, London, 1949), pp. 55–64.
18 Foy, 'The Ulster Volunteer Force', p. 71.

19 *Kelly's Handbook to the Titled, Landed and Official Classes*, 1914, p. 1233; obituary notice of Richardson in *The Times*, 11/04/1931 and Hew Strachan, *The Politics of the British Army* (Clarendon Press, Oxford, 1997) p. 112.
20 *Kelly's Handbook to the Titled, Landed and Official Classes*, 1914, p. 1128; obituary notice in *The Green 'Un* [Regimental journal of the Worcestershire Regiment], April, 1924, p. 5, obituary in *The Times*, 15/02/1924.
21 On Spender see Maxwell, 'The Life of Sir Wilfrid Spender, 1876–1960'. On the prestige of the Staff College in this period see Brian Bond, *The Victorian Army and the Staff College 1854–1914* (Eyre Methuen, London, 1972), p. 153 and I. F. W. Beckett, '"Selection by Disparagement": Lord Esher, the General Staff and the Politics of Command, 1904–14' in David French and Brian Holden Reid (eds), *The British General Staff: Reform and Innovation, 1890–1939* (Frank Cass, London, 2002), p. 43.
22 TNA, WO339/46427, personal file of Lieutenant Colonel T. V. P. McCammon.
23 TNA, WO339/3792, personal file of Lord Craigavon, undated memorandum [July 1915].
24 PRONI, D.1327/4/12, UUC papers, 'Headquarters' Staff Enrolment Forms' and PRONI, D.1238/115, O'Neill papers, UVF order 16, 11/11/1913.
25 PRONI, D.1327/4/12, UUC papers, 'Headquarters' Staff Enrolment Forms'.
26 PRONI, UUC papers, D1327/2/12.
27 PRONI, D.1238/150, O'Neill papers, UVF order 55, 23/05/1014.
28 PRONI, D.1238/9AK and 9AL, O'Neill papers, letters from J. S. Reade, Honorary Secretary, Co. Antrim committee to Captain Hon. Arthur O'Neill, 02/09/1913 and 10/10/1913.
29 PRONI, D.845/3, Jenkins papers, letter, J. S. Reade to A. P. Jenkins, 17/10/1913.
30 Morrison, *Modern Ulster*, p. 155.
31 *The Times*, 18/03/1914.
32 Beckett, *Riflemen Form*, p. 175 and Hugh Cunningham, *The Volunteer Force: A Social and Political History, 1859–1908* (Archon Books, Hamden, 1975), pp. 53–4.
33 Mackenzie, *The Home Guard*, p. 36.
34 PRONI, D.1238/101, O'Neill papers, UVF order 10, 07/02/1914.
35 PRONI, D.1238/120, O'Neill papers, memorandum, presumably by W. T. Adair.
36 Trimble, *The History of Enniskillen*, vol. II, p. 1068.
37 PRONI, D.1414/30, Battalion Orders for 1st (North) Tyrone Regiment. For details on Herdman see his obituary in *The Times*, 11/02/1949.
38 PRONI, D.1132/6/1, Lowry papers, typescript, 'Organisation of Section and Companies'.

39 DRO, D/Lo/C686(306) (I), Londonderry papers, letter, T. V. P. McCammon to the Marquis of Londonderry, 30/01/1914.
40 PRONI, D.3054/4/2, enrolment register for Derry City Regiment.
41 PRONI, Herdman papers, D.1414/20, printed handbill re. 1st (North) Tyrone Regiment.
42 Morrison, *Modern Ulster*, p. 165; PRONI, D.1238/130, O'Neill papers, UVF order 2, 19/09/1913; PRONI, D.1238/145, O'Neill papers, letter, Captain Hon. Arthur O'Neill to [W. T. Adair?], 20/05/1914 and PRONI, D.1238/97, O'Neill papers, UVF order 23, 14/03/1914.
43 Nuffield College, Oxford, Mottistone 22, ff. 193–4, Brigadier General Count Gleichen, 'The Ulster Volunteer Force', 14/03/1914.
44 PRONI, D.1238/149, O'Neill papers, memorandum, Adair to regimental commanders, 16/05/1914.
45 Nuffield College, Oxford, Mottistone 22, ff. 193–4, Brigadier General Count Gleichen, 'The Ulster Volunteer Force', 14/03/1914.
46 PRONI, D.1238/173, O'Neill papers, UVF order 70, 04/07/1914.
47 Nuffield College, Oxford, Mottistone 22, ff. 193–4, Brigadier General Count Gleichen, 'The Ulster Volunteer Force', 14/03/1914.
48 PRONI, D.1295/2/7, Spender papers, 'Transport Organisation of a County Battalion' and PRONI, D.3465/J/37/69, Madden papers, draft mobilisation orders for Co. Monaghan Regiment.
49 PRONI, D.1238/72, O'Neill papers, letter, Major General Adair to Captain Hon. Arthur O'Neil, 21/04/1914.
50 Bodleian Library, Oxford, MS. Asquith, 38, ff. 87–92, memorandum, 'Special Plans for Ulster' by David Harrell, 07/01/1914.
51 Morrison, *Modern Ulster*, p. 155.
52 Foy, 'The Ulster Volunteer Force', p. 54.
53 PRONI, D.1414/12, Herdman papers, letter, Carson to 'Fellow Covenanters'.
54 PRONI, D.1390/19/1, Charles Falls papers, John Sears's notebook, entry for 23/01/1914.
55 *The Times*, 18/03/1914.
56 Beckett, *The Amateur Military Tradition*, p. 213.
57 PRONI, D.1327/4/1, UUC papers, minute book of the Co. Down committee, 20/12/1912.
58 Morrison, *Modern Ulster*, pp. 158–9.
59 *The Times*, 18/03/1914.
60 Peter Dennis, *The Territorial Army, 1907–1940* (Royal Historical Society and The Boydell Press, Woodbridge, 1987), p. 12.
61 All details taken from PRONI, D.1327/4/1, UUC papers, Co. Down committee book.
62 PRONI, D.1238/160, O'Neill papers, memorandum from Captain W. B. Spender to all county secretaries, 11/06/1914.
63 PRONI, D.3465/J/37/78, Madden papers, letter, Rev. C. Mannerstack to Colonel Madden, 12/05/1914.

64 PRONI, D.1238/190a, O'Neill papers, UVF enrolment form.
65 *Northern Whig*, 13/07/1914.
66 *Northern Whig*, 20/07/1914.
67 Crozier, *Impressions and Recollections*, p. 149.
68 PRONI, D.1238/85, O'Neill papers, 'Instructions with Regard to Arms & Ammunition', issued by G. Hacket Pain, 09/05/1914 and PRONI, D.1238/160, O'Neill papers, memorandum by Adair to all battalion commanders, 13/06/1914.
69 PRONI, D/1132/6/17, R. T. G. Lowry papers, circular letter from Lord Northland to members of 4th Tyrone Regiment.
70 PRONI, D/1132/6/17, R. T. G. Lowry papers, return headed, 'No. 5 Section, Replies to Stinkers'.
71 PRONI, D.1238/156, O'Neill papers, circular letter, W. T. Adair to UVF members, undated but May 1914.
72 PRONI, D.1518/3/9, 'List A – 2nd Battalion, North Antrim Regiment, UVF' undated but mid-1914.
73 French, *Military Identities*, p. 221 and Crozier, *Impressions and Recollections*, p. 149.
74 PRONI, D.1238/115, O'Neill papers, UVF order 18, 02/11/1913.
75 PRONI, D.1238/92, O'Neill papers, UVF order 37, 09/04/1914.
76 PRONI, D.1238/124, O'Neill papers, memorandum from UVF HQ [undated but c. October 1913].
77 PRONI, D.1238/115, O'Neill papers, UVF order 20, 22/11/1913.
78 PRONI, D.1238/167, O'Neill papers, memorandum to all divisional, regimental and battalion commanders by Hacket Pain, 27/06/1914.
79 PRONI, D.1238/85, O'Neill papers, 'Instructions with Regard to Arms & Ammunition', issued by G. Hacket Pain, 09/05/1914.
80 PRONI, D.1238/16, O'Neill papers, circular to all divisional, regimental and battalion commanders from UVF HQ, 16/03/1914.
81 PRONI, D.1238/174, O'Neill papers, UVF special order, 04/07/1914.
82 PRONI, D.1238/144, O'Neill papers, circular memorandum from Lieutenant Colonel T. V. P. McCammon, 18/05/1914.
83 PRONI, D.1238/88, O'Neill papers, memorandum by Hacket Pain, 07/05/1914.
84 PRONI, D.1238/181, O'Neill papers, letter, O'Neill to Adair, 24/07/1914.
85 PRONI, D.1238/151, O'Neill papers, memorandum to all divisional, regimental and battalion commanders by Hacket Pain, 23/05/1914.
86 PRONI, D1327/4/21, report by James Craig [?], of a meeting held on 17/12/1913, cited in Patrick Buckland, *Irish Unionism 18851923: A Documentary History* (HMSO, Belfast, 1973), pp. 240–1.
87 PRONI, D.3465/J/37/71, Madden papers, letter, Gerald Madden to Jack Madden, 09/04/1914.
88 Maxwell, 'The Life of Sir Wilfrid Spender', p. 60.

89 PRONI, D.1295/2/8, Spender papers, 'Headquarters Defence Scheme', undated but early 1914.
90 PRONI, D.1295/2/8, Spender papers, 'Headquarters Defence Scheme', undated but early 1914.
91 PRONI, D.1295/2/7, Spender papers, 'Contingency No.1'.
92 PRONI, D.1295/2/7, Spender papers, 'Contingency No. 3'.
93 PRONI, D.1295/2/7, Spender papers, 'Contingency No. 4'. Similar advice was offered in PRONI, D.1238/139, O'Neill papers, 'Confidential Circular Memorandum to Divisional, Regimental, Battalion and Headquarters Corps Commanders Only', 14/05/1914, where it was suggested that by 'sheer weight of force' the UVF could overpower the attacking force.
94 PRONI, D.1238/139, O'Neill papers, 'Confidential Circular Memorandum to Divisional, Regimental, Battalion and Headquarters Corps Commanders Only', 14/05/1914
95 PRONI, D.1238/176, O'Neill papers, memorandum entitled, 'Refugees', 10/07/1914 and PRONI, D.1327/4/4, Murland papers, pamphlet, 'Ulster Refugee Committee' [July 1914].
96 PRONI, D.1327/4/4, Murland papers, letter, Dawson Bates to C. H. Murland.
97 Memorandum by Craig, 26/07/1913, cited in Josephine Howie, 'Militarising a Society: The Ulster Volunteer Force, 1913–14' in Yonah Alexander and Alan O'Day (eds), *Ireland's Terrorist Dilemma* (Kluwer Academic, Lancaster, 1986), pp. 222–3 and PRONI, D.1415/B/34, Craigavon papers, F. H. Crawford, 'The Arming of Ulster', p. 27.
98 PRONI, D.1238/8, O'Neill papers, memorandum by CO, Central Antrim Regiment, 01/03/1914.
99 PRONI, D.1238/164, O'Neill papers, letter, Adair to all regimental and battalion commanders, 22/06/1914.
100 PRONI, D.1238/185, O'Neill papers, memorandum, Adair to commanders of North and South Antrim Regiments, 25/07/1914.
101 PRONI, D.1238/9S, O'Neill papers, letter, Colonel H. T. Lyle to Captain Hon. Arthur O'Neill, 21/03/1914.
102 PRONI, D.3465/J/37/89, Madden papers, letter, J. F. W. Macleary to J. C. Madden, 26/06/1914.
103 PRONI, D/3160/1, John Regan, 'Memoirs of Service in the RIC and RUC', p. 73.
104 PRONI, D.1633/2/19, Lilian Spender diary, entry for 23/06/1914.
105 PRONI, D.3465/J/37/54, Madden papers, letter, Gerald Madden to Jack Madden, 23/12/1913.
106 PRONI, D.1507/A/11/17, Carson papers, letter, Lord Dunleath to Carson, 09/03/1914.
107 Alvin Jackson, 'British Ireland: What If Home Rule Had Been Enacted in 1912?' in Niall Fergusson (ed.), *Virtual History: Alternatives and Counterfactuals* (Picador, London, 1997).

108 Strachan, *The Politics of the British Army*, p. 112, citing a figure calculated by Jonathan Frew.
109 PRONI, D.1498/7, Richardson papers, 'Nominal Roll of Officers Recently Serving with UVF. Who Have Been Recalled to Army Service'.
110 PRONI, MIC/204/1, 'Records of The Queen's University of Belfast Contingent, Officer Training Corps, 1909–1950'.
111 Nuffield College, Oxford, MSS Mottistone 22/f. 171, HQ Irish Command report on Ulster Volunteer Force, c. September 1913 and PRONI, D.1238/165, O'Neill papers, UVF order 64, 20/06/1914.
112 TNA, WO141/26, miscellaneous RIC reports of illegal drilling.
113 PRONI, D.3054/4/2, J. M. Harvey papers, roll of Derry City Regiment, c. January 1914.
114 Morrison, *Modern Ulster*, p. 159.
115 Trimble, *The History of Enniskillen*, pp. 1070–2.
116 DRO, D/Lo/C682 (129), Londonderry papers, letter Lord Castlereagh to his mother, 14/10/1913, and PRONI, D.1498/7, Richardson papers, 'Nominal Roll of Officers Recently Serving with UVF. Who Have Been Recalled to Army Service'.
117 PRONI, D.1238/188, O'Neill papers, UVF order 80, 25/07/1914.
118 Morrison, *Modern Ulster*, pp. 158–9.
119 Foy, 'The Ulster Volunteer Force', p. 116.
120 *Belfast Evening Telegraph*, 09/04/1914 and 16/04/1914.
121 PRONI, D.3465/J/37/53 and 55, Madden papers, letters, Gerald Madden to Jack Madden, 06/11[?] /1913 and 26/12/1913.
122 TNA, CO904/27/2/II, programme entitled, 'Ulster Volunteer Force, Belfast Division, Official Arrangements, Inspection by Sir Edward Carson', 27/09/1913.
123 Nuffield College, Oxford, MSS Mottistone 22/f. 171, HQ Irish Command report on Ulster Volunteer Force, c. September 1913.
124 TNA, CO904/27/2/II, programme entitled, 'Ulster Volunteer Force, Belfast Division, Official Arrangements, Inspection by Sir Edward Carson', 27/09/1913.
125 PRONI, D.1327/4/2A, UUC papers, memorandum re. West Belfast UVF, undated.
126 PRONI, D.1327/4/2A, UUC papers, memorandum re. West Belfast UVF, undated.
127 Crozier, *Impressions and Recollections*, pp. 142–63.
128 PRONI, D.1633/2/19, Lilian Spender diary, entry for 10/06/1914.
129 PRONI, D.1498/7, Richardson papers, 'Nominal Roll of Officers Recently Serving with UVF. Who Have Been Recalled to Army Service'.
130 PRONI, D.1633/2/19, Lilian Spender diary, entry for 11/04/1914.
131 Crozier, *Impressions and Recollections*, p. 143.
132 For a more detailed discussion of this topic see Timothy Bowman, *Irish*

Regiments in the Great War: Discipline and Morale (Manchester University Press, 2003), pp. 111–18.
133 PRONI, D.3835/E/2/5/8, Farren Connell papers, letter, Nugent to his wife, 10/10/1915.
134 TNA, WO339/11239, personal file of Captain A. F. Penny and PRONI, D.1498/7, Richardson papers, 'Nominal Roll of Officers Recently Serving with UVF. Who Have Been Recalled to Army Service'.
135 PRONI, D.1238/121, O'Neill papers, memorandum by W. T. Adair, 25/10/1913.
136 PRONI, D.1238/91, O'Neill papers, UVF order 41, 16/04/1914.
137 PRONI, D.1238/91, O'Neill papers, UVF order 42, 16/04/1914.
138 PRONI, D.1238/97, O'Neill papers, UVF order 21, 14/03/1914.
139 PRONI, D.1238/165, O'Neill papers, UVF order 68, 20/06/1914.
140 PRONI, D.1238/98, O'Neill papers, UVF order 19, 07/03/1914.
141 On the TF in this period see, Beckett, *The Amateur Military Tradition*, pp. 198–222; Dennis, *The Territorial Army 1907–1940*, pp. 4–15; French, *Military Identities*, pp. 203–32; H. B. McCartney, *Citizen Soldiers: The Liverpool Territorials in the First World War* (Cambridge University Press, 2005), pp. 9–22; K. W. Mitchinson, *Defending Albion: Britain's Home Army 1908–1919* (Palgrave Macmillan, Basingstoke, 2005), pp. 13–33 and E. M. Spiers, *Haldane: An Army Reformer* (Edinburgh University Press, 1980).
142 PRONI, D.1390/19/1, Charles Falls papers, John Sears's notebook, references for August and September 1913.
143 PRONI, D.1238/100, O'Neill papers, UVF order 15, 14/02/1914.
144 PRONI, D.1518/3/9, Hamilton papers, return for 'A' Company, 2nd North Antrim Regiment, 14/02/1914.
145 PRONI, D.1390/19/1, Charles Falls papers, John Sears's notebook, entry for 08/03/1914.
146 PRONI, D.1390/19/1, Charles Falls papers, John Sears's notebook, entry for 24/01/1913.
147 PRONI, D.1390/19/1, Charles Falls papers, John Sears's notebook, entries for 20/03/1914 and 21/03/1914.
148 PRONI, D/1132/6/17, R. T. G. Lowry papers, note headed 'No. 1 Section, 'J' Company Dungannon Battalion'.
149 PRONI, D.1518/3/9, Hamilton papers, return for 'A' Company, 2nd North Antrim Regiment, 14/02/1914.
150 PRONI, D.1390/19/1, Charles Falls papers, John Sears's notebook, entry for 30/07/1913.
151 PRONI, D.1390/19/1, Charles Falls papers, John Sears's notebook, entries for 30/08/1913 and 17/12/1913.
152 PRONI, D.1238/8, O'Neill papers, memorandum by CO, Central Antrim Regiment, 01/03/1914.

153 PRONI, D.1518/3/8, Lyle papers, circular letter issued by Lieutenant Colonel H. J. Lyle.
154 PRONI, D.1518/3/8, Lyle papers, circular letter issued by General W. T. Adair.
155 *Northern Whig*, 29/01/1914.
156 PRONI, D.1390/19/1, Charles Falls papers, John Sears's notebook, entry for 27/08/1913.
157 PRONI, D.1390/19/1, Charles Falls papers, John Sears's notebook, entry for 28/01/1914.
158 PRONI, D.1238/9P, O'Neill papers, Adair to regimental commandant, 14/02/1914.
159 PRONI, D.1390/19/1, Charles Falls papers, John Sears's notebook, entry for 19/08/1913.
160 PRONI, D.1390/19/1, Charles Falls papers, John Sears's notebook, entry for 19/09/1913.
161 PRONI, D.1390/19/1, Charles Falls papers, John Sears's notebook, entry for 29/09/1913.
162 PRONI, D.1390/19/1, Charles Falls papers, John Sears's notebook, entries for 13/09/1913.
163 PRONI, D.1238/7, O'Neill papers, memorandum by W. T. Adair, 05/03/1914.
164 PRONI, D.1238/150, O'Neill papers, UVF order 52, 23/05/1914.
165 PRONI, D/1132/6/17, R. T. G. Lowry papers, returns re. trial mobilisation of No.1 Section, 'J' Company, 4th Tyrone Regiment.
166 *Northern Whig*, 24/07/1914
167 PRONI, D.1238/65, O'Neill papers, letter, Lieutenant Colonel T. V. P. McCammon to Captain Hon. Arthur O'Neill, 27/03/1914 and PRONI, D.1238/79, O'Neill papers, 'North Antrim Regiment: Numbers Who Completed the 3 Days Course of Instruction in Camp at Lissanoure'.
168 PRONI, D.1238/37, O'Neill papers, memorandum re. Camp of Instruction at Lissanoure Castle.
169 PRONI, D.1238/68, O'Neill papers, printed booklet, 'Ulster Volunteer Force, North Antrim Regiment, Lissanoure Camp', letter, Lieutenant Colonel T. V. P. McCammon to Captain Hon. Arthur O'Neill, 27/03/1914.
170 PRONI, D.1132/6/1, Lowry papers, circular to officers commanding companies, undated but August 1913.
171 PRONI, D.1238/65, O'Neill papers, letter, Lieutenant Colonel T. V. P. McCammon to Captain Hon. Arthur O'Neill, 27/03/1914.
172 PRONI, D.1238/60, O'Neill papers, letter, Colonel A. Pakenham to Captain Hon. Arthur O'Neill, 02/04/1914.
173 PRONI, D.1238/44, O'Neill papers, letter, Director, Bloomfield Bakery to Captain Hon. Arthur O'Neill, 11/04/1914.
174 PRONI, D.1238/52, O'Neill papers, telegram, Chichester to O'Neill, 03/04/1914.

175 PRONI, D.1238/58, O'Neill papers, letter, A. P. Jenkins to Captain Hon. Arthur O'Neill, 03/04/1914.
176 Bodleian Library, Oxford, MS Asquith 38, memorandum by H. H. Asquith, 'Government of Ireland Bill', undated but September 1913.

4

Parades and propaganda: the public face of the UVF

The whole issue of Unionist propaganda during the Third Home Rule crisis is a complex one, which to date has received very little consideration from historians. Michael Foy's important article on the subject shows the importance of picture postcards and cartoons in the Unionist campaign and suggests that Unionist propaganda was aimed at four different audiences: Ulster Unionists themselves, British public opinion, the Liberal government and Nationalist Ireland. Foy's article does illustrate the problems which the UVF brought to the Unionist propaganda campaign; from one perspective Ulster Unionists wanted to portray an army in being which was unified in its opposition to Home Rule, conversely, there was a desire to illustrate Ulster in artistic terms as a, more or less helpless, woman who required support from Unionists in Britain.[1]

Obviously, through press reports of its parades, the UVF was able to aid the Unionist propaganda machine in appealing to all of the four target groups which Foy identifies. However, it seems that UVF parades, especially relatively small ones held in rural communities, were designed primarily to bolster morale among UVF members themselves and to provide some opportunity for rank and file members to come into contact with battalion and regimental commanders and members of HQ; and indeed, to establish the authority of the latter. A number of local parades, church services and field days seem to have been designed to demonstrate that the UVF was a separate entity from either the Unionist Clubs or various Loyal Institutions, though, of course, the membership overlapped significantly. While historians of other Irish paramilitary movements (the Fenian movement of the 1860s and Blueshirt movement of the 1930s) have argued that these were based around social, specifically sporting, activities, the same cannot be said of the UVF.[2] Indeed Unionist members of football and rugby clubs explicitly stated in late 1913 and early 1914 that they would not be playing sports until the Home Rule crisis had passed and a number of clubs cancelled their fixtures to devote more time to UVF drilling.[3] In its activities the UVF drew heavily on British army and Orange Order practice, with members taking part in parades (some of the largest based on the presentation of regimental standards), church services, field days, mimic warfare and training camps. There are some examples of UVF sponsored concerts, sports days and magic lantern or film shows, but these are insignificant in terms of the total number of activities undertaken by the force.

The amount of information available on UVF parades varies enormously, with some units receiving very few column inches throughout their existence. By contrast the Enniskillen Horse received considerable media attention, not least because the *Impartial Reporter* was owned by the unit's CO W. C. Trimble. However, the rival but equally Unionist *Fermanagh Times* also featured approving articles on the unit. The *Fermanagh Times* did criticise Trimble in that they were given no advance notice of the parade times of the Enniskillen Horse. An article commenting on a parade concluded, 'There was a fairly large crowd of spectators at the field, but this number would have been four times as large had the public known where the inspection was to take place'.[4] The editorial in the same edition expanded on this:

> Mr. Trimble thought it proper, when addressing the Enniskillen Horse at their review on Saturday to state that efforts had been made to "create mischief between him and the men." We have no doubt Mr. Trimble meant the reference for us and it is the only reply – and an extremely indirect and deceptive one – vouchsafed to our article complaining that all information as to the work and movements of the Horse was confined to Mr. Trimble's own paper, the Impartial Reporter. The circumstances that all news was limited to that paper had been openly commented upon. We only gave public echo to statements often heard that Mr. Trimble laid himself open to the suspicion that he was thereby exploiting this praiseworthy Unionist movement for the benefit of his own personal newspaper.[5]

The earliest UVF parades were those which were carried out in July 1913 in North Down. These seem to have been to establish the position of Holywood, Co. Down, as having formed both the first Unionist Club in 1911 and the first UVF company in 1913.[6] UVF parades tended to be co-ordinated with periodically intense bursts of Unionist activity. Carson undertook a whirlwind review of a large number of rural UVF units in September 1913 (for the purpose of introducing Richardson and other members of the HQ staff), commemorating the anniversary of the signing of the League and Covenant on 28 September 1912. Carson undertook a similar tour during Easter 1914, presumably as during the holiday season most UVF members were available for parades and large turnouts could be expected. UVF parades were also numerous in the period surrounding the Twelfth of July Orange celebrations in 1914. Some UVF units certainly held parades to celebrate the relief of Derry and the Battle of the Boyne, while Empire Day and Guy Fawkes day also served as important commemorative days for certain UVF units.[7] The last major focus for UVF parades was in the autumn of 1914 when UVF units were paraded for the purpose of encouraging their members to enlist in the British army.[8] Parades were also built around important funerals: the deaths of Joseph Chamberlain, R. J. McMordie, the Lord Mayor of Belfast, and Lily Birney, a UVF nurse in Derry City, provided a focus for UVF parades. UVF members rarely took part, as such, in Orange Order parades or Unionist Club activities. An exception was on the Twelfth of July 1914 when in Bangor members of the UVF who were not Orangemen took part in the parade through the town.[9] At the Twelfth of July parades in Derry in 1914, UVF members armed with sticks acted as stewards and were complimented by the Unionist press for preventing a repeat of the rioting that had occurred the previous year.[10] At a Unionist demonstration in Coleraine in October 1913 the UVF appeared simply as a bodyguard to James Craig.[11] Most UVF parades were part of a larger Unionist demonstration with typically a parade being followed by an inspection of the UVF, speeches of a political character and, often, an entirely separate political meeting.

UVF parades varied enormously in size. The largest was that carried out on 28 September 1913 at the Royal Ulster Agricultural Society's show grounds at Balmoral, just outside Belfast, when as many as 12,000 (an RIC report noted 10,390 organised in 14 battalions) Belfast UVF members may have been on parade, with up to 25,000 spectators.[12] The *Northern Whig* reported this parade, stating with some hyperbole, 'The inspiring spectacle at Balmoral was one that will never fade from the memory of those who were privileged to witness it. Nothing approaching it in character and significance had ever been seen before in the history of Ireland'.[13] By contrast parades could be of relatively small numbers of men, for example when 70 UVF members from the Aughnacloy company of the 3rd Tyrone Regiment marched from their drill hall to the rectory grounds to be inspected by the adjutant of their battalion.[14] Carson was keen to emphasise rural support for the UVF and in one of his first UVF inspections it is noteworthy that he carried this out at the small village of Clough in East Down.[15]

As an example, it is worth outlining the structure of one parade which Carson attended, namely that at Armagh on Saturday 4 October 1913, which was itself controversial in that it was held in a mainly Nationalist city. Special trains, offering discounted tickets, had been organised to bring Unionists to this event emphasising that it was not just a display of local Unionist strength. As part of this demonstration the Co. Armagh UVF was inspected by Carson, following its march past the Royal School. After the inspection there was a public meeting chaired by J. B. Lonsdale, the local MP. At this meeting there were speeches by Carson, Lonsdale and F. E. Smith and an Orange Order style resolution 'We Hereby reaffirm our Solemn Resolve: "We will not have Home Rule"'. There was a strong religious element to this meeting as it opened with a hymn, 'Lord Thou Hast Been Our Refuge'. However, the religious element was rather curtailed as the Lord Primate of Ireland simply 'announced' this hymn, neither leading those assembled in prayer nor preaching a sermon of any sort. The meeting ended with the singing of the National Anthem, with the addition of a specially written verse, which sounded a strangely conciliatory note, given the audience:

> God bless our native land!
> May Heaven's protecting hand
> Still guard our shore.
> May peace her power extend,
> Foe be transformed to friend
> And Ulster's rights depend,
> On War no more.[16]

It is also worth quoting Lilian Spender's vivid account of what it was like to take part in a parade with the West Belfast Regiment as an indication of how popular these parades were:

> Almost the whole day the road was lined with a ragged, cheering crowd. Our car was next but one to Sir Edward's and the General [Richardson] came in for a lot of cheers on his own account.
> It was the most deafening, and wildly exciting experience I ever had. Be-shawled women waved a baby in one arm and a Union Jack in the other, and incredibly dirty and unkempt men waved caps and flags, and fairly danced with excitement. 'God love ye' quavered a toothless old crone, and 'God bless ye' shouted others. 'No Home Rule bawled the men, thrusting their faces almost into our car; 'Hooray' shrieked the children, most ear piercing of all.[17]

In general a UVF parade in a local area could rely on someone of some importance to attend. Carson's presence was undoubtedly the most sought after, showing the Unionist leader's support for, in some cases, outlying Unionist communities and guaranteeing considerable newspaper coverage. The phrase 'Carson weather' seems to have come into popular usage at this time, as a humorous reference to the torrential downpours which often accompanied Carson's reviews of UVF units.[18] However, as the Third Home Rule crisis continued Carson clearly tired of attending endless UVF displays and when unable or unwilling to attend a demonstration by the 1,800 strong Monaghan Regiment in July 1914 he sent the organiser the rather brief telegram, 'I wish you and the Volunteers every success at presentation of colours today'.[19] After Carson, Lieutenant General Sir George Richardson was probably the key figure that local organisers wanted to attend their parades. In the absence of Carson and Richardson, county, regimental and battalion commanders or MPs or Peers would often inspect units and if Carson and Richardson were present these notables would normally attend as part of a platform party. Occasionally, there were special guest reviewers, a very good example being in July 1914 when Brigadier General John Gough (brother of Brigadier General Hubert Gough who had become a Unionist hero through his part in the Curragh Incident) visited the Spenders and seems to have inspected some UVF units in North Down.[20] Similarly, Walter Long MP, the former Irish Unionist leader, inspected the North Antrim Regiment at Ballymena and the North Londonderry Regiment in Coleraine in July 1914.[21]

At a number of parades, the great and the good of Irish and British Unionism were often present, either as spectators or to present flags. Indeed, the importance of 'Big House' Unionism seemed to be reinforced by the fact that many of these reviews were conducted on the demesnes surrounding large country houses; for example, in August 1913 the Ballymoney UVF paraded at Leslie Hill Demesne, on Easter Monday 1914 the North Down Regiment of the UVF paraded at Clandeboye, the estate owned by the Marquess of Dufferin and Ava and in March 1914 the South Down Regiment held a field day at Narrow Water Castle.[22] However, reviews and parades were also held in the centres of towns and cities and, more rarely, at certain historic sites. An example of the latter occurred in July 1913 when Carson reviewed 2,000 UVF members from Bangor, Conlig, Carrowdore, Comber, Donaghadee and Newtownards at the historic cottage of Betsy Gray, one of the heroines of the 1798 Rebellion, at Six Roads Ends just outside Bangor.[23]

Other public areas were pressed into service as when the 5th East Belfast Regiment were presented with their colours at a ceremonial parade held at the Glentoran Football and Athletic Club grounds.[24]

'Big House' Unionism also tended to try to establish its position at the head of the UVF through the presentation of colours, which were generally purchased by and presented by the wives of prominent Unionists. For example, the colours presented to the 2nd North Down Regiment were purchased and presented by the Marchioness of Londonderry and Lady Dunleath and the East Down Regiment received their colours in early August 1914 from Lady Bangor.[25] An exception to this dominance of 'Big House' Unionism was the presentation of colours to the West Belfast Regiment by Stewart Blacker Quinn, an accountant and prospective Unionist parliamentary candidate for West Belfast.[26] Problems could arise over the presentation of colours. The idea of presenting colours seems to have originated with the Countess of Bective, who promised a King's colour to the Queen's Island UVF in August 1913 and this was reported to the membership then but the reorganisation of the UVF by Richardson in September 1913 around place of residence rather than workplaces meant that this colour was never presented.[27] Not all UVF units received colours but they were certainly presented to the 1st South Antrim Regiment, 1st North Belfast Regiment, 1st and 2nd North Down Regiment, 2nd East Down Regiment, 1st South Belfast Regiment, 1st and 2nd West Belfast Regiment, 5th East Belfast Regiment and 6th North Belfast Regiment, providing a focus for impressive parades on each occasion.[28]

Religion often played an important part in UVF parades, with the singing of hymns, a prayer and, in the case of the presentation of colours, a short religious service, consecrating the flags themselves. The role of the churches was most clearly shown through the number of army style church parades which were carried out by the UVF. These were particularly important in demonstrating the ecumenical nature of the UVF with Anglican, Presbyterian and Methodist clergy often officiating together and should be seen within the context of what Alan Megahey has identified as increasing ecumenism within the Irish Protestant churches in this period.[29] For example, at a church parade organised by the North Belfast Regiment at Belfast Cathedral on Sunday 1 February 1914 it was noted in the advance publicity that while Rev. T. G. Collins, the rector of St James's Church, would be the preacher, Rev. J. Maconaghie, the Minister of Fortwilliam Presbyterian Church, and Rev. Wesley Guard of Methodist Church, Belfast, would also take part in the service.[30]

While most church parades took place in churches or cathedrals, there were a few British army style drumhead services, such as that attended by over 3,000 members of the Belfast UVF at Forth River Football Grounds in July 1913 and that held by the 2nd Tyrone Regiment in Omagh in September 1913.[31] The focus of many open air religious ceremonies was the consecration of regimental colours by members of the clergy.[32] Church parades could also be useful for boosting UVF funds as it seems that at many collections were made for the Carson Defence Fund.

Most members of the clergy took suitable texts and argued that Home Rule would increase the power of the Catholic Church over Irish Protestants and often referred to historical examples which UVF members should see as a parallel to contemporary events. For example, at Westbourne Church when the Rev. W. Witherow preached to men of the East Belfast Regiment he stated,

> a Home Rule Parliament would mean the domination of Rome ... Therefore it followed we would be the slaves of slaves under a Romish Parliament which must be dominated by the Roman Catholic hierarchy. Ulster held the pass in 1688 and 1689, also in 1886 and 1893, and history would yet record the fact that in the years between 1912 and 1914, when men's hearts were failing them for fear of Home Rule, Ulster, once again, as of old and, like the brave, unconquerable Spartans at Thermopylae, held the pass against mighty odds, saved herself, saved Ireland from ruin, strife and bloodshed and saved the Empire from making a fatal blunder and an irreparable mistake.[33]

Rev. R. Ussher Greer, addressing men of the West Down Regiment, spoke to them of the importance of obedience to their officers and comradeship, comparing them with 'the crusaders of old'.[34] Church parades were carried out on a small scale by a number of units, meaning that members of the clergy involved were often addressing fairly small congregations. For example the Lisnaskea UVF company attended a church parade on 10 May 1914 and the tiny Clough company of the UVF showed the importance of church parades to them as they went to the trouble and expense of having their parade services printed in pamphlet form by the *Down Recorder*.[35]

Demonstrating his commitment to the Unionist cause and also his concerns that UVF members may act hastily, provoking trouble, the Lord Primate had a prayer printed for distribution to every Anglican member of the UVF which read:

> O Heavenly Father, hear, we pray Thee, the prayer of Thy children who call upon Thee in their time of danger and difficulty. Forgive me, I pray Thee,

for all my sins which I have so often committed against Thee, in thought, word and deed. Make me, 'ready to endure hardness as a good soldier of Jesus Christ.' Fill me with Thy Holy Spirit, that I may know Thee more clearly, and follow Thee more nearly. Strengthen and uphold me in all difficulties and dangers, keep me faithful unto death, patient in suffering, calm in Thy service, and confident in the assurance that Thou, Lord, wilt direct all things to the glory of Thy name and the welfare of my Church and country. Bless the King whom we serve, and all the Royal family. O Lord, grant me Thy grace that no word or act of mine may be spoken or done rashly, hastily or with anger towards those who differ from me. Bless all my comrades in the Ulster Volunteer Force and make me loving and gentle, obedient to my leaders, and faithful to my promises; and in Thine own good time bring peace to Ireland. All this I beg for Jesus Christ's sake. Amen.[36]

The consecration of colours was a high-profile activity which senior Protestant clergy keenly participated in, as in July 1914 when the Moderator of the General Assembly and the Dean of Connor consecrated the colours of the Central Antrim Regiment.[37] The government was highly critical of the involvement of senior clergy in the consecration of UVF colours, as when the Bishop of Down and Connor, the Right Rev. Dr D'Arcy carried out this ceremony at the presentation of colours to the 2nd North Down Regiment.[38] The Bishop defended his action stating,

I can assure him [Colonel J. E. B. Seely, Secretary of State for War] that his vehement charge of hypocrisy leaves me absolutely unmoved ... When a Bishop consecrates colours for a regiment of the Army he does so because he believes his country's cause to be a righteous and holy cause and because he believes the Army's main purpose is the maintenance of peace and not the shedding of blood.

The position of a Bishop consecrating colours for the Ulster Volunteers is exactly similar. The Volunteers stand for the Great Britain which all patriotic men love, for the traditions that have made Britain great, for the flag that has ever been the symbol of freedom and, as all Ulstermen believe, for the true well-being of all creeds and classes in Ireland.[39]

Funerals provided the focus for some UVF public demonstrations. When the Lord Mayor of Belfast, R. J. McMordie, died in March 1914 members of the UVF lined the route of the funeral procession.[40] When Miss Lily Birney, a member of the UVF Nursing Corps, was tragically killed in a house fire, a large contingent of the City of Derry Regiment formed outside her house, while the funeral service was conducted there, then some acted as pall bearers and the rest paraded behind her coffin to the City Cemetery.[41] The death of the leading Unionist politician, Joseph Chamberlain, in July 1914 lead to a drumhead service being held by the 1st South Antrim Regiment.[42]

Occasionally female Unionists would make their presence felt at UVF parades. This was largely in the traditional role of providing refreshments for UVF members but this seems to have occurred more frequently at small rural parades. In January 1914 refreshments were provided by Lady Brooke at Colebrooke House to men of the Cavanaleck UVF who had marched the four miles there.[43] Meanwhile in February 1914 Miss Murray-Ker served refreshments to the Newbliss company of the UVF following a route march and drill exercise and in March 1914 Mrs Robert Porter provided refreshments to the Bellisle UVF following a three-hour parade.[44] When the 2nd North Antrim Regiment paraded at Ballycastle in August 1914 they were treated to tea by the Ladies' Committee of the battalion.[45] However, at some UVF reviews, small female nursing detachments were on parade as at Ballyclare in September 1913 and Antrim Castle in April 1914, when Carson reviewed 60 and 80 members, respectively, of the ladies' nursing corps.[46] In the *Belfast Evening Telegraph* an illustrated feature noted the role of 'Ulster Women Despatch Riders' who were operating in Fermanagh.[47]

Few UVF parades seem to have involved many armed members before July 1914, when Richardson issued an order stating his belief that now was the time for all UVF members to carry their rifles. The first armed parades occurred in South Belfast, when UVF units from the notoriously militant Sandy Row area paraded and in Lisburn on 6 July 1914.[48] The first instance of the Donegal UVF mobilising with their rifles was reported as occurring on 25 July 1914, while the Rathfriland UVF company was presented with their rifles after their usual drill practice on 22 July 1914.[49] The Omagh UVF was presented with its rifles after drill practice on 21 July 1914 and then paraded, armed, through the town; similar scenes occurred in Bangor and Newry at the same time.[50] Not all UVF members were eager to parade bearing rifles. In Richill, Co. Armagh, the local UVF paraded as usual carrying dummy rifles on 8 July, but their CO sent them home to fetch their rifles before awarding medals for rifle shooting and putting them through a series of field manoeuvres.[51] Machine guns seem to have been of immeasurable propaganda value. At a review of the East Belfast Regiment, 'the two Colt-guns which appeared as well as Maxims, drew tremendous cheering from the crowds'.[52]

On parade most UVF members simply wore their civilian clothes with the addition of the UVF armband and lapel badge; indeed the current Orange Order supposedly wear bowler hats as this was the preferred headwear of Belfast UVF members in 1913–14. The YCV which first paraded with the UVF in June 1914, 'looked smart in their grey uniform' which as discussed in chapter 1 had been purchased by YCV members themselves.[53] Of UVF units proper, it appears that only some of the Belfast Special Service Force units were issued with British army style khaki uniforms.[54] Unusually, some uniformed spectacle was brought to a UVF parade in Lisburn when uniformed warders from Hillsborough Castle, wearing eighteenth-century style blue and red volunteer uniforms, took part in the parade.[55]

Parades were sometimes accompanied by music. At the massive UVF parade at Balmoral in September 1913 the Rescue Tent and Sirocco Bands (the latter based on the large engineering concern, the Sirocco Works in East Belfast, which specialised in the manufacture of ventilation equipment) played a collection of martial music, including 'Our Glorious Empire Day', 'The Old Brigade', 'The Hero of Trafalgar' and 'Let Me Like a Soldier Fall'. Musical accompaniment was made easier at this parade as those parading were marching round the Agricultural Show Grounds, while the band was able to remain stationary just beside the saluting point.[56]

UVF parades also saw some towns decorated, in a fashion normally used during the Orange marching season. At Dromore it was noted that, 'Bright arches with lines of fluttering streamers spanned the streets, flags flaunted everywhere, bands discoursed patriotic airs and from end to end the usually sober silent townlet presented a moving mass of people'.[57] At Ballyclare, the town was illuminated with Japanese lanterns, arches were hung across the streets displaying portraits of Carson and loyal mottos such as 'The Union We Will Maintain' and 'Remember Our Covenant' and flags were placed in the windows of many houses.[58]

Parades became another area in which UVF HQ attempted to establish its authority over UVF units, especially those in outlying rural areas. As late as July 1914, Richardson stated:

> It has come to the notice of the General Officer Commanding that various units have paraded for certain inspections and ceremonies without any reference to Headquarters. It must be understood, that unless special circumstances demand a Parade being held without such reference, application to hold such Parade must be submitted to Headquarters for approval, in accordance with the usual custom of the service.[59]

Despite the provocation implicit in UVF units parading in mainly Nationalist villages or towns, only rarely were Unionist demonstrations interrupted; for example in June 1914 when two suffragettes interrupted Sir Edward Carson's speech to a Belfast parade, albeit very briefly.[60]

Parades could provoke mixed reactions, as in the case of a parade carried out by the Enniskillen Horse on 13 June 1913. The *Fermanagh Times* correspondent was much impressed by this parade, stating, 'The discipline of the men, their upright smart, soldierly bearing and the ready and unhesitating way in which they immediately obeyed commands were all subjects of favourable criticism throughout the day and spoke well for the regular and systematic training which, we understand, every troop and squadron is receiving from experienced instructors'.[61] From a very different perspective, the local RIC District Inspector P. A. Marinan noted of this parade, 'In the few drill movements performed, however, I noticed great confusion and bad horsemanship; and although in general the troopers were of a good type physically and fairly well mounted, by no stretch of the imagination could the body be called an effective cavalry force ... the body is composed mainly of the farming class'.[62] The County Inspector, viewing the same parade, noted, 'The drill was indifferent; but, on the whole the men were well mounted, and their discipline was good'.[63]

The Nationalist press remained distinctly unimpressed by UVF parades. Carson's lengthy series of inspections conducted in September 1913 was dismissed by the *Irish News* as 'Carson Company's Provincial Tour' and it went on to suggest that many of the supposedly rural volunteers were actually members of the Belfast UVF Regiments who had travelled to rural areas for the purpose of swelling the numbers on parade.[64]

Apart from parades proper, field days and mimic battles became increasingly popular with the UVF leadership as the UVF became better organised and better trained. These were often held on the half day holidays which occurred in rural towns in Ulster or on Boxing Day, Good Friday or Easter Monday when as large a UVF turnout as possible could be counted on, although surprisingly a fair number seem to have been held in the winter of 1913/14 when, in generally poor weather, few spectators could be depended on. An example of mimic warfare was on Boxing Day 1913 when the 5th Tyrone Regiment marched from Castlehill demesne to Augher Castle, where two companies held the Castle, while five others attacked it.[65] On Easter Monday 1914 a number of UVF units were involved in field days of this nature. The 2nd South Down Regiment was involved in a series of manoeuvres at Mourne Park, the East Belfast Regiment carried out a similar demonstration at Orangefield, Belfast, and the Richill and Loughgall UVF companies carried out a war game of blue forces against red forces which took the form of a rearguard action.[66] Field days were becoming very popular by July 1914 when, on one weekend alone, the Portadown Battalion UVF and 3rd South Down Regiment carried out field work, which involved digging and attacking entrenchments.[67] Surprisingly, it appears that there were remarkably few injuries sustained at these various field days, at which UVF members were often armed. One death was attributed to the Loughgall company's field manoeuvres in April 1914, when a horse took fright and bolted, overturning the ammunition cart it was carrying and killing the 13-year-old boy driving it.[68] Despite the supposed role of these field days as training exercises, they clearly had a social element and in many cases obtained a large number of spectators. Thus when Lilian Spender watched a sham fight carried out by units of the South Antrim Regiment on 4 August 1914 she brought a picnic with her.[69] One of the major publicity stunts carried out by the UVF in regard to such training exercises was in the early hours of 28 July 1913 when members of the Co. Armagh Regiment in camp at Tynan Abbey grounds organised themselves into flying columns of motor transport and 'raided' Drogheda and Oldbridge, leaving notes nailed to railway and road bridges reading, 'CAPTURED BY ULSTER VOLUNTEER FORCE'.[70] A number of test mobilisations were carried out by UVF units, but these rarely had any publicity element, often being carried out in the hours of darkness.[71]

As with field days there was a clear conflict between the purpose of UVF camps of instruction in overcoming training deficiencies and in using them as propaganda exercises to impress visiting journalists. This does not seem to have been appreciated by UVF HQ as they, at UUC request, organised the admittance of certain photographers and cinematograph operators to all UVF Easter camps in 1914.[72] The *Belfast Evening Telegraph* carried a report on the Baronscourt camp of instruction, detailing the officers involved and printing photographs of some of the trenches dug.[73] Most UVF camps were fairly small in scale, being designed for the training of UVF officers and NCOs rather than units as a whole, which probably accounts for the relatively small amount of newspaper interest in most of them. This was only starting to change from mid-1914 onwards. For example in July 1914 Lieutenant General Richardson inspected the 2nd North Londonderry Regiment when it was encamped at Magilligan for three days.[74]

As noted at the outset of this chapter, the UVF was involved in few social activities, beyond drilling, marching and parading. The social aspects of Unionism – dinners, concerts, fetes, etc. – were generally organised by the Orange Order, UWUC or Unionist Clubs. However, there were a few notable exceptions. At the Tyrone Regiment camp in October 1913 it was hoped that concerts could be organised in the evenings and any man who could sing was asked to bring some music with him.[75] At Jordanstown School room, a concert was held in aid of both the Greenisland UVF Company and Unionist Club on the evening of Friday 30 January 1914, with General Sir W. T. Adair, the commander of Co. Antrim UVF units, presiding. After a lengthy speech from Adair on the organisation of the UVF in Co. Antrim and the development of the Ulster Medical Board, he presented badges to members of the Greenisland Company who had qualified for them by attending a sufficient number of drills. Following this, the men were entertained by a number of 'appropriate songs' not all sung by members of the UVF. Some of these were purely for entertainment value, such as 'Blackbird's Song' and 'A Maid Sings Light', but others, such as 'Ulstermen' and 'My Love, My Crown', had a deeper political significance.[76] A social at Seskinore, earlier in the same week, involved 'J' Company of the 2nd Tyrone Regiment entertaining the audience with a demonstration of drill, followed by a speech by Colonel McClintock and a musical programme.[77] In March 1914 'E' Company of the 6th North Belfast Regiment held a smoking concert in Merchant's Buildings, North Street; this included a programme of songs with pianoforte accompaniment and a number of political speeches.[78] A similar event was held in August 1914 when the Special Service Section of the East Belfast Regiment held a smoking concert in St John's School room, Ballynafeigh; this involved political speeches from the unit's CO, Lieutenant Colonel A. Hill-Trevor, and Colonel Hacket Pain but, curiously, does not seem to have included a musical programme of any sort.[79] The largest concert held by any UVF unit occurred in July 1914 when 'H' Company of the Young Citizen Volunteers organised a concert in the Ulster Hall in Belfast, in aid of battalion funds. The YCV regimental band played a number of tunes, notably, 'Songs of Great Britain and Ireland', described as a 'series of well known patriotic airs', and this was followed by artistes singing a number of songs such as 'Land of Hope and Glory', 'My Little Grey Home in the West' and 'The Death of Nelson'. The Lord Mayor of Belfast gave a short speech at this concert, which seems to have been the only definite political element of the proceedings.[80] Demonstrating newer types of entertainment the Tyrone battalion was entertained with magic lantern views of the UVF camp of instruction at Baronscourt in November 1913.[81] While it is clear that some film footage was taken of the UVF, it seems that when this was shown in Belfast it was simply in commercial cinemas, not to UVF units specifically.[82]

Even rarer than UVF concerts were UVF sports days, which seems surprising given the popularity of these in units of the British army. 'E' Company of the 1st North Antrim Regiment held a sports day at Cullybackey in July 1914. Events included a 100 yards and half mile flat race and a cycle race and there were a number of sideshows, including an Aunt Sally and quoits.[83] A more militaristic type of sporting day was organised by the 1st Armagh Regiment when it organised an inter-company shooting competition in July 1914.[84]

The term 'UVF' soon came to have a commercial value and in January 1914 Lieutenant Colonel T. V. P. McCammon warned UVF units:

> Attention has been drawn to the fact that certain traders are selling articles naming them UVF pattern, or giving them some similar description that might lead members of the UVF to think that they have received official approval.
>
> Members of the UVF, are cautioned that no authority has been given from Headquarters for this procedure, and that no boots or other articles labelled UVF have been officially approved ... it has been found that in some cases Equipment was being obtained by units of indifferent material, or at excessive prices.[85]

Some time after this directive had been issued Messrs Sharman D. Neill Ltd of Belfast offered cap badges at 1s 3d per dozen but 'The General Officer Commanding is still of opinion that no expenditure should be incurred on Head-dress until a Battalion is fully equipped with more necessary articles'.[86] An enterprising firm quickly marketed Union Jacks for the Ulster Volunteers, urging them not to go to the Balmoral parade in September 1913 without one.[87] Items of a less utilitarian nature were soon being produced for the UVF. From January 1914 W. &. G. Baird Ltd of Belfast were offering busts of Sir Edward Carson to members of the force costing between 7s 6d and £1 1s 0d depending on whether they opted for a marble or old silver finish.[88] A company called Picture Stamps was soon producing a series of Ulster stamps with the phrase 'We will not have Home Rule' and a portrait of Carson.[89]

While the Irish Republican tradition has fostered a number of well-known songs, the same cannot be said of the UVF in this period. The small number of songs and hymns which appeared in connection with the force were of little artistic merit and do not even seem to have been popular at UVF concerts or church services, much less surviving the demise of the movement. A Covenanter's Hymn was published on 28 September 1913, presumably to mark the first anniversary of Ulster Day. The third verse sounded a suitably militant note:

> God is our Strength. Though man betray
> Kinsmen and comrades, blood and bone;
> Though all forsake us – even they
> Who share our Faith, our Flag, our Throne –
> We shall not flinch; we will not bend.
> The oath that our forefathers swore
> Is ours to carry to the end,
> Confident on the God of War.[90]

A rather more catchy 'Volunteer Hymn' to be sung to the tune of the National Anthem appeared in April 1914.[91] A song entitled 'The Ulster Volunteers' was also written at this time. Of this it is worth quoting the first verse and chorus, which show the attempts by contemporary Unionists to emphasise the class alliance and Ulster-wide nature of the force:

> We've enroll'd in thousands,
> In the cause of right,
> To guard our homes, our liberties,
> Against the force of might.
> At the call of duty,
> The lab'rer, far-mer, peer,
> Have banded in to brotherhood,
> To face a common fear.
>
> *Chorus*
> Men from Dry, men from Down,
> Men from Donegal,
> Antrim men, Fermanagh men,
> Have rallied to the call
> Tyrone men, Cavan men,
> Men from Monaghan,
> Armagh men, brave Ulster men,
> All stand man to man,
> All are in the muster,
> All 'For God and Ulster',
> All are volunteers.[92]

Ada Shaw's song 'The Ulster Volunteers' was written in commemoration of the Balmoral parade of September 1913 and concluded:

> And if they meet a soldier's fate,
> And die in fair freedom's name,
> Then deathless glory shall be theirs,
> Honour and lasting fame.
> And never shall their memory fade
> In the mists of crowding years;
> God in His kindness guard and keep
> Our Ulster Volunteers.[93]

In conclusion, the typical UVF member's involvement in the force was likely to be dominated by carrying out drill and parading, with few more social activities available. This, as discussed in chapter 3, may explain the low turnout for UVF activities. It follows then that most spectators' experiences of the UVF would be in watching them parade either on a small scale in small towns or villages or at much larger city or county-wide demonstrations. Normally UVF members, at least pre-July 1914, would parade unarmed and would occasionally be accompanied by a marching band. However, the context of the parade could vary enormously depending on who was addressing or inspecting the parade, at what point in the Third Home Rule crisis the parade occurred and whether it was held in a majority Nationalist or Unionist area. UVF parades do not seem to have been carried out in any numbers after autumn 1914 and, as discussed in chapter 7, the revived UVF of 1920 does not seem to have organised 1913–14 style parades, though the Ulster Imperial Guards formed in that period clearly did. Beyond parades, some UVF members were involved in organising or attending UVF concerts, sports days or magic lantern shows, but these were the exception rather than the rule. Strangely the UVF of 1913–14 produced little lasting memorabilia; the songs composed to honour the force were of little artistic merit and were rarely performed, even at the time.

Notes

1 Foy, 'Ulster Unionist Propaganda against Home Rule 1912–14'.
2 R. V. Comerford, *The Fenians in Context: Irish Politics and Society 1848–82* (Wolfhound Press, Dublin, 1985) and Mike Cronin, *The Blueshirts and Irish Politics* (Four Courts Press, Dublin, 1997).
3 *Belfast Evening Telegraph*, 22/12/1913 and 23/12/13, *Northern Whig*, 29/01/1914.

4 *Fermanagh Times*, 19/06/1913.
5 *Fermanagh Times*, 19/06/1913.
6 *Belfast Evening Telegraph*, 18/07/1913.
7 *Belfast News Letter*, 21/04/1914 and *Northern Whig*, 11/08/1914.
8 *Northern Whig*, 18/11/1914.
9 *Northern Whig*, 14/07/1914.
10 *Northern Whig*, 15/07/1914.
11 *Belfast Evening Telegraph*, 18/10/1913.
12 *Belfast Evening Telegraph*, 29/09/1913, *Northern Whig*, 29/09/1913 and TNA, WO141/26, report by Acting Sergeant Edwards.
13 *Northern Whig*, 29/09/1913.
14 *Belfast Evening Telegraph*, 15/12/1913.
15 *Northern Whig*, 16/07/1913.
16 All details on the Armagh parade taken from PRONI, D/1855/1, Leslie papers, printed programme, 'Unionist Demonstration and Inspection of Ulster Volunteer Force of County Armagh by the Rt. Hon. Sir Edward Carson, K.C., MP, Dean's Hill, Armagh on Saturday 4th October, 1913'.
17 PRONI, D.1633/2/19, Lilian Spender diary, entry for 10/06/1914.
18 *Belfast Evening Telegraph*, 27/12/1913.
19 PRONI, D.1855/1, Leslie papers, telegram, Carson to Leslie, 28/07/1914.
20 PRONI, D.1633/2/19, Lilian Spender diary, entry for 23/07/1914.
21 *Northern Whig*, 11/07/1914 and 13/07/1914.
22 *Northern Whig*, 01/09/1913, *Belfast Evening Telegraph*, 15/04/1914 and *Belfast Evening Telegraph*, 27/03/1914.
23 *Belfast Evening Telegraph*, 25/07/1913.
24 *Northern Whig*, 13/07/1914.
25 *Northern Whig*, 02/02/1914 and PRONI, D.1633/2/19, Lilian Spender diary, entry for 03/08/1914.
26 PRONI, D.1633/2/19, Lilian Spender diary, entry for 06/05/1914.
27 *Belfast Evening Telegraph*, 29/08/1913.
28 DRO, D/Lo/C686(306) (I), letter, T. V. P. McCammon to the Marquess of Londonderry, 30/01/1914, PRONI, D.1633/2/19, Lilian Spender diary, entry for, 11/04/1914 and *Northern Whig*, 13/07/1914.
29 Alan Megahey, *The Irish Protestant Churches in the Twentieth Century* (Macmillan Press, Basingstoke, 2000), pp. 121–31.
30 *Northern Whig*, 31/01/1914.
31 *Belfast Evening Telegraph*, 28/07/1913 and *Northern Whig*, 30/09/1913.
32 *Northern Whig*, 02/92/1914.
33 *Belfast Evening Telegraph*, 04/11/1913. For similar views of 'Rome Rule' see report on a sermon preached by Rev. Canon Peacocke to Bangor UVF, *Northern Whig*, 27/01/1914.
34 *Belfast News Letter*, 28/04/1914.

35 PRONI, D.1390/19/1, Charles Falls papers, John Sears's notebook, entries for 10/05/1914 and PRONI, D.1263/6, Hall papers, 'Parade Services' in Clough Presbyterian Church, 18/03/1914 and 05/04/1914.
36 *Belfast Evening Telegraph*, 03/04/1914. David Simpson Quigley's printed copy of this is held in NLI, Ms.27,988.
37 *Northern Whig*, 13/07/1914.
38 *Northern Whig*, 02/02/1914.
39 *The Times*, 02/05/1914.
40 *Belfast Evening Telegraph*, 30/03/1914.
41 *Northern Whig*, 16/07/1914.
42 *Northern Whig*, 06/07/1914.
43 PRONI, D.1390/19/1, Charles Falls papers, John Sears's notebook, entry for 28/01/1914.
44 *Northern Whig*, 05/02/1914 and PRONI, D.1390/19/1, Charles Falls papers, John Sears's notebook entry for 06/03/1914.
45 *Northern Whig*, 06/08/1914.
46 *Belfast Evening Telegraph*, 22/09/1913 and 14/04/1914.
47 *Belfast Evening Telegraph*, 20/12/1913.
48 *Northern Whig*, 07/07/1914.
49 *Northern Whig*, 25/07/1914 and 27/07/1914.
50 *Northern Whig*, 22/07/1914 and 23/07/1914.
51 *Northern Whig*, 09/07/1914.
52 PRONI, D.1633/2/19, Lilian Spender diary, entry for 28/07/1913.
53 PRONI, D.1633/2/19, Lilian Spender diary, entry for 11/06/1914.
54 PRONI, D.1633/2/19, Lilian Spender diary, entry for 11/06/1914.
55 *Belfast Evening Telegraph*, 23/07/1913. On being granted the town and fort of Hillsborough in the 1660s Sir Arthur Hill was permitted to raise a small force, practically a private army, to garrison it. By 1914 the castle warders seem to have been about 20 in number, mostly elderly ex-servicemen. See the display at Hillsborough Courthouse for details of this unusual formation.
56 TNA, CO904/27/2/II, printed pamphlet, 'Ulster Volunteer Force, Belfast Division, Official Arrangements, Inspection by Sir Edward Carson and the General Officer Commanding UVF in the Agricultural Show Grounds, Balmoral, Saturday 27th September 1913'.
57 *Northern Whig*, 19/09/1913.
58 *Northern Whig*, 22/09/1913.
59 PRONI, D.1855/1, Leslie papers, UVF order 75, 18/07/1914.
60 PRONI, D.1633/2/19, Lilian Spender diary, entry for 11/06/1914.
61 *Fermanagh Times*, 19/06/1913.
62 TNA, CO904/27/1, 'Enniskillen Horse', report by DI P.A. Marriman, 15/06/1913.
63 TNA, CO904/27/1, 'Enniskillen Horse', memorandum, CI, RIC to Under Secretary, Dublin Castle.

64 *Irish News*, 19/09/1913 and 22/09/1913.
65 *Belfast Evening Telegraph*, 27/12/1913 and *The Times*, 29/12/1913.
66 *Belfast Evening Telegraph*, 14/04/1914.
67 *Northern Whig*, 06/07/1914.
68 *Belfast Evening Telegraph*, 15/04/1914.
69 PRONI, D.1633/2/19, Lilian Spender diary, entry for 04/08/1914.
70 *Belfast Evening Telegraph*, 28/07/1913.
71 *Northern Whig*, 03/08/1914.
72 PRONI, D.1238/92, O'Neill papers, UVF order 36, 09/04/1914.
73 *Belfast Evening Telegraph*, 12/10/1913.
74 *Northern Whig*, 24/07/1914.
75 PRONI, D.1132/6/1, Lowry papers, pamphlet, 'UVF, The Tyrone Regiment, Advance Orders for Camp of Instruction'.
76 *Northern Whig*, 31/01/1914.
77 *Northern Whig*, 31/01/1914.
78 *Belfast Evening Telegraph*, 28/03/1914.
79 *Northern Whig*, 03/08/1914.
80 *Northern Whig*, 01/07/1914.
81 *Belfast Evening Telegraph*, 22/11/1913.
82 TNA, CO904/27, printed circular letter, 24/05/1913.
83 *Northern Whig* 27/07/1914.
84 *Northern Whig*, 03/07/1914.
85 D.1238/109, O'Neill papers, UVF order 3, 10/01/1914.
86 PRONI, D.1238/96, O'Neill papers, UVF order 26, 21/03/1914.
87 *Belfast Evening Telegraph*, 25/09/1913.
88 *Belfast Evening Telegraph*, 11/11/1913 and 01/01/1914.
89 *Belfast Evening Telegraph*, 22/12/1913.
90 *Northern Whig*, 03/10/1913.
91 *Belfast News Letter*, 27/04/1914.
92 'The Ulster Volunteers: Song with Chorus', words by the Rev. Arthur Davis, music by 'Unionist' (Joseph Williams Ltd, London, 1914).
93 *Northern Whig*, 30/09/1913.

5

Arms, equipment and finance

This chapter assesses three different but closely related issues which directly influenced the training and military capabilities of the UVF. The issue of gunrunning is one that will be dealt with fairly briefly in this chapter. It was the key element of A. T. Q. Stewart's *Ulster Crisis* and little subsequent research seriously challenges his interpretation of events. Other issues surrounding UVF arms do, however, require reappraisal such as the legal framework in which the arming of the force was conducted, the type and numbers of firearms obtained and the ultimate fate of these weapons. With regard to finance, full access to the, admittedly incomplete, UUC financial files for this period does allow for a reinterpretation of this aspect of Unionist resistance to Home Rule. While previous works, from Unionist apologias to Marxist reinterpretations, have stated that the UVF was very well funded (the figure of £1,000,000 available is oft cited[1]) this does not actually seem to have been the case. While UVF funds were carefully dispersed it seems that the movement never had access to more than £150,000 and a perennial problem for UVF HQ, in trying to assert its authority, was its inability to provide adequate funding for most key requirements. This situation meant that the matter of equipment, from uniforms to food rations, was largely left to local initiatives and like so much else concerning the UVF was left open to wide regional variations.

Previous works on the UVF have neglected to consider the place of the force within the vibrant gun culture that existed in Edwardian Britain. Joyce Lee Malcolm in her important work on the subject, notes that firearms ownership was linked with the concept of individual liberty and that the 1870 firearms legislation, which introduced gun licences, was widely breached, largely as police forces saw it as an excise, not a criminal matter.[2] Firearms ownership was also increasing at a time when crime rates were falling, so contemporaries did not make the direct connection between illegal firearms ownership and crime, which police forces do today.³

Before 1920 there were few legal restraints on the carrying of firearms in the United Kingdom as a whole, though some restrictive Irish legislation existed. The Irish Attorney General noted that the Peace Preservation Act (Ireland) of 1881 was not renewed in 1906 and thus, the only Act in force in Ireland which interfered with the use or carrying of arms was the Gun Licence Act of 1870. He went on to note, in August 1913, 'the prohibition is only for the use or carrying of the gun and does not prevent the possession of firearms or subject the possessor to the licence duty. Moreover, this is a Revenue Act which must be enforced exclusively by the Excise Authorities ... Therefore, the Act of 1870, for the purposes of the present consideration, is of no practical use'.⁴ This important legal question over the powers of the RIC to act in excise cases was to drag on for months. Only in July 1914 was Sir John Simon, the English Attorney General, to state definitively that the RIC (but not the Dublin Metropolitan Police) had the same powers as customs officers to seize arms, making the observation that the RIC was not slow to act over illegal distilling which was also an excise matter.⁵

The Attorney General went on to suggest that those UVF members carrying arms could be tried

> under statute of 2 Edw. III, cap. 3, in three counts: first for going armed not being one of the King's servants or one of his ministers executing his precepts, and in a second count for going armed in public without lawful occasion in such a manner as to be a nuisance and to alarm the public, and in the third count for discharging a loaded revolver to the danger of the public as was the case in The King v. Meade, Carnarvon Assizes, 5/6/1903 ... It occurs to me that this case of The King v. Meade may be made use of in connection with these armed processions, parties going armed to meetings, and persons discharging firearms from trains, but we have always to contend with the difficulty of finding Grand Juries who will be willing to act and find true Bills, and of finding Petty Juries who will do their duty.⁶

As late as September 1913 the Attorney General was suggesting that some of those identified carrying arms at a UVF demonstration in Ballynahinch should be prosecuted for not having gun licences and for illegal drilling. However, Birrell refused to act on this advice.⁷ In increasing desperation the Irish Attorney General also suggested that UVF members who had participated in the Baronscourt Camp and had openly carried arms in field training there could be tried for 'obstructing the public highway' for their activities near Ardstraw Bridge.⁸

UVF members seem to have been entirely clear about their legal rights. Lieutenant Colonel John Madden complained, at length, to the RIC County Inspector for Monaghan, stating

> I wish to bring to your notice the way the police are behaving here. I understand they are trespassing through my place without any leave from me.
>
> Only yesterday the Sergeant in Scotchouse came in and watched the drill of a section of volunteers who were drilling in my pleasure ground, _ of a mile from the boundary of the place; concealed in a wood. This is an unwarrantable liberty, and I have to give you notice that I shall forcibly remove any police sergeant or constable entering my place in future ... I have also to complain that your Sergeant chose to come up into my yard during my absence in Dublin the other day, ostensibly to look at my motor car, but really to try + cross examine my chauffeur as to whether I had any arms in my home. I may say that naturally I have arms in my house of various sorts, + always have had, + I should like to know what law there is against my having as many as I choose.[9]

County Inspector Tyache responded civilly but firmly to this letter stating that his sergeant had understood that he was free to enter Madden's estate at any time and that the sergeant spoke to Madden's chauffeur only about a defective tail light on Madden's car.[10] In replying, Gerald Madden made it clear that he would not allow the RIC to search his car for arms unless they produced a search warrant.[11]

Similarly, the legality of importing arms into Ireland was a grey area, at least until December 1913, and the legal powers with which the government could act against UVF gunrunning were surprisingly limited. Outlining the situation in April 1913 the Solicitor General noted, 'Importation of Arms from abroad may be prohibited by Proclamation or Order in Council under section 43 of Customs Laws Consolidation Act 1876 ... Supplying of Arms for certain purposes might conceivably be dealt with under the old Riot Act of the Irish Parliament ... [and] Prerogative Power of Lord Lieutenant. Only to be used in very extreme cases. Its limits have never been defined'. The Solicitor General went on to note that goods imported under the wrong description in a cargo manifest could be held under the Customs Laws Consolidation Act of 1876.[12] Offering further advice in December 1913 the Law Officers suggested that if a 'criminal purpose' was clear then arms could be seized 'by the direction of the Executive Government' following the issuing of a proclamation similar to that issued by the Irish government on 11 March 1793.[13] This latter advice was apparently offered in response to the government's decision to issue two Royal Proclamations on 4 December 1913. One of these forbade the importation of arms and ammunition, apart from those intended solely for sporting purposes, mining or any other 'unwarlike' purpose into Ireland, while the second prohibited the carriage by sea of military arms and ammunition.[14] However, even after this proclamation had been issued, the government was reluctant to act against Unionist gunrunning. An Admiralty memorandum of May 1914 stated, 'Officers of the Navy are not as such authorised to search vessels for prohibited arms, but they may be employed on this duty with the concurrence of the Commissioners of Customs'.[15]

Thus the Liberal government abided by a very liberal interpretation of firearms legislation throughout the Ulster crisis. Indeed, the legal authority under which the government made its largest seizure of 4,500 rifles destined for the UVF in Hammersmith in June 1913 was the Gun Barrel Proof Act of 1868 which had been introduced to protect British industry rather than British lives. The UVF could have retrieved these weapons for a fine of £2 per rifle as, being of Italian origin and imported from Hamburg, they had not received the required quality control from the Gunmakers' Company as required by the 1868 Act. However, this was not done, largely as the rifles seized had cost considerably less than £2 each. While F. H. Crawford was surprised that the government had made use of such a little known Act, it is possible that this action was taken by the government under pressure from the Court of the Gunmakers' Company, which had taken an interest in the foreign firearms being imported into Ulster as early as November 1911.[16]

The issue of 'hawks' and 'doves' in the UVF's ruling councils became very clear over the armaments issue. As Alvin Jackson has noted the decision to arm the UVF was taken reluctantly and was an attempt to bolster morale which was seen as wavering in early 1914.[17] Fred Crawford's rather melodramatic account of the Larne gunrunning even suggests that when the 20,000 guns brought in during this enterprise were on the high seas UVF HQ ordered him not to land the guns as planned; presumably in the wake of the Curragh Incident which served to make their presence less important.[18]

What seems clear is that UVF HQ was under pressure from local units to import and distribute arms. A deputation of UVF members from Co. Antrim, consisting of General Sir William Adair, the divisional commander and his three regimental commanders, saw Carson and Craig on 20 January 1914. At this meeting the Co. Antrim officers

Arms, equipment and finance 139

expressed, 'very great dissatisfaction ... at the inadequate supply of arms – even for instructional purposes'. They stated that the entire county had just 150, .303 carbines and 50 Vetterli rifles, the latter with no ammunition, for a force of 10,700 men. The officers went on to note that their men were tiring of basic drill and that the ex-army officers promised from England had not arrived. They also stated that other counties had received more rifles and ammunition and demanded an explanation for this.[19] Other county committees, if not quite so militant in their approach, were starting to ask awkward questions about the issuing of arms. The Co. Down committee asked if UVF HQ would issue arms directly or provide funds to the county committees so that they could make their own arrangements.[20] Thus it seems that the provision of arms became an issue necessary for UVF HQ to maintain its authority over county committees and local commanders.

Who then, can be identified as hawks? Crawford, who directed most of the gunrunning operations, noted that his efforts were consistently supported by James Craig, who, after all, provided him with the finance for his missions. It also seems from Crawford's account that Colonel R. H. Wallace, Colonel T. E. Hickman, Lord Leitrim, Lord Farnham, Sir William Bull and, perhaps more surprisingly, Bonar Law and Walter Long were fellow hawks.[21] Carson ultimately backed Crawford's mass gunrunning operation of April 1914; however, by this time Carson was aware that he was, in J. C. Beckett's memorable phrase, 'a prisoner of his own people', conscious that he had to back militant action or risk the disintegration of Ulster Unionism.[22]

The doves then are, by implication, those who did not support Crawford's endeavours. Lieutenant General Sir George Richardson and Lieutenant Colonel T. V. P. McCammon were presumably the senior UVF HQ officers who issued the countermanding orders to Crawford. Colonel G. H. Hacket Pain was later to be credited with organising the Larne gunrunning, although Crawford certainly saw him as a dove.[23] Captain W. B. Spender's role is similarly ambivalent. He seems to have carried out the bulk of the staff work which was necessary for landing the rifles at Larne, Bangor and Donaghadee and, in retrospect, certainly identified himself with the hawks by writing a glowing foreword to Crawford's, *Guns for Ulster*.[24] However, it seems that in mid-April 1914 it was Spender who was dispatched to order Crawford not to land arms.

There were, of course, doves at the local level and this became obvious over the question of which UVF volunteers should be armed. As discussed in chapter 3, Colonel Oliver Nugent saw his force in Co. Cavan as effectively a police force, while Colonel Sharman Crawford, a leading figure in the Co. Down UVF, stated that arms would not necessarily be issued to every member of the force.[25] The Larne gunrunning should not be seen as a decisive victory for the hawks within the UVF. It was July 1914 before UVF HQ ordered the distribution and carrying of arms, issuing an order stating, 'It has been decided that, at the discretion of the COs, the time has come when arms may be carried openly by members of the Ulster Volunteer Force, and that any attempt to seize arms from individuals who may be carrying them in accordance with these instructions is to be resisted, in accordance with former instructions issued on this subject'.[26] As discussed in chapter 4, this was the occasion for a number of UVF parades where members were publicly presented with their rifles but, as discussed below, many UVF COs simply stored rifles in armouries, conscious of the problems that mass arming could produce.

Gunrunning long preceded the formation of the UVF in January 1913. There had certainly been some gunrunning during the First and Second Home Rule Bills. The problems in assessing the nature and extent of gunrunning are varied. Firstly, Crawford's and Adgey's accounts are both self-serving and were written years after the events described. Secondly, the police interest in gunrunning varied over time and place; noticeably few English or Scottish police forces seem to have taken any interest, the exceptions being the Metropolitan Police and Durham Constabulary, the former being involved in the Hammersmith seizure and, through Special Branch, keeping a watching brief on gunrunning as a whole, and the latter force seizing 150,000 rounds of ammunition at Stockton on Tees, under section 74 of the Explosives Act, 1875.[27] Thirdly, there always seems to have been a conflict among Ulster Unionists over how gunrunning should be conducted. This was seen most clearly in the Larne gunrunning as Major F. H. Crawford wrote, 'The Unionist papers ought to be squared so that they will not refer to it at all, at least for some days after. This will give you a better chance of getting redistributed later'.[28] However, Crawford's wishes were ignored, presumably as the Unionist leadership wanted to maximise the publicity value of his enterprise. It is therefore likely that arms, far from being run in under a veil of secrecy were, whenever possible, flaunted for maximum publicity.

It appears that the RIC first became aware of guns being brought into Ulster in relatively large numbers by Unionists in December 1911, when, with some press attention, 24 Martini-Henry rifles and 1,000 rounds of ammunition were delivered to Orange Lodges in Co. Londonderry.[29] It seems that James Craig was first involved in gunrunning at this time and Fred Crawford appears to have started his activities in July 1911.[30]

Given the grey legal area in which the arming of Ulster Unionists was conducted it is not surprising to find that, at least initially, Unionists relied on established gunsmiths in Belfast to meet their requirements. In November 1913, the RIC noted that 2,200 rifles had been imported into Ulster, in that month alone, by Adgey and Murphy, Hunter and Son, W. D. Ryall, E. E. Tyack and C. D. Williams, arms dealers. It was also noted that Birmingham arms dealers who were trading with Ulster refused to give the names of their customers.[31] The Earl of Lanesborough brought a certain degree of panache to the UVF gunrunning in that he purchased 175 Martini Enfield .303 rifles from Harrods Department Store in London, which appear to have been delivered to the Earl of Erne in Enniskillen.[32]

Most of the rifles issued to the UVF were brought into Ulster by Major Fred Crawford who was the UVF's Director of Ordnance. Initially he worked with Sir William Bull MP and Bull's brother-in-law, Captain H. A. Budden. Bull and Budden set up a front firm, John Ferguson and Company, which was based in the large stable yards adjoining the Windsor Castle Hotel in Hammersmith. They also operated through a legitimate firm of motor body builders, F. M. Foyer & Co. Ltd, again based in Hammersmith and owned by Bull's former chauffeur. Crawford's arrangements with Bull, Budden and Foyer were initially successful; it was through this Hammersmith operation that Crawford imported six Vickers machine guns and thousands of rifles into Ulster. Disaster struck on 9 June 1913 when the Metropolitan Police seized 4,500 rifles, which they held under the 1868 Proof Act. In later years Crawford became convinced that Budden, an alcoholic with financial troubles, had informed on the operation in return for a financial reward. During 1913, when Crawford relied on the Hammersmith operation, he also had a much smaller clearing house operating in Newcastle upon Tyne, through which he imported 400 rifles.[33]

Crawford's largest gunrunning success was the major operation of April 1914 which culminated in the landing of a large number of rifles at Larne, Bangor and Donaghadee. The events of this audacious enterprise have been recounted in detail elsewhere and need only be dealt with briefly here.[34] In essence, Crawford purchased 20,000 rifles and 2,000,000 rounds of ammunition in Hamburg in February 1914 and embarked them on a Norwegian vessel, the SS *Fanny*, on 2 April 1914.

Following a circuitous route and trans-shipment of the rifles and ammunition onto a coal vessel, the SS *Clyde Valley*, on 19–20 April, the cargo was unloaded in the three Ulster ports on 24/25 April 1914. The importance of the so-called Larne gunrunning was partly that it showed what the UVF could achieve. The UVF was mobilised throughout Ulster, with local units seizing Larne, Bangor and Donaghadee, quickly overawing the local police, coastguards and customs officials. Telegram and telephone systems were short circuited which meant that no police or army reinforcements could be summoned, a crucial task given that a battalion of British troops was based at Palace Barracks in Holywood, a mere seven miles from Bangor. In addition a careful deception plan was effectively executed by 2,500 UVF members under the command of Colonel Couchman. This group met the SS *Balmerino* when it docked in Belfast and drew RIC and customs attention to this vessel, which in fact carried no arms at all. Perhaps the major success of this operation was that only one death occurred during it, when a coastguard, H. E. Painter, died of a heart attack at Donaghadee, having cycled furiously to wake his CO.

It seems amazing that the Larne gunrunning was able to proceed given that the British Acting Vice Consul in Hamburg, E. G. Cable, had warned the Foreign Minister on 12 April that the SS *Fanny* was British owned and spoken of, in Hamburg, as a gunrunner.[35] At least one RIC officer felt that the arms could have been easily seized, stating in his memoirs:

> The gun-running is always said to have been carried out in such a masterly fashion that the RIC were caught napping, and all the arms distributed before police were aware as to what was happening. This was not so in my case at any rate. Sometime during the day in question I heard that arms were to be brought that evening to the house of Mr. J. Porter-Porter, of Belleisles. I did not know what to do and could not get instructions. It would have been very easy to seize the arms as they all seemed to be in packages and, of course, useless for immediate use. I brought just a few men to Mr. Porter-Porter's demesne. When I got to the front gate I knew the information was correct, as he and his wife were both there. I sat on the other side of the road and a jocose conversation was kept up. After a time along came the cars with their packages in the back, and in they went to Belleisle. I knew a number of the drivers and some of them waved as they passed. The arms were delivered and there was no interference at any time.[36]

However, the operation was not flawless. There was a shortage of transport at Larne, with General Adair the UVF commander in Co.

Antrim asking for any available transport (including horse drawn wagons and hand carts) to be sent to Larne; as a result it is not clear how far the guns were transported from Larne, Bangor and Donaghadee in the crucial hours following their unloading. Many of the cars and lorries entering and leaving the harbours did nothing to disguise their number plates, which meant that the RIC could quickly ascertain who had been involved and the likely destinations of the rifles landed. It also seems that Crawford had not recruited enough sailors to properly crew the *Clyde Valley* and that crucial harbour facilities had not been secured (in Bangor water had to be fed to the *Clyde Valley* by the district council's fire cart). This all meant that the unloading proceeded much more slowly than had been planned, with the unloading at Bangor and Donaghadee, which should have been carried out under cover of darkness, not completed until 8.30 a.m.[37]

Other gunrunning operations were carried out through 1912–14 and it appears that Crawford had no part in these. R. J. Adgey operated a shop, which appears to have mainly been a pawnbrokers, but which also dealt in second-hand firearms. As such he had been involved in selling arms to individual Unionists from the beginning of the Ulster crisis. The extent of Adgey's involvement in supplying the UVF is unclear, but he claimed to have imported 'many' rifles into Ulster disguised as hardware or secreted in bleaching powder barrels and in November 1914 the RIC understood him to have imported 1,188 Martini Enfield rifles in that month alone.[38] W. P. Johnston, who was interviewed by A. T. Q. Stewart, claimed to have been involved in importing hundreds of rifles into Ulster from Manchester, under the cover of his family's textile printing business.[39] It also seems likely, based on reports of the seizures of arms, that Messrs Samuel Lawther and Co. of Belfast, J. W. Buchanan of Strabane, Abraham Combe of Dromore, Lord Leitrim and M. Archdale of Ballinacumber were involved in gunrunning, though they may simply have been acting as fronts for Crawford and Adgey's activities.[40] As late as July 1914 the UVF appears to have been attempting to obtain rifles from sympathetic British army personnel and Staff Sergeant Ensell of the King's Own Yorkshire Light Infantry was charged with stealing five rifles from his battalion's armoury in Dublin, with the intention of supplying them to Dublin UVF members.[41]

The quality of guns which the UVF possessed varied enormously and, as Charles Townshend has stated, this would have created a, 'logistical nightmare' in any conflict and this seems to have been the case given the unwillingness of UVF units to agree to any sensible redistribution of arms.⁴² This was despite Colonel Hacket Pain's suggestion, made in May 1914, that, 'failing an inter-county agreement it appears that two courses only are feasible to minimise the general mixing up of the two types of rifles available in most counties. First, by mutual inter-Regimental agreement in the Counties to collect into battalions of one Regiment the whole of one type ... The Second course should be to arm the men of the "marching Battalions" of the Regiment with what is considered the most suitable rifle and handing over the other type of rifle to the men left for protection duty'.⁴³ By mid-1914 the UVF appears to have been equipped with a variety of Lee Metford, Martini Henry, Mauser, Steyr and Vetterli rifles, all taking different types of ammunition. Indeed, Adgey argued that one of the key reasons behind the Larne gunrunning was the realisation that if a large number of similar rifles were not brought in together then the UVF would continue to be armed in a piecemeal fashion.⁴⁴ Most rifles were of the single shot variety and a large minority were Vetterli rifles, which were purchased from the bargain basement of the international arms market, having been withdrawn from service in the Italian army in 1887.⁴⁵ Brigadier General Count Gleichen was utterly dismissive of the military value of these Italian rifles noting, 'they were not good, but weedy + weak + only cost 5 francs apiece, including belt and bayonet!'⁴⁶ It was probably the poor quality of these rifles which made redistribution of arms throughout the UVF, as suggested by Colonel Hacket Pain, impossible as no county committee wanted to risk their units being re-equipped solely with these Italian rifles, while their more highly prized British, German and Austrian rifles were sent elsewhere.

The number of firearms which the UVF possessed is impossible to calculate. As noted above, firearms control was very lax in Edwardian Ireland, at least until late 1913, and revolver ownership was certainly widespread.⁴⁷ A. T. Q. Stewart has stated that in July 1914 the force had 37,048 rifles.⁴⁸ This is a curiously precise figure given the efforts made by local UVF commanders to obtain (and, of course, retain) rifles, without reference to UVF HQ. Alvin Jackson has come to an estimate of around 40,000 rifles in UVF hands by July 1914, while Josephine Howie suggested a figure of 60,000 rifles by early May 1914.⁴⁹ This, of course, reflects confusion among contemporaries on how many rifles the UVF had available. The RIC seems to have felt that the UVF possessed 24,879 by 31 March 1914, the Dublin Castle administration seems to have believed a figure of 51,595 by 31 May 1914 and, incredibly, given his background in military intelligence, Count Gleichen seems to have given

Arms, equipment and finance 145

credence to estimates of 80,000 rifles in UVF hands.[50] An RIC report of February 1917 (compiled at a time when the UVF was co-operating with the RIC to ensure that no UVF arms fell into Irish Volunteer hands) suggested that the UVF then had access to 53,130 rifles, though, as discussed below, this figure is probably an under-estimate given the unwillingness of UVF members to hand in rifles to central armouries.[51] In absolute terms, including rifles of all calibres and vintages, Howie's figure of 60,000 would seem credible. What can be concluded definitely is that the UVF 'field force' of 25,000 men could all have been armed with modern rifles and probably all 100,000 members of the force could have been armed with firearms of some sort, if revolvers and shotguns in private ownership are taken into account.

Table 5.1. The distribution of rifles and machine guns per county 1917

Area	Lee Enfield (magazine)	Martini Enfield (single loader)	German and Austrian	Italian	Other makes	Machine guns	TOTAL
Co. Antrim	2152	896	6606	55	101	0	9810
Co. Armagh	397	416	447	2920	0	0	4180
Belfast	6030	3353	1657	700	630	11	12381
Co. Cavan	188	746	311	41	88	0	1374
Co. Donegal	193	1578	5	8	0	0	1784
Co. Down	1002	1493	5043	130	859	0	8527
Co. Fermanagh	134	186	118	1830	50	0	2318
Londonderry (City)	805	205	800	0	60	0	1870
Londonderry (County)	366	575	860	1362	20	0	3183
Co. Monaghan	21	0	720	712	255	0	1678
Co. Tyrone	705	3471	1844	5	0	0	6025

Source: See note 51.

The distribution of arms is interesting and while confirming that the arming of the Ulster Volunteers was carried out in a piecemeal fashion also suggests that political rather than military decisions were important in deciding how to arm particular units (see Table 5.1). It is noticeable that the 'frontier' counties did not receive the best equipment, as one would have expected, with a disproportionately high number of the despised Italian rifles present in Counties Armagh, Fermanagh, Londonderry and Monaghan. It is also noticeable that Co. Antrim, whose county committee, as discussed above, was particularly hawkish, received very few of the Italian rifles, despite the fact that the county was relatively secure, in terms both of being well behind any likely Unionist 'front line' and of having a small Catholic minority. The figures for Belfast are interesting as while the highest number of rifles was in the city, along with the entire compliment of machine guns, the numbers of rifles are disproportionately low, given the large numbers of UVF personnel in the city and the fact that the Special Service Force was centred on the Belfast regiments.

With the outbreak of the Great War, the UVF played an important role both in the creation of the 36th (Ulster) Division and in home defence duties, as discussed further in chapter 6.[52] The rapid expansion of the British army in late 1914 saw a crisis develop regarding the quantity of rifles available, with a national reserve of only 70,000 being held in store.[53] This meant that many New Army and TF units were provided with pitifully few rifles for training purposes.[54] However, the 36th (Ulster) Division was placed in a fortunate position, as the then Major Wilfrid Spender, GSO II with this formation noted, 'Whilst the Division remained in Ulster it found its association with the UVF very useful in many ways, not only were rifles and machine guns provided for training – a fact which inspecting Generals thought it wiser not to notice – but some musketry was also made possible'.[55]

The Belgian army initially showed some interest in the UVF arms. However, James Craig was only prepared to give (contemporaries all agree that this would have been a free gift) rifles to the Belgians if the British government repealed the Home Rule Bill which had been placed on the statute book in September 1914. Not surprisingly, such a high price was unacceptable to the British government.[56] An element of the UVF arsenal was sold, when on the outbreak of war 2,000,000 rounds of ammunition were sold to the British government at a price of 90s per 1,000 rounds, which Adgey claimed was the cost price.[57]

During the Great War, most of the UVF weapons remained with the UVF which recast itself as a home defence force. In the chaotic situation which engulfed the UVF in 1914–15 Adgey and some subordinates tried to collect the UVF arms into central arsenals, where they could be carefully oiled, greased and stored for the duration. However, Adgey noted that he was unable to collect more than 25,000 rifles and 10,000,000 rounds of ammunition into these armouries.[58]

Arms, equipment and finance 147

Following the Easter Rising, the British authorities became concerned at the amount of weapons available in Ireland. In August 1917 the INV headquarters was raided and a number of rifles seized. This led Lieutenant General Sir Bryan Mahon, GOC, Ireland to reflect:

> The possession of a large number of arms by the Ulster Volunteers is a source of irritation to the National Volunteers whose arms were lately seized. The pretext of seizing arms does not exist in the case of Ulster as it is unlikely that they will get into undesirable hands, though a *coup de main* by the Sinn Fein Party for the seizure of some of them is not impossible.
>
> It is also recognised that the risk of the stoppage of work in the Munitions Factories in the North prevents the taking of these arms by force. The only solution appears to be an arrangement by which they would be voluntarily surrendered to the Military.[59]

The UVF authorities themselves were concerned about arms seizures in October 1917. The CO of the 5th Tyrone Regiment wrote to his company commanders,

> I have received an order from Head Quarters requiring special + immediate attention to the protection of arms + ammunition.
> I shall be glad if you will answer the questions which I enclose – return to me by Reg[istere]d. post as soon as possible …
> 1. Are you satisfied that all rifles + ammunition in your district are so situated that they cannot fall into the hands of undesirable people.
> 2. If not, what immediate step will you take to insure their safety.
> 3. Have the bolts been removed from Rifles + hidden apart from them, it is most essential that this should be done …
> 6. Kindly specify each place where Rifles and Ammunition in your District are stored in quantity + state what provision is made to ensure their safety.[60]

Edward Shortt, the Chief Secretary, wanted to over-rule Mahon in August 1918 and secure UVF arms in military custody, by force if necessary.[61] However, Field Marshal Lord French, the Lord Lieutenant, concurred with General Mahon's views stating in September 1918, 'The temper of the Belfast workers is such that a single false step might cause grave industrial trouble'.[62] Therefore, the voluntary scheme outlined by Mahon was implemented.

UVF officers who wished to do so could deposit their unit's weapons in armouries, which would be protected by British troops. The weapons were not therefore seized in any sense of the word as the UVF retained ownership of the arms. By October 1918 the Chief Secretary reported that 50,000 rifles and 11 machine guns, mostly UVF weapons, had been handed over to the military.[63]

In April 1919 Lieutenant General Sir George Richardson resigned as GOC of the UVF. In his last order, presumably acting in accordance with the wishes of the Ulster Unionist leadership, he stated, 'Existing conditions call for the demobilisation of the Ulster Volunteers'.[64] Surprisingly, this 'stand down' does not seem to have caused any consideration to be given to what would happen to the arms owned by the UVF. A. T. Q. Stewart has provided a colourful account of the fate of the UVF arsenal in which he states that most of the rifles were used to equip the British officered Ethiopian levies who restored Emperor Haile Selassie to his throne in 1941.[65] Unfortunately Stewart's account has little basis in fact; most of the UVF arsenal remained rusting in Lisburn until 1940 when some were issued to Home Guards in Northern Ireland with the bulk being used as scrap. Having noted this, it is clear that a number of UVF rifles remained in private hands after 1920 and as recently as 2002 the author saw a number for sale at a militaria fair in Bangor, Co. Down.

Many of the Loyalist forces raised in 1920–22 and, of course, the reformed UVF, were armed with old UVF arms and Sir James Craig noted in a cabinet memorandum, 'The Loyalists have in a measure disarmed themselves by voluntar[il]y placing a large proportion of the UVF Arms under the Military ... It is noteworthy that in the areas where the UVF units have retained their Arms, no serious disturbances have hitherto arisen'.[66] It seems likely that, following consideration of this memorandum, the British government released many of the arms under its control to these vigilante groups and to the USC, when it began its formation in October 1920. Indeed, by 1922, the number of rifles in store was not the 50,000 quoted by Shortt but just under 20,000. Some UVF equipment which had never been handed over to the British government quickly came under the control of some of the fringe paramilitary groups. For example, the thousands of rounds of ammunition hidden in Colonel Fred Crawford's bleach works were being guarded by members of the extreme Ulster Imperial Guards by August 1920.[67] It appears that contingency plans were made to issue the 20,000 rifles remaining in government storage to members of 'B' Division of the USC in November 1921 in the event of the Anglo-Irish Truce breaking down, as by this time sufficient numbers of modern rifles had not been secured in Great Britain to arm the entire force. At this time, the rifles were being stored with their bolts removed, which rendered them unserviceable.[68]

Already by 1922 the UVF weapons remaining in government storage (now transferred from the War Office to the Ministry of Home Affairs of the new Northern Ireland government) were something of an embarrassment. Writing in June 1922, Colonel F. S. Pountney from the Office of the Military Adviser to the Northern Ireland government noted:

> Now that Service Rifles for the whole of the Ulster forces are available, there is no reason whatever for the retention of the various patterns of weapons belonging to the UVF, which are costing something like £15,000 a year to store and guard, besides taking up the services of a number of valuable men.
>
> I suggest that the whole of these rifles, together with the ammunition belonging to them, be taken out to sea and sunk in deep water.
>
> This would be the cheapest way of getting rid of them, as they are quite unsaleable, and we should be at once relived of an unnecessary responsibility.[69]

Pountney's sensible advice was greeted with horror by civil servants, one firmly stated, 'No. If this was done the whole of Ulster would be up in arms. This is a matter for the P.M.' While another indignantly wrote, 'Evidently the Military Adviser's staff don't think much of the UVF arms I think the D.[eputy] C.[ommissioner] might say whether it is a fact that guarding them costs £15,000 a year. This seems an inflated estimate'. Such optimism proved to be misplaced. Queried on this matter the Inspector General of the Royal Ulster Constabulary (RUC) noted that 27 men were required to guard these rifles and that they were being stored in rented premises in East Belfast.[70] The arms were, as a result of these queries, transferred to the RUC stores depot at Sprucefield, near Lisburn.

Two years later the issue of the UVF rifles emerged again, this time at Cabinet level. At the Cabinet meeting on 17 November 1924, H. M. Pollock, the Minister of Finance, circulated a memorandum stating that, 'providing cover for these Arms entailed an expenditure of some £250, which the Arms themselves were not worth'.[71] However, the Cabinet decided that it would not be expedient to dispose of the arms. Unsatisfied with this conclusion, Pollock wrote to Richard Dawson Bates, the Minister for Home Affairs, informing him that either the guns would have to be stored as 'lumber' (presumably this meant that they should not be securely housed in any building) or that the Ministry for Home Affairs would have to find somewhere to store them, within existing accommodation. Dawson Bates tersely replied that the Cabinet had clearly wanted the guns to be stored safely.[72] The fact that they remained housed at Sprucefield seems to suggest that the Minister for Home Affairs had the final say on this matter.

The debates surrounding the Firearms (Amendment) Act (Northern Ireland) of 1926 suggest that a significant number of UVF rifles remained in private hands. Up until early 1926 an easy way for Unionists to legally possess firearms was to enrol in 'C' Division of the USC. Raised in 1920 'C' Division was an emergency reserve formation and members were not required to carry out any duties but were entitled to possess firearms for self-defence. Thus membership of it enabled Unionists to avoid both the cost of a firearms licence and, possibly, the police enquiries which went along with the granting of this. The decision to stand down 'C' Division of the USC in 1925 left the Unionist government in the unwelcome position of having a number of its most ardent supporters holding firearms illegally. The solution to this was the Firearms Act of 1926 which enabled people to posses a firearm that they could retain in their own home, by paying an initial fee of 2s 6d followed by 1s per annum, considerably cheaper than the charges made under the 1920 Firearms Act. Speaking during the debate on this new legislation, Viscount Massereene and Ferrard stated, 'There may be persons who for sentimental reasons desire to keep arms in their houses, but have no desire to carry them'.[73] Meanwhile, J. F. Gordon, a Unionist MP stated that people may have wanted to retain such arms, 'As a souvenir'.[74]

In April 1927 the guns kept in government storage were again discussed, this time at a 'conference', which presumably included former members of the UVF and the Ministers for Finance and Home Affairs (no minutes of the conference itself survive). Following this conference a civil servant noted:

> The articles are not the property of the Ministry and I think it would be a very doubtful procedure if the Ministry were to take any action in regard to selling the articles by tender and I think it would be preferable if these articles could now be handed over to an accredited agent of the UVF for disposal ... The arms have been in the custody of the Ministry for some years and a question which is sure to arise on disposal is whether the Ministry should receive anything as custodian over that period.[75]

In August 1927 it was decided that arrangements for sale should be left to Colonel Frederick Crawford, the famous gunrunner. A. P. Magill, a senior civil servant stated, 'The transaction will thus be so far as we are concerned a hand over to Col. Crawford and parties under his authority acting on behalf of the UVF and we shall have no responsibility in regard to cash'.⁷⁶ The timing of this move may have been related to Crawford's job prospects. Crawford had joined the Northern Ireland Civil Service but on a temporary rather than permanent contract and, faced with the necessity of making cuts, the establishment officer proposed to dispense with his services after 31 December 1927. James Craig seems to have believed that Crawford's previous services to the Unionist cause deserved a reward and it seems that a post was created for him within the civil service, giving him the responsibility for dealing with the disposal of the UVF arsenal.⁷⁷

A tendering process was started in September 1927 and initially it looked as if the problem would soon be resolved. In February 1928, R. J. Adgey, still in business as a rifle agent in Belfast, was negotiating to purchase 5,000 Steyr Rifles (1904), 5,000 Model 1888 [Mauser] Rifles, 10,000,000 cartridges, 1 Maxim machine gun and 60 Lee Enfield rifles.⁷⁸ Adgey claimed that the guns were for export to Venezuela, but it was believed that their real destination was to be China and the export license was withheld by the Home Office.⁷⁹ Finding that the guns were destined for China, Crawford ended negotiations at this point.

Some sales did go ahead in the 1926–33 period and these, perhaps, suggest why R. J. Adgey stated in his memoirs, 'I just want to add that I have heard it said that I had made a fortune out of my work for the UVF I here want to say that I gave almost two years of my time to this work for the Ulster Provisional Government for which I never expected payment or reward, nor did I receive one penny beyond railway fares and hotel expenses'.⁸⁰ Such rumours, regarding Adgey's profiteering, would seem to be quite believable as Adgey was the only individual to purchase any of the UVF arms in the entire 1920–45 period, purchasing 54 rifles and 1,138,356 rounds of ammunition for export to Belgium, Australia and South Africa. In many cases, costs were written off against vouchers, which could well have been those issued to UVF officers when putting their rifles into store in 1918.⁸¹ Furthermore, Adgey appears to have been able to purchase rifles at very low prices, for example in 1933 he purchased 50 rifles for £27 10s 0d, a very low price when we consider that in 1940 the scrap value of these rifles was estimated at £2 12s 6d each and that in March 1914 the Earl of Lanesborough purchased 175 similar rifles from Harrods Department Store for £2 5s 0d each.⁸²

Belatedly, in October 1930, the issue of UVF arms was raised by Nationalist MPs at Stormont. It appears that the matter had come to a head both as W. R. Horend was involved in a court case in London regarding his attempted gunrunning to China, and the Public Accounts

Committee reports of 1928 and 1929 had made some cryptic references to the large number of military stores available at Sprucefield.[83] In the Northern Ireland House of Commons, Cahir Healy, a Nationalist MP, voiced his concerns that these guns could be used against Christian missionaries in China.[84] After 1930 this brief interest faded; the Public Accounts Committee did not revisit the issue of stores at Sprucefield and the Nationalist opposition let the matter drop.

Following the failed attempts to sell off all of the UVF arms in the 1920s, by 1937 civil servants were making the same sort of suggestions which Colonel Pountney had made in 1922. One noted in May 1937, regarding 10,381 of the rifles:

> It is suggested that as the removal of the wood stocks would cost more for time than the stocks would realise, the rifles should be piled up and burnt. This would be much the cheapest way to make the rifles unserviceable and the barrels and metal work could thus be offered for disposal as scrap ... There are about 9,000 odd Mauser and Mannlicher rifles, UVF property which I have not included in the above.[85]

Following this, in January 1938, W. A. Magill of the Ministry of Home Affairs wrote to Sir Wilson Hungerford, Chairman of the UUC stating:

> I wonder is there any possibility of getting rid of the UVF rifles at Sprucefield? ... I don't myself see that there is the slightest use in keeping them any longer and I think that from the point of view of £. s. d. it would be better to break them down and get what we could for them now, rather than to keep them indefinitely.[86]

Despite these concerns the rifles remained at Sprucefield; the lack of any further correspondence for the 1938–39 period suggests that Hungerford must have met, informally, with either Dawson Bates or Craigavon to arrange to leave matters as they were.

The outbreak of war did not see any sudden revival of interest in the UVF rifles. Only in March 1940 did the weapons issue again emerge. However, the Ministry of Home Affairs was still at pains to point out that it did not own the guns. A minute of 14 March 1940 noted, 'Mr. R. J. Adgey is the official agent appointed by the UVF authorities for the disposal of their stocks of arms + amm[u]n[ition]. + we should not press them to agree to hand over to the mil[itar]y any articles which have any commercial value'.[87] By the end of March 1940, Sir Wilfrid Spender noted that the War Office had agreed to take over all unserviceable arms and deal with them as scrap.[88] Lieutenant Colonel A. R. G. Gordon, the parliamentary secretary to the Ministry of Finance, who had undertaken some civil defence responsibilities (and who resigned on 19 June 1940 in disgust at the Northern Ireland government's poor contribution to the war effort[89]) wrote to Dawson Bates on 6 June stating that there was a great shortage of rifle steel in the UK and asking, 'Is it not possible for those to whom these rifles belong to immediately offer them as a gift to the Imperial Government?'[90]

Finally, in the dark days after Dunkirk, 3,147, 264 rounds of obsolete German and Italian ammunition, 11,088 rifles, 10,597 sword bayonets and 13 machine guns were sold to the Ministry of Supply for £33,985 2s 11d; the cheque was made out to Sir Richard Dawson Bates, personally. (The closure of parts of the UUC papers at PRONI has made it impossible to deduce the final destination of this money.) The price per rifle was calculated at a surprisingly high £2 12s 6d.[91]

Not all of the UVF guns in the Sprucefield store were sold at this time: 8,788 rifles of British .303 calibre patterns, including 959 ancient Lee Metford rifles, complete with bayonets were kept back for use by the Local Defence Volunteers in Northern Ireland. Initially, this force was under the control of the Northern Ireland government, affiliated to the USC. When in 1942 it became the Ulster Home Guard under the direct control of the War Office, Colonel Fred Crawford put in a claim for £23,496 for the cost of the remaining arms. Prolonged negotiations ensued, with the War Office offering 25 shillings per rifle and Crawford offering to settle for £11,000 for the lot. Finally, the War Office invoked the Compensation (Defence) Act 1939 and purchased these remaining rifles for £8,743 in mid-1942.[92] A final batch of 1,019 UVF rifles stored in Derry were purchased at the same time for £1,050; this amount being made payable to the USC commandants in the City of Derry. Surprisingly, it was to be May 1944 before the rifles from Derry were sent to the Central Ordnance Depot at Weedon, having been rediscovered only when the Sea Cadets in Northern Ireland had requested some obsolete firearms for drill purposes.[93]

UVF HQ, while issuing rifles and ammunition to a large number of units, seems to have provided very little additional equipment. A number of UVF units were provided with uniforms of some sort and it seems likely that they were provided by HQ in at least some cases.[94] Headquarters also became aware of the problems that could be caused by their purchase of equipment. In April 1914 Colonel Pakenham had to write, in some embarrassment, to Captain Hon. Arthur O'Neill explaining that he could now not let the North Antrim Regiment have the palliasses which he had been using at the South Antrim camp of instruction as these were owned by HQ and had been promised to the North Down Regiment.[95] Thus it seems that, apart from rifles and some uniforms, the only items supplied to most UVF units by HQ were the various certificates of efficiency and UVF bronze lapel badges.

Local UVF units then had to provide much of their own equipment and supplies, including for many some firearms; this was recognised by HQ which compiled a list of approved suppliers.[96] In the North Antrim Regiment a Board of Equipment was set up which seems to have purchased leather bandoliers, belts and bayonet frogs, haversacks and puttees sufficient to equip 1,000 men at the cost of 3s 5d per man. This committee was also responsible for providing canvas armlets for the regiment and these, stating the battalion number and regiment, seem to have been acquired by all UVF units.[97] In Co. Monaghan an equipment fund raised £300 to provide equipment for poorer UVF members who could not afford to purchase their own.[98]

The supply of foodstuffs was organised on an even more informal basis. In Pomeroy, Co. Tyrone, the local UVF seems to have come to a financial agreement with one or possibly two local grocers. These grocers agreed to supply oatmeal, flour, tea, jam, potatoes, cheese and sugar to the UVF at a specific set price; these goods would then be stored at Pomeroy House. The merchants undertook to purchase back unused foodstuffs at full invoice price but would receive 1d per £1 of goods stored each month.[99] However, in Co. Antrim the provision of foodstuffs was left to individual volunteers who were told to keep sufficient supplies of tinned food, chocolate, tea and bread to last them for two days always available in their homes.[100] Presumably, in the event of a prolonged mobilisation, the UVF would have requisitioned foodstuffs, but how easily these could have been found in remote rural districts for the fairly large UVF forces which would have assembled there is a moot point.

As noted above UVF funds were not as substantial as has been assumed. Trying to assess the funds that the UVF had available is, quite simply, an impossible task. The UVF had a number of accounts in banks in Belfast, London and Paris and the confusion is complicated by the number of separate internal UVF paying out accounts which also existed; for example, the Ulster Signalling and Dispatch Riding Corps had its own account. The written accounts are also of little use as Stewart Blacker Quinn, who compiled them, was a member of the UUC and UVF and made it clear that he had not seen receipts for all the monies listed. It also seems that most of the funds raised ultimately found their way into the UVF Patriotic Fund, which doled out various sums of money to UVF members who had seen active service during the Great War and their dependants into, at least, the mid-1960s.[101]

What does seem clear, from the available UUC records, is that Colonel Sharman Crawford was the man in day to day control of UVF finances and in the critical period between December 1913 and May 1915, £89,256 11s 4d seems to have passed through his hands in connection with UVF expenses. It also seems that the expenses of the UVF were generally very low; two large elements of expenditure were Lieutenant General Sir George Richardson who was paid £1,500 per annum and, when Adgey set up the centralised armouries at the start of the Great War, it seems that these cost £2,800 per annum to rent. The largest single expenditure made by the UVF was, of course, the purchase and transportation of the guns used in the Larne gunrunning, which seems to have cost something in the region of £60,000; the funds for this do not appear to have been controlled by Sharman Crawford, but by James Craig directly. In 1967 an Income Tax return showed that there was still £43,867 9s 1d in UVF funds, most of it invested in British Electricity Stock. UVF funds were used for some unexpected and unintended purposes: in 1915 Michael O'Leary, the VC winner, received a gift of £25, Unionist delegates to the Irish Convention of 1917–18 received financial support amounting to £880 16s and 10d and by the 1960s at least £5,000 had been loaned to Fermanagh Unionist Association from these funds.[102]

UVF fund raising operated through a number of different funds. The largest appears to have been the Sir Edward Carson Unionist Defence Fund established in January 1912, which raised money from individuals and business concerns throughout Ulster and provided the money used by Sharman Crawford. However, Carson was disappointed by the amount raised by this fund and wrote in March 1914:

> Let those who are well off or comparatively well off, in accordance with the means they have, contribute what they can ... The wage earners of our democracy show a fine example in all the inconvenience they are prepared to undergo, in abandoning pleasure and such leisure as they have at the end of a hard day's work, in preparing themselves for any consequences that may ensue, in their determination to resist this conspiracy against their civil and religious liberties. They give us feely and willingly all that they have to help us to win the fight, and those who are in better circumstances may well find, in watching such sacrifices, the keynote to what they ought themselves to do.[103]

A major problem for the Carson Fund was, of course, that it was competing with a number of other UVF local funds and also with ordinary donations to the Unionist party, Unionist Clubs and Orange Order. In particular, it was noted at a meeting at UVF HQ in May 1914 that contributions to the Carson Fund had fallen away over the course of the year due to competition from county arming and equipping funds. A new appeal was made to rectify this situation.[104] Another central UVF fund was an Indemnity Fund established in September 1913. The purpose of this fund was to provide financial support for those killed or wounded while serving in the UVF. By January 1914 this fund claimed to have £1,043,816 available but, crucially, these were in the form of pledges which would only be paid when the UVF mobilised.[105]

The UVF Patriotic Fund was largely a creation of the Great War, designed to provide financial help to UVF members disabled by their war-time service and their dependants. Ultimately, the fund received £97,515 16s 4d in subscriptions and by June 1927, £39,683 6s 9d in interest payments had been added to this. The fourth subscription list appeared in the press in July 1916; by this stage £32,513 5s 1d had been raised, £8,855 6s 2d in the fourth subscription alone. This list is of interest as the bulk of donations came from individuals, most noticeably in door-to-door collections held in Banbridge, Lurgan and Dromore, which raised £750 7s 11d, £433 13s 6d and £60 18s 0d respectively. Linen firms can be identified as contributing £690 but it is unclear whether these were company donations or collections made among the workforces. It is noticeable that this fund, in some cases, saw a redistribution of funds within the UVF; the 1st East Belfast Regiment contributed £25 and 'C' Company of the 5th North Belfast Regiment, following a successful concert, £50. Servicemen, some of whom probably benefited from the fund, also made contributions, for example the 19th Royal Irish Rifles donated £17 7s 0d the proceeds of a sports day and concert. Most of the fund was paid out to ex-servicemen and their families and by June 1927, expenditure already stood at £93,134 8s 9d. Of this expenditure, the only sum not directly paid to ex-servicemen appears to have been £1,207 3s 10d which was a contribution towards the Ulster Division Memorial built at Thiepval with another £239 15s 11d set aside as a contribution towards the caretaker's wages.[106]

It therefore seems that the UVF was worse funded and better armed than previous accounts have allowed. UVF weapons would not have enabled the force to engage in a prolonged fire-fight with the British army, due to the poor quality of many rifles and a shortage of ammunition, but were more than adequate to over-awe or, if necessary, over-power, the RIC and INV in Ulster. If the situation had deteriorated into guerrilla warfare the UVF would have been incomparably better armed than the IRA of 1919–21. UVF rifles remained of symbolic value into the 1930s and only reluctantly were they finally scrapped during the Second World War. During the crisis period of 1914, UVF arms were not allocated on any rational basis; regiments in likely conflict areas were worse armed than units based in Unionist heartlands, which had more political influence. UVF finance was very limited and this helps to explain why UVF HQ was unable to impose its authority on local units. Headquarters reluctantly provided rifles but everything else from tinned food to transport wagons was left to local committees and officers to organise on their own initiative.

Notes

1 McNeill, *Ulster's Stand for Union*, p. 157, Ervine, *Craigavon*, p. 245 and Belinda Probert, *Beyond Orange and Green*, p. 44.
2 Joyce Lee Malcolm, *Guns and Violence: The English Experience* (Harvard University Press, London, 2002), pp. 95–141.
3 V. A. C. Gattrell, 'The Decline of Theft and Violence in Victorian and Edwardian England' in V. A. C. Gattrell, Bruce Lenman and Geoffrey Parker (eds), *Crime & the Law: The Social History of Crime in Western Europe since 1500* (Europa Publications, London, 1980).
4 TNA, CO904/182, 'City of Belfast. Importation of Arms' by John F. Moriarty, 23/08/1913.
5 TNA, CO904/182, letter, Sir John Simon to Augustine Birrell, 31/07/1914.
6 TNA, CO904/182, 'City of Belfast. Importation of Arms' by John F. Moriarty, 23/08/1913.
7 TNA, CO904/182, 'Armed Party of the Ulster Volunteers Manoeuvring on the Public Road Near Baronscourt', 17/06/1914.
8 TNA, CO904/182, 'Armed Party of the Ulster Volunteers Manoeuvring on the Public Road Near Baronscourt', 17/06/1914.
9 PRONI, D.3465/J/37/62, Madden papers, letter, John C. Madden to CI E. M. Tyache, 24/02/1914.
10 PRONI, D.3465/J/37/67, Madden papers, letter, CI E. M. Tyache to John C. Madden, 03/03/1914.
11 PRONI, D.3465/J/37/72, Madden papers, letter, Gerald Madden to Jack Madden, 30/04/1914.
12 TNA, CO904/182, 'Importation of Arms: Summary of Solicitor General's Opinion of 9th April, 1913' and Bodleian Library, Oxford, MS. Asquith 38, 'Ulster – Carriage of Rifles 1913, Attorney General's Opinion'.
13 TNA, CO904/182, memorandum, 21/12/1913.
14 *The Times*, 06/12/1913.

15 TNA, LO3/512, 'Powers of the Navy in Regard to the Searching of Vessels Suspected of Importing Arms into Ulster', 19/05/1914. This was perhaps a recognition that many naval officers were sympathetic to the Ulster Unionist cause, see Ian Beckett and Keith Jeffery, 'The Royal Navy and the Curragh Incident', *Bulletin of the Institute of Historical Research*, 62, 147, 1989.
16 Details of the Hammersmith raid are taken from the manuscript notes in Sir William Bull's copy of McNeill, *Ulster's Stand for Union*, PRONI, D.3813/3. See also TNA, CO904/28/2, letter, D. C. Lee, clerk to the Gunmakers' Company to Secretary of State for War, 03/11/1911.
17 Alvin Jackson, 'Unionist Myths, 1912–1985', pp. 174–5.
18 PRONI, D.1415/B/34, Craigavon papers, F. H. Crawford, 'The Arming of Ulster', pp. 35–45.
19 'Statement on the arms question laid before Sir Edward Carson and James Craig 20 January 1914, by a deputation of Co. Antrim volunteers, consisting of General Sir William Adair', PRONI, D.1238/108, cited in Buckland, *Irish Unionism 1885–1923*, p. 243.
20 PRONI, D.1327/4/1, Co. Down committee book, entry for 08/04/1914.
21 PRONI, D.1415/B/34, Craigavon papers, F. H. Crawford, 'The Arming of Ulster', pp. 2–45.
22 J. C. Beckett, 'Carson – Unionist or Rebel' in J. C. Beckett, *Confrontations: Studies in Irish History* (Faber and Faber, London, 1972), p. 166.
23 See Hacket Pain's obituary in *The Green 'Un* (Regimental Journal of the Worcestershire Regiment), 1926.
24 Crawford, *Guns for Ulster*, pp. vii–xii. This work appears to have been effectively ghost written by Crawford's son and I have relied on Crawford's fuller and contemporary account held in PRONI, D.1415/B/34 in this chapter.
25 PRONI, D.1327/4/1, Co. Down minute book, 20/12/1912.
26 *Northern Whig*, 02/07/1914.
27 On the Stockton on Tees seizure see TNA, CO904/28/3, letter, Chief Constable of Durham to Commissioner, RIC, Belfast, 10/07/1914.
28 PRONI, D.1700/5/17/16A, Crawford papers, letter, Crawford to Spender, 21/04/1914.
29 TNA, CO904/28/1, report by DI E. S. Cory, 11/12/1911, *Irish Times*, 07/12/1911 and *Northern Whig*, 01/12/1911.
30 PRONI, D.1415/B/38/1, Craigavon papers, Lady Craigavon's diary, entry for 08/12/1911 and PRONI, D.1700/5/17/2C–E, Crawford papers, various letters, Crawford to Craig, July and August 1911.
31 TNA, CO904/119, Section entitled 'Arms' in Inspector General's report for November 1913.
32 PRONI, D.1939/27/27, Earl of Erne papers, receipt from Harrods, 27/03/1914.

Arms, equipment and finance 159

33 All details from PRONI, D.1415/B/34, Craigavon papers, Fred Crawford, 'The Arming of Ulster', pp. 5–35.
34 See Stewart, *The Ulster Crisis*.
35 Letter, E. G. Cable to Sir Edward Grey, 12/04/1914, TNA, CO904/29/1.
36 PRONI, D/3160/1, John Regan, 'Memoirs of Service in the RIC and RUC', p. 76.
37 Stewart, *The Ulster Crisis*, pp. 176–212; *Belfast Evening Telegraph*, 25/04/1914, McNeill, *Ulster's Stand for Union* and PRONI, D.1415/B/34, Craigavon papers, Fred Crawford, 'The Arming of Ulster'.
38 Adgey, *Arming the Ulster Volunteers*, pp. 2–25 and TNA, CO904/28/2, report by Sergeant J. Edwards, 06/11/1914.
39 Stewart, *The Ulster Crisis*, pp. 99–100.
40 *Fermanagh Times*, 05/06/1913, *Northern Whig*, 18/06/1913 and *Northern Whig*, 07/07/1913.
41 *Northern Whig*, 23/07/1914.
42 Townshend, *Political Violence in Ireland*, p. 255.
43 PRONI, D.1238/148, O'Neill papers, memorandum from Hacket Pain to Adair, 16/05/1914.
44 Adgey, *Arming the Ulster Volunteers*, p. 14.
45 John Whittam, *The Politics of the Italian Army 1861–1918* (Croom Helm, London, 1977), p. 194.
46 Nuffield College, Mottistone 22/f. 193–4, report by Brigadier General Count Gleichen, 'The Ulster Volunteer Force', 14/03/1914, see also Count Gleichen, *A Guardsman's Memories* (William Blackwood and Sons, London, 1932), p. 366
47 TNA, CO904/28/1, report by DI P. McHugh, Londonderry, 27/08/1913 in file entitled, '1886–1913 Arms Importation and Distribution'.
48 Stewart, *The Ulster Crisis*, p. 248.
49 Alvin Jackson, 'British Ireland: What If the Home Rule Had Been Enacted in 1912?', in Niall Ferguson (ed.), *Virtual History: Alternatives and Counterfactuals* (Macmillan, London, 1997), p. 220 and Josephine Howie, 'Militarising a Society', p. 221.
50 Breandan MacGiolla Choille (ed.), *Intelligence Notes, 1913–16* (State Paper Office, Dublin, 1966), p. 34; NLI, Ms.26, 154, Joseph Brennan papers, 'Summary of Arms Believed to Be in the Possession of Unionists in Ulster on 31st May, 1914 by Counties' and Nuffield College, Mottistone 22/f. 193–4, report by Brigadier General Count Gleichen, 'The Ulster Volunteer Force', 14/03/1914.
51 TNA, CO904/29/2, 'Return of Rifles in Possession of Ulster Volunteer Force', 28/02/1917.
52 For a detailed discussion of this issue, see my 'The Ulster Volunteer Force and the Formation of the 36th (Ulster) Division'.
53 Peter Simkins, *Kitchener's Army: The Raising of the New Armies, 1914–16* (Manchester University Press, 1988), p. 279.

54 Simkins, *Kitchener's Army*, p. 291.
55 PRONI, D.1295/2/1A, Spender papers, 'The UVF and 36 Division', p. 25.
   See also, Cyril Falls, *History of the 36th (Ulster) Division*, p. 14.
56 Adgey, *Arming the Ulster Volunteers*, pp. 30–1 and PRONI, D.1295/2/1A, Spender papers, 'The UVF and 36 Division', p. 8.
57 Adgey, *Arming the Ulster Volunteers*, pp. 63–5.
58 Adgey, *Arming the Ulster Volunteers*, pp. 29–31.
59 TNA, WO32/9515, 'Administration of Defence of the Realm Act in Ireland', letter, Mahon to H. E. Duke, 05/11/1917.
60 PRONI, D.1132/6/7, Circular letter from T. MacGregor Greer to company commanders, 5th Tyrone Regiment, 19/11/1917.
61 Eunan O'Halpin, *The Decline of the Union: British Government in Ireland 1892–1920* (Gill and Macmillan, Dublin, 1987), p. 169.
62 IWM, 75/46/12, French papers, letter, French to David Lloyd George, 04/09/1918.
63 IWM, 75/46/12, French papers, telegram, Chief Secretary of Ireland to Under Secretary, 14/10/1918.
64 NAM, 8210–88, Richardson papers, 'UVF order 100' and PRONI, D.1507/A/29/30, Carson papers, letter, Richardson to Sir Edward Carson, 29/04/1919.
65 Stewart, *The Ulster Crisis*, p. 249.
66 Mervyn Dane, *The Fermanagh 'B' Specials* (Impartial Reporter, Enniskillen, 1970), p. 4 and PRONI, CAB5/1, cabinet memorandum by Sir James Craig, 01/09/1920.
67 PRONI, D.640/11/1, Colonel Fred Crawford's diary, entry for 27/08/1920.
68 PRONI, D.640/11/1, Colonel Fred Crawford's diary, entries for 05/11/1921 and 14/11/1921.
69 PRONI, HA/32/1/144, 'Disposal of Arms + Ammunition of UVF', memorandum, Pountney to Solly Flood, 07/06/1922.
70 PRONI, HA/32/1/144, 'Disposal of Arms + Ammunition of UVF', letter, A. P. Harrison for Inspector General RUC to Secretary, Ministry of Home Affairs, 01/09/1922.
71 PRONI, CAB/4/131, cabinet conclusions.
72 PRONI, CAB/4/131, letter, Pollock to Dawson Bates, 02/12/1924.
73 *Northern Ireland Senate Debates* (Belfast, 1926), c. 279.
74 *Northern Ireland House of Commons debates* (Belfast, 1926), c. 1430.
75 PRONI, HA/32/1/505, 'UVF Ammunition Held on Charge at Sprucefield, Disposal of.', minute by H. C. Montgomery to Assistant Secretary, Home Affairs, undated.
76 PRONI, HA/32/1/505, 'UVF Ammunition Held on Charge at Sprucefield, Disposal of.', minute by A. P. Magill, 23/08/1927.
77 PRONI, PM9/17, letter, Blackmore to Craig, 25/08/1927.
78 PRONI, HA/32/1/505, 'UVF Ammunition Held on Charge at Sprucefield,

Arms, equipment and finance   161

Disposal of.', letter, W. A. M. Magill, Ministry of Home Affairs to A. Locke, Home Office, 01/02/1928.
79 PRONI, HA/32/1/505, 'UVF Ammunition Held on Charge at Sprucefield, Disposal of.', letter, Harold Sate, Home Office to Magill, Ministry of Home Affairs, 07/02/1928, *Daily Mirror*, 06/07/1928 and *The Times*, 17/10/1930.
80 Adgey, *Arming the Ulster Volunteers*, p. 12.
81 Returns in PRONI, HA4/1/81, 'UVF Arms and Ammunition, Disposal of'.
82 PRONI, HA4/1/81, 'UVF Arms and Ammunition, Disposal of', export licence, 04/07/1933 and PRONI, D.1939/27/27, Earl of Erne papers, receipt from Harrods, 27/03/1914.
83 *Report of the Public Accounts Committee* (Belfast, 1928), pp. 76–8 and *Northern Ireland House of Commons Debates* (Belfast, 1930), c. 2107.
84 *Northern Ireland House of Commons Debates* (Belfast, 1930), c. 2107.
85 PRONI, HA4/1/81, 'UVF Arms and Ammunition, Disposal of', letter, ? to 'Dear Montgomery', ?/05/1937.
86 PRONI, HA4/1/81, 'UVF Arms and Ammunition, Disposal of', letter, Magill to Hungerford, 11/01/1938.
87 PRONI, HA4/1/81, 'UVF Arms and Ammunition, Disposal of', minute by ?, 14/03/1940.
88 PRONI, HA4/1/81, 'UVF Arms and Ammunition, Disposal of', letter, Spender to Hungerford, 21/03/1940.
89 David Harkness, *Northern Ireland since 1920* (Gill and Macmillan, Dublin, 1983), p. 90.
90 PRONI, HA4/1/81, 'UVF Arms and Ammunition, Disposal of', letter, Gordon to Dawson Bates, 06/06/1940.
91 PRONI, HA4/1/81, 'UVF Arms and Ammunition, Disposal of', letter, Director, Warlike Stores, War Office to Ministry of Home Affairs, 20/05/1942.
92 PRONI, HA4/1/81, 'UVF Arms and Ammunition, Disposal of', letters, Crawford to Secretary, Ministry of Home Affairs, 05/03/1942; Director, Warlike Stores, War Office to Ministry of Home Affairs, 20/05/1942; Assistant Secretary, Ministry of Home Affairs to Director, Warlike Stores, 27/05/1942 and letter, Richard Lewton, Ministry of Supply to Sir Richard Dawson Bates, 26/06/1942.
93 PRONI, HA4/1/81, 'UVF Arms and Ammunition, Disposal of', Wright to Montgomery, 29/05/1944.
94 Crozier, *Impressions and Recollections*, p. 149.
95 PRONI, D.1238/60, O'Neill papers, letter, Colonel A. Pakenham to Captain Hon. Arthur O'Neill, 02/04/1914.
96 PRONI, D.1238/9E, O'Neill papers, 'Equipment List of Approved Suppliers' by Captain W. B. Spender, 29/01/1914.
97 PRONI, D.1238/9A, O'Neill papers, memorandum from officer commanding 1st Battalion, North Antrim Regiment to officer commanding

North Antrim Regiment, 02/03/1914. A selection of UVF amulets is on display in the Ulster Museum, Belfast.
98 PRONI, D.3465/J/37/87, Madden papers, letter, Laider Irwin to Mrs Madden, 02/06/1914.
99 Draft agreement in PRONI, D/1132/6/11.
100 PRONI, D.1238/9Q, O'Neill papers, memorandum from Commandant Co. Antrim to Regt. + Batt. Commanders, 11/02/1914.
101 The files relating to this fund are presently held by the Somme Heritage Centre, Newtownards, and are closed to researchers due to the Data Protection Act. I am grateful to Craig McGuicken, the former director of the Somme Heritage Centre, for advice on this matter.
102 This section on finance is largely based on the incomplete UVF accounts for 1913–67 in the UUC collection at PRONI, D.1327/14/6/1–10.
103 PRONI, D.1327/2/10, 'Sir Edward Carson Unionist Defence Fund Minute Book', letter, Carson to R. M. Liddell, 06/03/1914.
104 PRONI, D.1238/143, O'Neill papers, memorandum by W. T. Adair, 16/05/1914.
105 Ervine, *Craigavon*, p. 245.
106 The details on the UVF Patriotic Fund are taken from *Northern Whig*, 28/07/1916 and PRONI, PM9/17, letter, Richard Dawson Bates to James Craig, 28/07/1927.

6

War and decline, 1914–19

With the outbreak of the Great War, Ulster Unionists were, as J. O. Stubbs has stressed, 'imprisoned by their patriotism'.[1] The leaders of the UVF who during the entirety of the Third Home Rule crisis had spoken of their loyalty to Britain had little choice but to offer the services of the UVF to the British government on the outbreak of war; partly as the basis of a new army division (the 36th (Ulster) Division) and partly as a home defence force. However, this was not to be an unconditional offer. Ulster Unionists wanted the newly formed division to have its own distinctive badge, the title 'Ulster' in its name, local battalion titles and the appointment of officers, sympathetic to the Unionist cause; concessions which were largely granted by the War Office. Similarly, the Ulster Unionist leadership refused to have the UVF organisation which remained as a home defence force, incorporated in either the TF or the VTC as its services would then be largely lost to Unionism. What is clear though is that UVF enlistment in the British army was not as impressive as some contemporary Unionists accounts would have us believe and, more importantly, the UVF organisation in Ulster seems to have quickly become moribund. Few home service units were training or parading by spring 1915 and, ironically, the response of the UVF to the Easter Rising in 1916 was for the organisation to become even less active. This chapter will examine the changes in the UVF officers corps, which occurred at the outbreak of war, the home defence role undertaken by the force, the material benefits offered by the UVF to the British army, the recruitment of members of the UVF into the British army and the connections between the UVF and the 36th (Ulster) Division.

The outbreak of war brought chaos to the UVF, as retired and reserve officers continually left to take up commands in the rapidly increasing British army. As the bottom of the barrel was increasingly scraped to obtain officers for the newly formed Kitchener armies and expanding TF, the UVF was left with an officer corps which consisted of the unacceptably senior, elderly, unfit, incompetent and utterly inexperienced. This saw a rapid turnover of COs at the start of the war. The best example of this is in the Belfast and North Down Divisions which lost their divisional commanders, Colonel G. H. H. Couchman and Major General C. H. Powell respectively, to the 36th (Ulster) Division in October 1914; they were replaced by Brigadier General Molesworth, who combined these commands until he was recalled to army service in December 1914, he was then replaced with Captain W. L. Down, who was recalled to active service with the Royal Navy in early 1915.[2] With Down's departure, this key post was left unfilled, which meant that UVF battalion commanders were responsible only to Richardson directly. Lieutenant General Sir George Richardson held his command of the UVF throughout the Great War due to his advanced age and, more importantly, his advanced seniority. If sent to the Western Front in command of the 36th (Ulster) Division he would have outranked every corps commander there. At the battalion level experienced officers were quickly recalled to colour service and civilians filled the key positions of commanding officer and adjutant in most units, pending the return of their permanent incumbents.[3]

The services of many officers were quickly lost on a permanent basis to the UVF and the 36th (Ulster) Division. Of course, many of these experienced officers were quickly killed. The first appears to have been Captain R. C. Orr of the Somerset Light Infantry who had been adjutant of the 1st North Antrim Regiment; he was quickly followed by Captain Arthur O'Neill, MP, who had commanded the North Antrim Regiment, and Viscount Northland, who had commanded the 4th Tyrone Regiment.[4] On the outbreak of war many officers who had been involved in the UVF, such as the Earl of Clanwilliam and Lord Castlereagh, rejoined their former regiments. Clanwilliam, who had rejoined the Household Cavalry as a captain, was requested by Lieutenant General Richardson for a position in the 36th (Ulster) Division in early September and served for a short period, as a major, with the 13th Royal Irish Rifles before returning to the Royal Horse Guards on 5 November 1914.[5] Castlereagh (soon to succeed as the Marquess of Londonderry on his father's death) spent his entire wartime service in the Royal Horse Guards, although it seems that he too had the option of serving in the 36th (Ulster) Division.[6] In all Lieutenant General Sir George Richardson specifically requested 64 named, serving, reserve and retired officers for appointments in the 36th (Ulster) Division in September 1914. By

January 1915, just 15 of these officers had been appointed to the Division.[7] Thus many officers, recalled to their former units, quickly relinquished any connections they had with the UVF, preferring to serve in their old regiments than the newly formed 36th (Ulster) Division.

Unfortunately for the UVF organisation that remained in Ulster, the 36th (Ulster) Division soon denuded it of experienced senior and staff officers. Thus Major General C. H. Powell (appointed GOC) had been CO of the North Down Regiment; Brigadier General G. H. H. Couchman (appointed as commander of 107th Brigade) had been the CO of the Belfast Special Service Force, Brigadier General G. W. Hacket Pain (appointed as commander of 108th Brigade) had been the Chief of Staff, Brigadier General T. E. Hickman (appointed as commander of 109th Brigade) had been the Inspector General, Lieutenant Colonel James Craig (appointed AAQMG) had been the QMG and Captain Wilfrid Spender (appointed general staff officer (GSO) II) had been the UVF's senior staff officer. However, at battalion command level the pattern was much more varied. Of the 13 battalion COs, only seven had been involved in the UVF. In the 107th Brigade, only one of the COs, Lieutenant Colonel H. T. Lyle of the 8th Royal Irish Rifles served in the UVF. Indeed, of the officers appointed as COs in this brigade, two were still serving officers, namely Colonel H. C. Bernard, Indian Army, posted to the 10th Royal Irish Rifles and Lieutenant Colonel G. H. Ford-Hutchinson, Connaught Rangers, posted to the 15th Royal Irish Rifles.[8] The other CO in the brigade was Lieutenant Colonel G. S. Ormerod, who had retired from the Royal Munster Fusiliers as a major as long ago as 1904.[9]

The lack of qualified COs quickly caused problems in UVF units. As Lilian Spender noted of the Donegal Regiment, 'Mr. Sclater was busy going the round of his Reg[imen]t. of the UVF, he having just been gazetted to the Command of it [temporarily] vice Lord Clanwilliam who has got his orders [to rejoin the Royal Horse Guards]. Being a civilian, he feels very important, and is rather fussed but very pleased'.[10] The situation was more problematic in the case of the 3rd South Down Regiment. As the CO of this unit had been recalled to military service UVF HQ seems to have suggested that the battalion could be run by a committee until the end of the war. This was rejected by elements of the unit who noted that men from Rathfriland would not accept a president from Castlewellan as the effective CO, stating, 'We created the Battalion here. We got the men together, we did all the hard work + to put it straight we want no outside figurehead'.[11] UVF HQ appears to have washed its hands of the whole affair at this point and left it to local negotiations to decide how the battalion was managed; it seems to have folded shortly after this. While the major contribution of the UVF to the British war effort was to be its role in the formation of the 36th (Ulster) Division, the Unionist leadership was keen to preserve the UVF as a viable force itself, conscious that the Home Rule issue and partition would be revisited when the war ended. There were also genuine fears of a German naval raid on Ulster and so the UVF was recast as a home defence force.[12] UVF HQ initially instructed battalion commanders to either parade (in rural areas) or canvas (in Belfast) their men to find out if they would be prepared to serve a) in Ulster only, b) anywhere in the United Kingdom, or c) overseas, and men were assured that they would serve on the same basis as the TF in Great Britain.[13] Presumably this exercise was carried out so that UVF HQ could ascertain what sort of military forces it could offer the British Government.[14] Therefore it is significant that the results of this canvas were never made public, but it is clear that, at least in Belfast, the results were falsified. Major F. P. Crozier, who helped to compile the Belfast returns, freely admitted:

> There was difficulty in obtaining the signatures of the men to serve 'unconditionally anywhere' in a Division, not because they did not want to go, but on account of the accursed Irish question. They feared the South ... I now plead guilty to putting many a 'yes' in the more patriotic column in order to swell the numbers for publication.[15]

Meanwhile, in rural areas, it appears that men were asked, by a show of hands on parade, to demonstrate their willingness to serve overseas.[681] It would seem unlikely that, in full view of his comrades, a UVF member would want to present his reasoned, if unpatriotic, view that the fate of his farm was more important than the formation of a new British army unit, much less his view that, at this time of national crisis, the British government probably still could not be trusted over the Home Rule issue.

Carson, whatever the views of rank and file UVF members, was conscious of the need to retain the UVF as an effective force in Ulster for political reasons. Thus he wrote to Lieutenant General Richardson, shortly after the outbreak of war:

> Knowing as I do the loyalty and devotion of my friends in the Ulster Volunteer Force and on the Ulster Unionist Council, I am sure that many of them, whom age or physical causes debar from an arduous campaign, will, with Ulster pluck and regardless of personal consequences, consider it

their duty to tender their services to the new Ulster Division of Lord Kitchener's Army.

I earnestly beg of you as G.O.C., UVF to make it known to all such Applicants for commissions or enlistment that it is my strongly expressed desire that such should remain with their several units of the UVF in Ulster and devote themselves to further recruiting and increasing the efficiency of the Force which remains.

I can assure them that the efficiency of the UVF for the defence of our shores, and the training of Drafts for the supply of men to the new Division now being formed is as patriotic and as needful for the preservation of our great Empire as service with the colours.[17]

While the departure of experienced officers and enlistment of enthusiastic UVF members into the 36th (Ulster) Division saw many UVF units effectively cease to exist by autumn 1914, clearly some units did remain in existence, certainly into spring 1915. The CO of the 2nd North Antrim Regiment was making arrangements to inspect his companies at work at various times over the winter of 1914/15 and urged his men to keep their rifles in good order.[18] In November 1914 UVF HQ was urging units to devote more time to rifle practice and stated that half the cost of ammunition would be met by HQ.[19] In early 1915 UVF HQ tried to inject some enthusiasm into the movement with a defensive scheme in which the UVF would defend Belfast and the shores of Counties Antrim and Down from a threatened German naval raid and this plan was later extended to cover the whole of Ulster. The order giving notice of this scheme stated, 'It is hoped that every available member of the UVF will make a point of paying diligent attention to all orders referring to above scheme, so as to render himself efficient'.[20] Some local UVF units did put together invasion planning; elements of the South Down Regiment made preparations for the defence of Dundrum, Newcastle, Annalong, Newry and Carlingford Lough in the event of a German landing there.[21]

However, by early 1915 it was clear that the UVF was ceasing to function as any sort of effective military force. In January Carson issued a message to the Belfast Regiments of the UVF urging them, 'not to relax your efforts, to keep up your numbers and to keep up your efficiency. I know there is a great deal of drudgery about it, especially when men's minds are turned to other matters, and when the original object for which you were formed seems for the moment to be in abeyance. But recollect that the danger which you were organised to confront is yet a danger in front of you'.[22] In May 1915 Carson wrote to Richardson:

> As I understand you are to meet the Divisional, Regimental and Battalion Commanders of the UVF I shall be very glad if you would state to them my opinion of the absolute necessity of keeping our Ulster Volunteers, so far as organisation is concerned as perfect as possible. I do not think it is either necessary or advisable at the moment to try and press the members to do too much hard work, as I am aware that a great deal of labour is required at the present time, but at the same time, I should certainly hope that it will be possible to keep our men together by having at least once a week a parade for however short a time … I rely upon all commanders to do their best in difficult circumstances and at the same time with as little inconvenience as possible to our volunteers.[23]

UVF HQ, as a result of this, seems to have made ammunition and finance available to local units in the hope that they would organise shooting competitions for their members.[24] However, by June 1915 the major concern of UVF HQ became the security and maintenance of UVF rifles. This saw some conflict as the demands of enthusiastic volunteers could not always be reconciled with the security of arms. In March 1915 the North Belfast Regiment asked for permission for their men to keep their rifles in their own homes, rather than in armouries, but this was denied and the North Belfast Regiment seems to have ceased to function shortly after this event.[25] The UVF did have a minor political role during the war, in that its HQ council asked for the extension of the National Registration Bill to Ireland in July 1915.[26]

Of course the only threat which the UVF faced during the war was not from German raiders but from Irish Republicans, and the reaction of the UVF to the Easter Rising was far from impressive. When the Rising broke out, Richardson placed the UVF at the disposal of the British military authorities. However, in concrete terms this seems to have largely consisted of 1,148 UVF members being sworn in as special constables in Belfast, UVF guards being placed on vulnerable armouries, the protection of the wireless station at Ballycastle and the loan of UVF rifles to a Royal Army Medical Corps detachment at Dundalk.[27] At the local level some UVF commanders did take action. The Monaghan Regiment was put on stand-by during the Easter Rising as John Leslie wrote to Gerald Madden, one of his battalion commanders, 'Yes get pickets ready to turn out in the drill hall. Do not use arms unless the other side have already begun firing which I do not expect of them. Let the police know you are ready to help them. The men at Ballyboy + Castle Blayney should be warned to keep out of the towns'.[28] Curiously the Easter Rising lead to the UVF becoming more rather than less moribund as at the end of May

1916 Lieutenant General Richardson suspended all drills, presumably to prevent Republicans gaining clear intelligence of where UVF arms had been deposited.[29] By summer 1917 even the UVF HQ council had practically ceased to function as it held no meetings between 13 August 1917 and 11 January 1918; there was then no meeting until three were held between 12 and 22 August 1918, concerned with the safety of arms, and none again until 10 May 1920.

At the start of the war and indeed into mid-1915, UVF HQ was keen to have the force 'recognised' by the War Office, presumably meaning that it would qualify for government assistance – financial and material – and the attachment of some regular officers for training purposes.[30] However, the War Office refused to do this on the advice of the Irish Office, presumably taking the view that however serious the threat of a German naval raid was on Ireland, the arming and training of a political militia by the government was not an appropriate response.[31]

Throughout the first two years of the war there were external attempts made to incorporate the UVF in either the TF (which until early 1916 had only a home service liability) or the VTC. In April 1915 Colonel Eustace Jameson, writing with the support of the Irish Parliamentary Party (IPP), urged the British government to extend the Territorial system to Ireland where it could incorporate the UVF and INV.[32] Carson and Richardson both objected to this scheme. Richardson stated, 'If the Territorial Force in Ireland is kept up after the War, the UVF will cease to be under the Command of the Ulster Leaders'.[33] Richardson was also concerned that, 'A Territorial Force would be a grand excuse for these slackers and our object at present is to push them direct into the real army'.[34] Possibly on the back of Jameson's proposal Lord Wimborne, the Lord Lieutenant of Ireland, was keen to incorporate both the INV and UVF into the TF, claiming that he had IPP support but noting that the 'individualism' of previous times would have to be surrendered by the forces.[35] This was a view echoed by Sir Matthew Nathan, the Under Secretary at Dublin Castle, and General Friend, the GOC in Ireland.[36]

Attempts to incorporate the UVF in the VTC met with similar opposition from the Ulster Unionist and UVF leadership. UVF attitudes to the VTC do, however, seem unusual, given the amount of inspiration which they provided to this new force and the fact that VTC units were actually formed in Ireland. Percy Harris, a prominent Liberal member of the London County Council, wrote to *The Times* shortly after the outbreak of the war calling for the establishment of a new volunteer corps for London. He suggested that this corps should be independent of the War Office and funded by the London Boroughs, citing the UVF as a model.[37] Initially the UVF did seem supportive as a number of VTC units in Great Britain, especially those in the London area, received concrete support from the UVF in the form of wooden dummy rifles.[38] However, when VTC units were formed in Ireland this attitude changed; in November 1914 UVF HQ had refused to lend 200 rifles to the Trinity College Dublin OTC.[39] In April 1915 Richard Dawson Bates wrote to Carson, 'Of course the whole object of this Organisation [the Irish Association of the VTC] is to do harm to the UVF, where possible. This Organisation boasts of having obtained recognition when we could not'.[40] Keith Mitchinson believes that Carson was responsible for a Private Members Bill introduced into the House of Lords in October 1915, which aimed to revive the Volunteer Act of 1863, running out of parliamentary time as he did not want the INV to receive official recognition as this would again have put him under pressure to incorporate the UVF in the VTC.[41] It seems that the VTC was soon poaching UVF members; Hugh Mulholland, a solicitor in Lisburn, wrote to Carson to inform him that he had joined the Belfast Battalion of the VTC while remaining a member of the Lisburn UVF and asked him what the official position of the UVF was regarding the VTC.[42] It is noticeable that of the 2,434 VTC members in Ireland in February 1916, the largest single unit was the Belfast Defence Corps with 917 members and the VTC recruited well in the Unionist suburbs of Dublin, which had provided the personnel for the Dublin UVF unit.[43] In March 1916 Richardson, conscious that VTC units had been successfully formed in Ireland, again rejected proposals for the UVF to become incorporated in the Irish VTC.[44]

As late as May 1916 A. W. Samuels, one of the Irish Law Officers and a convinced Unionist, revisited this issue and suggested that the old Irish county militia should be revived and this would enable the British government to enrol the UVF and INV for home defence only under the Crown, without incorporating them in the TF or VTC.[45] Essentially these schemes all failed as Ulster Unionists were opposed to the incorporation of the UVF in either the TF or VTC as they would risk loosing control of the UVF and there was a danger that UVF and INV members would end up serving in amalgamated units. Unionists were also reluctant to give any support to the demands of the INV to be recognised by the government in their desire to illustrate the superior nature of Ulster Unionist compared to Irish Nationalist support for the British war effort.

With regard to equipment, UVF sources provided valuable supplies to the 36th (Ulster) Division. Shortly after the outbreak of war James Craig obtained 10,000 uniforms from Moss Brothers in London for the division, paid for out of UVF funds.[46] This meant that, unlike many other New Army units, men of the 36th (Ulster) Division did not have to drill for months in civilian clothes, the infamous 'Kitchener blue' uniforms, or obsolete scarlet jackets.[47] Also, UVF sources enabled battalions in the 36th (Ulster) Division to have access to rifles for training purposes, equipment which many other Kitchener units were not to possess until the beginning of 1915.[48] An important contribution from the UVF to the British army was the UVF hospitals; these consisted of two hospitals in Ulster, one in the grounds of The Queen's University of Belfast and the other at Dunbarton House, Gilford, Co. Down, which as early as May 1915 were providing beds for 214 patients. It was noted that the doctors and probationary nurses working in these hospitals were all members of the UVF, the doctors giving their services to the War Office at no cost. Later in the war, the UVF funded a hospital at Pau, France. In 1920, the UVF hospitals in Ulster amalgamated, moving to 'Craigavon', James Craig's former home in East Belfast. In 1949, after complex negotiations between the Stormont and Westminster governments, the UVF hospital came under National Health Service control and it continues to function as the Somme Hospital, a nursing home for ex-servicemen, to this day.[49]

However, the UVF was not always prepared to lend useful items of equipment to units of the 36th (Ulster) Division; when Lieutenant Colonel Ambrose Ricardo asked for the loan of some Maxim guns for the 9th Royal Inniskilling Fusiliers, his request was denied.[50] More bizarrely in August 1915 the UVF arranged to send 16,000 sand bags to the 36th (Ulster) Division.[51] Some local UVF units also started their own comforts funds; in Co. Antrim, General Adair set up a fund to supply fresh milk to the 36th (Ulster) Division.[52]

While the Ulster Unionist leadership approached the War Office very quickly after the outbreak of war, seeking to have the UVF incorporated into the British army, initially Kitchener seemed determined to continue Irish recruiting purely under War Office direction, without the involvement of political factions in Ireland. However, on 29 August 1914 he recognised, due to the poor recruitment returns for the 10th (Irish) Division, that recruiting in Ireland would have to involve a substantial political element.[53] Kitchener therefore reconsidered his position regarding an Ulster Division and it was officially approved following further meetings with Unionist politicians, discussed below.

For a time it appears that the Ulster Unionist political leadership was highly optimistic about the numbers of recruits which could be obtained and was seriously considering forming two divisions from the UVF.[54] However, the truth was that UVF members were not that inclined to enlist. In terms of rural recruiting in Ulster, it is worth noting that recruitment levels were not, in general, significantly higher than those in other rural counties in Ireland, suggesting that UVF membership had a fairly minimal impact on a man's decision to enlist, though in many cases directly deciding his choice of unit.[55] It is also likely that recruitment levels in rural Ulster, like those in South Western Ireland, did not peak until 1915, when the 36th (Ulster) Division had been formed.[56] It seems likely that rural farmers, keen to play a part in the war effort, would have joined the UVF itself, rather than the 36th (Ulster) Division. Home defence duties, if hardly the stuff to impress one's grandchildren, did at least enable sole proprietors to maintain their farms during the war. Therefore it appears that only the personnel surplus of industrial Belfast, from which, of course, a large part of the UVF had been drawn, enabled the 36th (Ulster) Division to become a viable entity. Another problem regarding recruiting for the 36th (Ulster) Division was that it did not gain support from the British League for the Support of Ulster and the Union. In September 1914 the Honorary Secretary of the League was using his contacts within this organisation to obtain recruits for Lord Willoughby de Broke's reserve regiment of Warwickshire Yeomanry.[57]

Nevertheless, the recruitment record of the UVF during the Great War appears to have been a reasonably good one. David Fitzpatrick has calculated that during the course of the entire war, nearly 31,000 members of the Ulster Volunteers, nearly one-third of the pre-war membership, joined the British armed forces.[58] Unfortunately, in his eagerness to map and tabulate UVF recruiting figures, Fitzpatrick has neglected to mention the highly speculative information on which these were based. Detailed figures compiled by Dublin Castle and based, it seems, on RIC reports showed that 25,265 UVF members had enlisted in the British army from 4 August 1914 to 15 April 1916, including 4,352 reservists. The pattern followed seemed to mirror the general experience of British and Irish recruiting with 16,435 members enlisting (including the reservists) by 15 December 1914.[59] However, A. P. Magill noted that there were serious deficiencies in these figures. He reflected on a return of October 1914 that suggested that 15,500 UVF members had enlisted by that date, 'The above figures are only guesswork as regards the division of the totals between R.[oman] C.[atholic]s + Protestants + National + Ulster Volunteers'.[60] He was even more blunt concerning the returns for November 1914, stating, 'The Volunteer figures in enclosed are not right for they assume that all the reservists & recruits who have reported or joined since the war began were volunteers. This is obviously not the case'.[61] Nevertheless, if we assume that these figures were based on educated guesswork and that the UVF membership followed wider Irish and British recruiting trends in 1916–18 the figure of 31,000 would seem to be an appropriate best estimate. However, if we reflect that the Unionist press, UVF HQ and sympathetic RIC officers (who seem to have been responsible for these returns) were suggesting that the UVF was making a major contribution to Irish recruiting, then the figure of 31,000 may well be a significant over-estimation.

What is interesting, of course, is the extent to which UVF members were not predisposed to join the 36th (Ulster) Division. If we take 31,000 as the number of UVF personnel who went into the British army then probably only a bare majority went into the 36th (Ulster) Division which, as discussed below, recruited slowly and by mid-1916 was relying on replacements from Great Britain. Scottish and Canadian units recruited well in Belfast, and it seems likely that many men, who had been UVF members, joined regiments which had been stationed in Ulster in 1914 as this had been their closest contact with the British army.[62] Some opted for units such as the Army Service Corps, either as they thought their specialist skills could best be utilised there or they were attracted by higher pay, and the Irish Guards was also a popular choice, presumably given its social and military prestige. The diversity of units joined by UVF members is illustrated by the case of 'E' Company of the 2nd North Antrim Regiment. By September 1916, 74 members of this unit had enlisted in British army units; 54 of these had enlisted in the 12th Royal Irish Rifles, the unit allied to their UVF regiment, but others had joined the Irish Guards, 10th Royal Inniskilling Fusiliers, 18th Royal Irish Rifles and Army Service Corps.[63] A number of UVF personnel, impatient with Carson's political haggling with the War Office, joined the 10th (Irish) Division, which started recruiting well in advance of the 36th (Ulster) Division.[64]

Traditional accounts of the formation of the 36th (Ulster) Division, which have been echoed by more recent works, suggest it was formed very quickly after the outbreak of war and purely from the pre-war UVF. Writing in 1920, Ramsay Colles stated:

the War Office decided that the simplest and best plan would be to create a separate division for the Ulster Volunteers, and as far as possible allow their own officers who were competent and had already received a military training, to command them, the War Office of course, retaining the right to appoint the divisional staff, commanding officers, and the senior officers of the battalions. It should, of course, be remembered that a large number of the men who had been acting as officers for the previous two years in the Ulster Volunteers had served in the army, and many of them were actually on the reserve of officers, while others were young men from the Public Schools, who had already passed through the Officers' Training Corps.[65]

Echoing this view and writing what was, effectively, the official history of the 36th (Ulster) Division, endorsed by the Northern Ireland government, Cyril Falls stated

> The Ulster Division was not created in a day. The roots from which it sprang went back into the troubled period before the war. Its life was a continuance of the life of an earlier legion, a legion of civilians banded together to protect themselves from the consequences of legislation which they believed would affect adversely their rights and privileges as citizens of the United Kingdom.[66]

However, Kitchener was initially reluctant to form a division from the UVF. An initial meeting between Sir Edward Carson, James Craig and Lord Kitchener, the Secretary of State for War, appears to have ended inconclusively. Kitchener seems to have rejected all of the Unionist demands. The idea of granting the title 'Ulster' to the new division appears to have caused him particular concern.[67] Therefore authorisation for the formation of the 36th (Ulster) Division was only given on 28 October 1914, following a number of further meetings with the Ulster Unionist leadership and by which stage it was obvious that Irish political pressure was required to boost Irish recruiting figures.[68] In the series of meetings between the Ulster Unionists and the War Office, it appears that Carson was promised a number of concessions, principally that regular officers involved in the UVF would be posted to the 36th (Ulster) Division but also that UVF regimental names could be used in battalion names and that the division would have the distinctive 'Red Hand' of Ulster, which had been used on UVF insignia, as its badge.[69]

While Kitchener had acceded to Unionist demands, these were easily met within the context of the formation of new army units and the concessions granted to Ulster Unionists were similar to those made to interest groups in Great Britain at the same time. This was not a point which was understood by many Irish Nationalists at the time. IPP members clearly believed that the Ulster Unionists had gained concessions for the 36th (Ulster) Division which they had been unfairly denied with respect to the 16th (Irish) Division.[70] Captain Stephen Gwynn, an officer in the 16th (Irish) Division and IPP MP, noted,

> Does anyone suppose that Sir Edward Carson had no voice in the staffing of the Ulster Division? He had at all events received from the first a clear promise that all professional soldiers who had been officers in the Ulster Volunteers would be officers in the Division and that any who had been mobilised should be restored to their associates in the Division.[71]

Just as historians have tended uncritically to accept Unionist claims of the overlap between the UVF and the 36th (Ulster) Division, so too much credence has been given to these complaints from Irish Nationalist politicians. For example, David Fitzpatrick has stated, 'On 3 September [1914], he [Carson] unconditionally offered 35,000 members of the UVF for overseas service, whereupon a well-disposed War Office approved formation of the 36th. (Ulster) division whose enlistment, initial training, and officer corps were closely controlled by the UVF command'.[72] In fact, the distinctive titles granted to English 'Pals' units, for example, the 14th Royal Warwickshire Regiment (1st Birmingham), were not substantially different from those granted to units in the 36th (Ulster) Division, such as the 9th Royal Irish Rifles (West Belfast Volunteers). One could argue that the UVF simply subsumed the recruitment and consequent patronage roles carried out by great landowners, local authorities, political parties, sporting clubs and leading businessmen in other parts of the United Kingdom. Indeed, concessions to the 36th (Ulster) Division appear minor, given those granted to the 38th (Welsh) Division, which enjoyed the patronage of David Lloyd George.[73]

Despite Kitchener's eventual endorsement, the 36th (Ulster) Division faced serious recruiting problems, for three major reasons. Firstly, many of the most enthusiastic and experienced Ulster Volunteers had already been recalled to the colours or had joined up by the time the Division was formed; most notably army reservists who were involved in the UVF had to return to their former regiments on the outbreak of war.[74] Secondly, and more importantly, by September 1914 some serious concern had already been voiced by UVF members who questioned the exact nature of the 'contract' which the Ulster Unionist leadership had entered into with the War Office. One UVF officer telegrammed Carson to enquire, 'Can we assure men before giving names for United Kingdom or foreign service no danger of Home Rule Bill passing while they are away?'[75]

These concerns were not only being voiced among the UVF officer class; one volunteer, writing in a leading Belfast newspaper stated:

> The Volunteers are to be asked tomorrow if they are willing to serve abroad. It may be assumed that those who will agree to do so will be the youngest and most efficient men. It is highly probable that many of them will never return. When the war is finished, and the Home Rule situation has to be faced again, the UVF will be without many of its most useful members, and as a fighting force it will be less formidable. Therefore I ask you, is it desirable that any Volunteer should offer himself for foreign service?[76]

Finally, Ulster Unionists had over-estimated the extent to which UVF members would be prepared to join the British army. In early September 1914, Lieutenant General Sir George Richardson was proposing to form two Ulster divisions for Imperial Service.[77] The bitter truth for Ulster Unionists was that UVF recruiting was to be on a rather smaller scale than they had expected and liable to strong regional variations, which meant that the insistence on a connection between specific UVF regiments and specific Ulster Division battalions was to lead to recruiting problems for many rural units.

The enlistment of UVF members into the 36th (Ulster) Division was, in some ways, similar to the experience of TF units in Great Britain. The TF, established in 1908, on the outbreak of war was a purely home defence force. However, with the deteriorating military situation, members of the TF were asked to take the Imperial Service Obligation, agreeing to serve overseas. There was a great variation between units in the acceptance of this. For example, while practically all members of the 5th Black Watch and over 90 per cent of those in the 8th Scottish Rifles (Cameronians) volunteered for overseas service, in the 5th Scottish Rifles (Cameronians) there were scarcely any volunteers as men were concerned that their battalion would be broken up if it served overseas.[78] Of most relevance to the case of the UVF and the 36th (Ulster) Division is the experience of the 51st (Highland) Division of the TF. While, on a show of hands, 75 per cent of men showed their willingness to serve overseas, when men were asked to attest, individually and in writing, an entire brigade opted for home service![79] One suspects that many UVF commanders in rural areas suffered a similar experience when asking their men to join the 36th (Ulster) Division, as this was clearly done on a show of hands while the UVF unit was on parade.[80]

One further problem caused in the formation of the 36th (Ulster) Division was the decision to open recruiting for the 107th (Belfast)

Brigade before commencing recruiting for rural battalions. This brigade was reported as 'practically complete' by Lieutenant General Sir George Richardson, as early as 10 September 1914.[81] Given that urban recruiting had proved remarkably easy in Britain during the first months of the war, this decision has been seen as an act of political posturing, attempting to expose supposed deficiencies in Nationalist recruitment.[82] The practical effect of this measure was to raise artificially high expectations about how easily and quickly the 36th (Ulster) Division would be completed. Indeed, it is worth noting that the 107th Brigade was raised during the highest levels of enlistment recorded in Britain, namely between 25 August and 9 September 1914.[83]

Table 6.1. demonstrates the recruiting difficulties faced by units of the 36th (Ulster) Division, recruiting in rural areas, by early October 1914. It is clear that while the 13th Royal Irish Rifles was well over the stipulated battalion establishment of 1,007 officers and other ranks, the 11th Royal Inniskilling Fusiliers was just over company strength. As late as December 1914 the situation was little better. By then the Ulster Division was still stated to be 1,995 under-strength. Recruiting notices were to be

Table 6.1. The strength of battalions of the 36th (Ulster) Division, 3 October 1914

Battalion	Officers	Other ranks
8th Royal Irish Rifles (East Belfast)	15	1065
9th Royal Irish Rifles (West Belfast)	19	1102
10th Royal Irish Rifles (South Belfast)	17	1119
15th Royal Irish Rifles (North Belfast)	12	1048
11th Royal Irish Rifles (South Antrim)	16	666
12th Royal Irish Rifles (Mid Antrim)	20	668
13th Royal Irish Rifles (1st Co. Down)	23	1246
9th Royal Irish Fusiliers (Armagh, Cavan and Monaghan)	20	940
9th Royal Inniskilling Fusiliers (Tyrone)	7	643
10th Royal Inniskilling Fusiliers (Derry Volunteers)	21	740
11th Royal Inniskilling Fusiliers (Donegal and Fermanagh)	15	471
14th Royal Irish Rifles (YCV of Belfast)	17	1038

Source: This table is based on figures given in the *Belfast Evening Telegraph*, 03/10/1914. The 16th Royal Irish Rifles (2nd County Down), the divisional pioneer battalion, was not formed until the 20th. October 1914 and thus is absent from this return. S. N. White, *The Terrors, 16th (Pioneer) Battalion, Royal Irish Rifles* (Somme Association, Belfast, 1996), p. 1.

read out to all UVF units on parade to try to address this short-fall, with a UVF order stating, 'the G.O.C. hopes that Regimental and Battalion Commanders will take every opportunity to point out to the men the necessity of responding to this appeal so as to complete the Division'.[84]

These recruiting problems demonstrated the difficulties in adapting the 'Pals' system of recruitment to many of the rural battalions of the 36th (Ulster) Division; the figures for the Derry battalion may also be a reflection on how poorly organised the UVF was in Derry City. In late October 1914, Lieutenant Colonel Ambrose Ricardo, 9th Royal Inniskilling Fusiliers, had the following handbill distributed among members of the Tyrone UVF:

> Carson says 'Quit yourselves like men.'
> Kitchener's Army.
> 9th. Service Battalion Royal Inniskilling Fusiliers (Tyrone Volunteers).
> The Tyrone Battalion at Finner Camp is now 864 strong. 300 more are required to complete.
> Come and join your comrades. If the Ballot Act is put into force you will not be able to choose your regiment.
> Hire this time with your Chums to fight against your Country's enemies. £9 for the half year with free food and clothing. AND YOUR WIFE AND CHILDREN WILL BE PROVIDED FOR; no delay now in receiving Separation Allowance.
> IN THE TYRONES you will find GALLANT COMRADES AND A COMFORTABLE REGIMENT. SURE PROMOTION FOR SMART MEN.
> TRAIN NOW FOR EMPIRE AND ULSTER.[85]

Privately, Ricardo stated, 'We have done fairly well, but require 300 men to complete if we do not get these at an early date there is a great risk of our being filled up from outside which would be a great slur on our country [sic]'.[86] The CO of the 2nd North Antrim Regiment made a similar appeal, on behalf of the 12th Royal Irish Rifles, stating, 'The War in Europe offers to young fellows possibilities of useful service to their King and Country, combined with opportunities for personal distinction and adventure, such as have not been afforded since the Napoleonic Era'.[87]

Continuity between the UVF and the battalions of the 36th (Ulster) Division varied significantly. While most of the other ranks in the 13th and 15th Royal Irish Rifles appear to have come from the pre-war UVF, this was by no means a universal experience.[88] In the case of the 14th Royal Irish Rifles, for which a complete register of next of kin addresses survives, it is clear that many recruits came from outside the battalion's recruiting area (Belfast): 20 per cent came from elsewhere in Ireland, 29 per cent from Great Britain and 1 per cent from overseas, principally the USA.[89] However, this experience is unrepresentative of the 36th (Ulster) Division as a whole as it is clear that most of its members came from Ulster if not always the UVF.[90] Formed on the basis of the pre-war YCV of Belfast, it is likely that the 14th Royal Irish Rifles would have appealed to Unionist middle-class recruits throughout Ireland and also to Ulster Unionist supporters in Britain.[91] Among rural battalions, the 11th Royal Inniskilling Fusiliers was unusual in that it relied on non-Irish recruits to fill its ranks; indeed 'C' company was formed by the British League for the Support of Ulster and the Union among Ulster Unionist sympathisers in Great Britain and one full company was raised in Glasgow.[92]

Recruiting was thus recognised as a serious problem for the 36th (Ulster) Division and, indeed, General Mackinnon, GOC Western Command received reports, in February 1915, that the 36th (Ulster) Division was recruiting, without permission, in Liverpool.[93] Stressing the urgency of the recruiting situation, Major General Powell, then the GOC of the 36th (Ulster) Division, wrote to Carson in March 1915:

> We are arranging the details for a very strenuous Recruiting Campaign throughout the length + breadth of Ulster, working in close contact with the UVF organisation.
>
> Will you very kindly address all your M.P. Colleagues up here that they must cooperate in this Campaign to the very utmost: that they must stump Ulster + go [up?] the highways + byways + stir up these sticky countryfolk. I would like to talk to each and all of these M.P.s. They must speak straight, forceable, words about the war to these audiences and especially to the women folk.
>
> Would it be too much to ask you to come over during the Easter recess + give a few speeches in the Country Districts of Ulster? I feel sure it would help a lot.[94]

The one area in which gradation between the UVF and the 36th (Ulster) Division can now be fairly accurately assessed is in the officer corps of these two formations, due to the release of officers' personal records at The National Archives, Kew, in the WO339 and WO374 series. These records are by no means complete, having been partially destroyed by enemy action in the Second World War; however, of the 344 officers appointed to infantry battalions in the 36th (Ulster) Division by January 1915 the files of 67 per cent survive.

The officers' personal records demonstrate that UVF membership was important, but not crucial, in officer selection for the 36th (Ulster) Division. Table 6.2 demonstrates that the importance of UVF membership in officer appointments varied considerably between units. In most of the rural units (especially the 11th Royal Inniskilling Fusiliers, 12th and 13th Royal Irish Rifles and 9th Royal Irish Fusiliers) UVF membership played an important role in officer selection and, indeed, a man's appointment as an officer may have been directly related to his ability to bring recruits from his UVF unit with him into the division. However, in the Belfast raised battalions, with the exception of the 14th Royal Irish Rifles (YCV), few officers had UVF experience; a situation which is not surprising given the difficulties which were found in officering Belfast UVF units, as discussed in chapter 3. However, it is also worth reflecting that there were clear differences of opinion within the UVF and 36th (Ulster) Division regarding who should be granted commissions. Richardson wrote to Carson, stating:

> I desire to point out, from a Military point of view, the great desirability of appointing the Officers who have been doing duty with these men, who have worked with them, who know them, and may have served with them since the Ulster Volunteers were organised. The personality of these Officers, it is superfluous to observe, will doubly add to the military efficiency of the Division.[95]

By contrast F. P. Crozier, appointed as the senior major in the 9th Royal Irish Rifles and former commander of the Special Service Company of the West Belfast Regiment, UVF, took the view that non-Ulstermen would make the best officers in the division. He reflected:

> Colonel Ormerod [the CO of the 9th Royal Irish Rifles] and I speedily came to the conclusion that if the battalion was to become really good, we should obtain other blood from the officer class in England in order to set up a better standard among our officers. To say this is not to cast a reflection on the Belfast officers – far from it – but it is correct to say, just as a prophet has no honour in his own country, so no middle-class men, drawn from the same town as the rank and file, to be made into officers *en masse*, do not carry, or pull, as much weight as efficient, or even mediocre, strangers. Their accents are too similar, unless they have been at school elsewhere, and their private histories are too well known among themselves and the rank and file.[96]

There were, of course, even for one of the last New Army divisions to be formed, some more normal channels through which officers could be obtained. Thus, for example, the OTC provided 51 junior officers for the division even though, as discussed in chapter 3, few OTC cadets seem to have been involved in the pre-war UVF.

War and decline 181

Table 6.2. The UVF membership of officers appointed to the 36th (Ulster) Division by January 1915

Unit	Number of surviving files	UVF officer	UVF other rank
8th Royal Irish Rifles	22	2	4
9th Royal Irish Rifles	17	4	0
10th Royal Irish Rifles	18	0	3
15th Royal Irish Rifles	18	1	2
11th Royal Irish Rifles	15	8	2
12th Royal Irish Rifles	18	14	0
13th Royal Irish Rifles	24	10	4
9th Royal Irish Fusiliers	14	7	2
9th Royal Inniskilling Fusiliers	18	3	4
10th Royal Inniskilling Fusiliers	22	5	2
11th Royal Inniskilling Fusiliers	17	9	2
14th Royal Irish Rifles	14	6	3
16th Royal Irish Rifles	15	3	3

Source: Based on a systematic analysis of the surviving officers' personal files in TNA WO339 and WO374 series.

Those with UVF command experience could be commissioned into the army at a relatively high rank, although having no military service before joining the UVF. This was the case with G. R. Irwin, who Lieutenant Colonel S. W. Blacker nominated to a captaincy on the basis that he had been adjutant of the 1st Armagh Regiment, and with A. P. Jenkins who Lieutenant Colonel H. A. Pakenham nominated to a captaincy on the basis that he had commanded the UVF battalion in Lisburn, Co. Antrim.[97] Both men were directly commissioned as captains. However, UVF officers were not automatically nominated for higher rank, for example Major the Earl of Leitrim nominated C. F. Falls to a mere second lieutenancy, despite the fact that Falls had commanded the 3rd Fermanagh Regiment.[98] A more prominent example of the claims of a UVF officer being ignored is in the case of William Copeland Trimble. Trimble, as noted previously, had been responsible for forming the Enniskillen Horse. When a service squadron of the 6th Inniskilling Dragoons was formed as part of the 36th (Ulster) Division, Trimble expected to become its commander and claimed to have been promised the command by Brigadier General T. E. Hickman. However, he was passed over, a not surprising decision, given his advanced age (he was 62) and lack of any formal military experience.[99]

In most cases the forms nominating a candidate for a commission were completed by the battalion CO, stating, 'I certify that I am well acquainted with _____ and can recommend him as a suitable candidate in all respects for appointment to a temporary commission in the Regular Army for the period of the war in the rank of _____'. Most COs seem to have completed this section following a brief interview with the candidate. Certainly, in many cases COs endorsed forms for men whom they did not know at all well; indeed, Lieutenant Colonel Ambrose Ricardo frequently crossed out, 'well' before signing the nomination.[100] In certain circumstances battalion COs did not complete all the nomination forms for their battalion. In the 107th Brigade, Brigadier General Couchman generally endorsed the applications of men applying for commissions in his brigade, presumably as his four battalion commanders were not appointed until his brigade had been formed for some time. Lieutenant Colonel James Craig, as the senior staff officer in the division, also endorsed a relatively large number of applications to various units, although there is little to suggest that he knew the applicants.[101] Despite orders stating that the COs of UVF units should send their recommendations for commissions to UVF HQ, it seems that HQ simply forwarded these applications to the War Office; there is certainly nothing to suggest that Richardson recommended the bulk of UVF officers for commissions in the 36th (Ulster) Division and it also seems that the War Office simply tended to confirm selections made by battalion COs.[102]

It is significant that the 36th (Ulster) Division, far from being well trained and able to take the field in August 1914, was not sent abroad until October 1915, while other New Army divisions, formed without the benefit of an existing paramilitary structure, for example the 14th (Light) Division, were on active service as early as May 1915.[103] This seems to confirm the argument advanced in chapter 3 that there were many serious deficiencies with the officering and training of the UVF in 1913–14.[104]

Despite the effective standing down of the UVF remaining in Ulster in May 1916, the force theoretically remained in being throughout the Great War. It was to be 1 May 1919 before the UVF 'demobilised' when Richardson stood down as its GOC.[105] Why Richardson choose this date is unclear, especially as VTC units in Great Britain did not disband until much later in 1919. In his final orders to the UVF Richardson stated:

1) Existing conditions call for the demobilisation of the Ulster Volunteers.
2) The Force was organised, to protect the interests of the Province of Ulster, at a time when trouble threatened. The success of the organisation speaks for itself, as a page of history, in the records of Ulster that will never fade.
3) The work connected with the UVF called for the exercise of tact, temper + discretion, on the part of all ranks. It is with pride that I fail to recall any single instance when the UVF were tried + found wanting.
4) The dedication of our great 'Leader', inspired all ranks, to 'play the game'.
5) In publishing this order, I take the opportunity of conveying to the Divisional, Regimental and Battalion Commanders – The Officers, N.C.O. + Men, my deepest gratitude + appreciation of services liberally + loyally given, during a critical period, extending over 5 _ years.

In these orders, Richardson then went on to thank specific units – the ladies involved, corps of despatch riders and medical officers.[106] Shortly after this, there was an attempt made to revive the YCV in Belfast and this received support from the then Lord Mayor of the city. However, the attempt failed, as Carson lacked enthusiasm for the reformation of this unit, merely advising its organisers to write to Dublin Castle for advice. Not surprisingly, Dublin Castle, then pre-occupied with attempts to disarm the Irish Volunteers, was not keen to see the re-emergence of armed Unionism.[107]

While the experience of the UVF during the Great War has tended, rightly, to be over-shadowed by the actions of the 36th (Ulster) Division it is clear that, for a short time, UVF units did remain in being. However, their rapid decline seems difficult to explain, given the enthusiasm for the VTC in Great Britain. It may be that the increased volume of work in the Belfast shipyards and heavy engineering firms in Belfast simply denied leisure time to those who would have been the backbone of the Belfast regiments, while the increasing demands on agriculture saw the demise of rural battalions. However, it seems more likely that UVF units were formed round a relatively small number of former army officers and enthusiasts; just the men lost to the movement shortly after the outbreak of the war when they were recalled to their former regiments or volunteered for service in the 36th (Ulster) Division or other units of the British army. The UVF clearly had an important role in the formation and officering of the 36th (Ulster) Division but we should not assume that all volunteers for this division were members of the UVF. The UVF made important contributions to the British war effort, but what does seem strange, given the events of 1913–14 and 1920–22, is that when faced with Irish Republican military activity the UVF leadership became completely inactive. Indeed, the picture left of UVF units remaining in Ulster in 1914–18 is a curious one: Lieutenant General Sir George Richardson seems to have sat neglected and neglecting in his Headquarters in Belfast while inexperienced civilians struggled and, in the vast majority of cases, failed to retain the UVF in existence at the local level.

Notes

1 J. O. Stubbs, 'The Unionists and Ireland, 1914–18', *Historical Journal*, 33, 4, 1990, p. 871.
2 PRONI, D.1327/4/5, UUC papers, UVF order 153, 19/12/1914.
3 PRONI, D.1327/4/5, UUC papers, UVF order 157, 09/01/1915.
4 PRONI, D.1327/4/5, UUC papers, UVF order 158, 09/01/1915 and order 5, 06/02/1915.
5 PRONI, D.1498/7, Richardson papers, 'Nominal Roll of Officers Recently Serving With the UVF Who Have Been Recalled to Army Service' and 'Provisional Organization of the "Ulster Division"' and Royal Ulster Rifles Museum, Anon., 'Historical Records of the 13th. Service Battalion, RIR', p. 18.
6 Fleming, *The Marquess of Londonderry*, pp. 19–75.
7 TNA, WO141/26, 'Miscellaneous Papers Regarding "Drilling" by Civilians in Ireland' and TNA, WO141/1, 'Intelligence Reports re. The UVF, 1913–14' and PRONI, D.1498/7, Richardson papers, Richardson to Carson, 10/09/1914.
8 War Office, *Army List*, July 1914, column 170 and 226.
9 War Office, *Army List*, October 1908, column 2012b.
10 PRONI, D.1633/2/19, Lilian Spender diary, entry for 01/08/1914.
11 PRONI, D.1327/4/3, UUC papers, letter, A. Oswald and A. Richardson to Lieutenant General Sir George Richardson, 04/02/1915.
12 PRONI, D.1327/4/2, UUC papers, UVF HQ minute book, entry for 21/12/1914.
13 PRONI, D.1327/4/3, UUC papers, memorandum by Hacket Pain to all divisional, regimental and battalion commanders, 07/08/1914 and Crozier, *Impressions and Recollections*, p. 156.
14 A copy of this form is in Liddle Collection, University of Leeds, the papers of Private R. Grange, 13th Royal Irish Rifles.
15 Crozier, *A Brass Hat in No Man's Land*, pp. 36–7.
16 PRONI, D.1507/A/8/2, Carson papers, UVF special order, by Colonel G. Hacket Pain, 02/09/1914.

17 PRONI, D.1855/1, Leslie papers, printed (which suggests wide circulation) letter, Carson to Richardson, 09/09/1914.
18 PRONI, D.1518/3/9, Hamilton papers, orders for 2nd North Antrim Regiment, 09/11/1914.
19 PRONI, D.1327/4/4, Murland papers, memorandum to UVF divisional and regimental commanders, 02/11/1914.
20 PRONI, D.1327/4/5, UUC papers, UVF special order 1, 16/01/1915 and UVF special order 2, 23/01/1915.
21 PRONI, D.1540/3/102 and 106, Hall papers, written orders by Captain Hall, undated but early 1915 and 'Ulster Defence Scheme', 16/01/1915.
22 PRONI, D.1518/3/8, Lyle papers, speech, Carson to Belfast UVF, 09/01/1915.
23 PRONI, D.1327/2/12, UUC papers, Carson to Richardson, 19/05/1915.
24 PRONI, D.1327/4/2, UUC papers, UVF HQ minute book, entry for 03/06/1915.
25 PRONI, D.1327/4/3, UUC papers, 'Resolution Passed at Meeting of UVF Headquarters Council', 25/03/1915.
26 PRONI, D.1327/4/2, UUC papers, UVF HQ minute book, entry for 01/07/1915.
27 PRONI, D.1327/4/2, UUC papers, UVF HQ minute book, entries for 28/04/1916, 08/05/1916 and 15/05/1916 and PRONI, D.1518/3/8, Hamilton papers, memorandum, Adair to Hamilton, 30/05/1916.
28 PRONI, D.3465/J/37/81, Madden papers, letter, John Leslie to Gerald Madden, undated but clearly Easter Monday 1916.
29 PRONI, D.1327/4/2, UUC papers, UVF HQ council minute book, entry for 29/05/1916.
30 PRONI, D.1327/4/2, UUC papers, UVF HQ council minute book, entry for 31/12/1914, UUC papers; PRONI, D.1507/A/11/12, Carson papers, letter, Richardson to Carson, 02/02/1915 and PRONI, D.1507/A/11/30, Carson papers, letter, Richardson to 'Sir' [Secretary, War Office?], 29/04/1915.
31 PRONI, D.1507/A/12/2, Carson papers, letter, Richardson to B. B. Cubitt, 05/05/1915 and PRONI, D.1507/A/12/32, Carson papers, letter, Dawson Bates to Carson, 26/05/1915.
32 PRONI, D.1327/4/17, Carson papers, letter, Colonel Jameson to Viscount Esher, 08/04/1915.
33 PRONI, D.1327/4/17, Carson papers, letter, Richardson to Carson, 05/07/1915 and PRONI, D.1327/4/2, UUC papers, UVF HQ minute book, entry for 05/07/1915.
34 PRONI, D.1327/4/17, Carson papers, letter, Richardson to Carson, 05/07/1915.
35 Bodleian Library, Oxford, Nathan 448, ff. 73–5, letters, Wimborne to Nathan, 06/06/1915 and 09/06/1915.
36 Bodleian Library, Oxford, Nathan 463, f. 458, letter, Nathan to Lord Wimborne, 08/06/1915.

37 *The Times*, 06/08/1914, cited in Mitchinson, *Defending Albion*, pp. 68–9. On the VTC see also Anon., *The Volunteer Force during the Great War: Official Record of the Central Association Volunteer Regiments* (P. S. King and Son, London, 1920), I. F. W. Beckett, 'Aspects of a Nation in Arms: Britain's Volunteer Training Corps in the Great War', *Revue Internationale d'Historie Militaire*, 63, 1985 and J. M. Osbourne, 'Defining Their Own Patriotism: British Volunteer Training Corps in the First World War', *Journal of Contemporary History*, 23, 1988.
38 Mitchinson, *Defending Albion*, p. 116.
39 PRONI, D.1327/4/2, UUC papers, UVF HQ council minute book, entry for 16/11/1914.
40 PRONI, D.1507/A/11/33, Carson papers, letter, Dawson Bates to Carson, 30/04/1915.
41 Mitchinson, *Defending Albion*, pp. 120–2. See also Bodleian Library, Oxford, Ms. Nathan, 449, f. 297, letter, Augustine Birrell to Matthew Nathan, undated but c. October 1915.
42 PRONI, D.1507/A/13/6, Carson papers, letter, Mulholland to Carson, 26/08/1915 and *Northern Whig*, 17/08/1915.
43 PRONI, D.1507/A/15/12, Carson papers, Irish Unionist Alliance, 'Notes from Ireland', 01/02/1916 and Bodleian Library, Oxford, Ms. Nathan 463, f. 318, letter, Matthew Nathan to H. O'Mahony, 19/05/1915.
44 PRONI, D.1327/4/2, UUC papers, UVF HQ minute book, entries for 13/03/1916 and 20/03/1916.
45 Bodleian Library, Oxford, Ms. Asquith 37, ff. 6–7, letter, A. W. Samuels to H. H. Asquith, 18/05/1916.
46 Patrick Buckland, *James Craig* (Gill and Macmillan, Dublin, 1980), p. 36 and Ervine, *Craigavon*, p. 298.
47 Falls, *The History of the 36th (Ulster) Division*, p. 6 and G. A. Cooper Walker, *The Book of the Seventh Service Battalion, The Royal Inniskilling Fusiliers* (Brindley & Son, Dublin, 1920), p. 3.
48 Simkins, *Kitchener's Army*, pp. 290–1. Two photographs on display at the Somme Heritage Centre, Newtownards, show recruits in the 36th (Ulster) Division training with obsolete Lee Metford and Mauser rifles, provided by the UVF. See also Foy, 'The Ulster Volunteer Force', p. 208.
49 UVF Headquarters, *Ulster Volunteer Force Hospital Christmas Book, 1915* (UVF, Belfast, 1915); TNA, PIN15/3590 'Ulster Volunteer Hospitals, Galwally + Belfast Capitation' and TNA, PIN15/3591, 'Ulster Volunteer Force Hospital'.
50 PRONI, D.1327/4/2, UUC papers, UVF HQ council minute book, entry for 04/02/1915.
51 PRONI, D.1518/3/8, Hamilton papers, memorandum, UVF HQ to divisional, regimental and battalion commanders', 26/08/1915.

War and decline

52 PRONI, D.1518/3/8, Hamilton papers, letter, Hamilton to Adair, 19/10/1915.
53 TNA, WO162/20, Kitchener papers, memorandum on recruiting, 29/08/1914.
54 PRONI, D.1633/2/19, Lilian Spender diary, entry for 02/10/1914.
55 'Statement Giving Particulars Regarding Men of Military Age in Ireland', xvii, [8390], H.C. 1916, 581.
56 Fitzpatrick, *Politics and Irish Life*, pp. 110–11.
57 NAS, GD391/22/6, letter, T. Comyn Platt, Honorary Secretary, British League for the Support of Ulster and the Union to John Stewart Peter, 25/09/1914.
58 David Fitzpatrick, 'The Logic of Collective Sacrifice: Ireland and the British Army, 1914–18', *The Historical Journal*, 38, 4, 1995, pp. 1028–9. On some of the problems with Fitzpatrick's figures see Keith Jeffery, *Ireland and the Great War* (Cambridge University Press, 2000), pp. 6–8.
59 NLI, Ms. 26,154, Joseph Brennan papers, recruiting figures to 15/04/1916.
60 Bodleian Library, Oxford, Ms. Nathan 457, f. 156, 'Returns Up To 15th October 1914'.
61 Bodleian Library, Oxford, Ms. Nathan 457, f. 155, letter, A. P. Magill to Matthew Nathan, 22/11/1914.
62 Bodleian Library, Oxford, Ms. Nathan 325, letter, A. P. Magill to Matthew Nathan, 24/09/1915.
63 PRONI, D.1518/3/9, Hamilton papers, 'Men of "E" (Bushmills) Company, 2nd North Antrim Regiment UVF in Regular Army', n.d. but c. September 1916.
64 Foy, 'The Ulster Volunteer Force', p. 206, Eric Mercer, 'For King, Country and a Shilling a Day: Recruitment in Belfast during the Great War, 1914–18' (unpublished M.A. dissertation, The Queen's University of Belfast, 1999), p. 5 and *Belfast Evening Telegraph*, 06/10/1914, p. 8.
65 Colles, *The History of Ulster from the Earliest Times to the Present Day*, p. 246.
66 Falls, *The History of the 36th (Ulster) Division*, pp. 1–2. More recent works which repeat Colles and Falls's views are Tom Johnstone, *Orange, Green and Khaki: The Story of the Irish Regiments in the Great War, 1914–18* (Gill and Macmillan, Dublin, 1992), p. 216 and Phillip Orr, *The Road to the Somme: Men of the Ulster Division Tell Their Story* (Blackstaff Press, Belfast, 1987), p. 45.
67 Hugh Montgomery Hyde, *Carson: The Life of Sir Edward Carson, Lord Carson of Duncairn* (William Heinemann, London, 1953), pp. 377–9.
68 Johnstone, *Orange, Green and Khaki*, p. 216 and PRONI, D.1507/A/8/4, Carson papers, letter, Carson to Ruby Frewen, 03/09/1914.
69 TNA, WO339/39413, personal file of Major P. K. Kerr Smiley, letter, Hickman to General Robb, War Office, 20/02/1915.

70 Terence Denman, *Ireland's Unknown Soldiers: The 16th (Irish) Division in the Great War 1914–18* (Irish Academic Press, Dublin, 1992), pp. 38–58 and Dennis Gwynn, *The Life of John Redmond* (G. G. Harup, London, 1932), pp. 389–90.
71 Stephen Gwynn, *John Redmond's Last Years* (Edward Arnold, London, 1919), p. 173.
72 David Fitzpatrick, *The Two Irelands, 1912–39* (Oxford University Press, 1998), p. 52.
73 Colin Hughes, *Mametz: Lloyd George's 'Welsh Army' at the Battle of the Somme* (Orion Books, Gerrard's Cross, 1990), pp. 29–30, Clive Hughes, 'Army Recruitment in Gwyneed, 1914–16' (M.A. thesis, University of Wales, 1983), pp. 71–194 and Clive Hughes, 'The New Armies' in I. F. W. Beckett and Keith Simson (eds), *A Nation in Arms: A Social Study of the British Army in the First World War* (Manchester University Press, 1985), p. 106.
74 Fitzpatrick, 'The Logic of Collective Sacrifice', pp. 1028–9.
75 PRONI, D/1507/A/7/6, Carson papers, telegram from unnamed UVF officer to Carson, 08/08/1914. See also, Thomas Hennessey, *Dividing Ireland, World War I and Partition* (Routledge, London, 1998), pp. 56–8.
76 *Belfast News Letter*, 07/08/1914, cited in Orr, *The Road to the Somme*, p. 40.
77 PRONI, D.1507/A/8/1, Carson papers, letter, Richardson to Carson, 02/09/1914.
78 Edward Spiers, 'The Scottish Soldier at War' in Hugh Cecil and Peter Liddle (eds) *Facing Armageddon: The First World War Experienced* (Leo Cooper, London, 1996), p. 316 and I. F. W. Beckett, 'The Territorial Force', in Beckett and Simpson (eds), *A Nation in Arms*, p. 134.
79 Beckett, *The Amateur Military Tradition*, p. 229.
80 PRONI, D.1327/4/4, Murland papers, UVF special order, 02/09/1914 and *Northern Whig*, 10/08/1914.
81 PRONI, D.1498/3, Richardson papers, telegram, Richardson to Carson, 10/09/1914.
82 Keith Grieves, *The Politics of Manpower, 1914–18* (Manchester University Press, 1988), p. 14 and Mercer, 'For King, Country and a Shilling a Day', pp. 6, 9.
83 I. F. W. Beckett, 'The British Army, 1914–18: The Illusion of Change', in John Turner (ed.), *Britain and the First World War* (Unwin Hyman, London, 1988), p. 102.
84 PRONI, D.1518/3/8, Lyle papers, UVF order 148, 15/12/1914.
85 Royal Inniskilling Fusiliers Museum, Enniskillen, Box 12, UVF recruiting correspondence, handbill. The expression 'hire' in this handbill suggests that it was particularly aimed at agricultural labourers, attending hiring fairs at this time of year.
86 Royal Inniskilling Fusiliers Museum, Enniskillen, Box, 12, UVF recruiting correspondence, letter, Ricardo to Mr Robinson, ? October 1915.

War and decline

87 PRONI, D.1518/3/9, Hamilton papers, orders for 2nd North Antrim Regiment, 09/11/1914.
88 Royal Ulster Rifles Museum, Belfast, Anon, 'Historical Records of the 13th. Service Battalion, R.[oyal] I.[rish] R.[ifles] part 3', pp. 1–3 and IWM, J. H. Stewart-Moore, 'Random Recollections', p. 7.
89 These figures are based on Royal Ulster Rifles Museum, Belfast, 'Membership of the 14/Royal Irish Rifles (Y.C.V.)'. It is unclear when this book was compiled, but the fact that deaths are not recorded, suggests that it was before this unit left for overseas service.
90 Nicholas Perry, 'Maintaining Regimental Identity in the Great War: The Case of the Irish Infantry Regiments', *Stand To!*, 52, 1998, pp. 6 and 11.
91 NAM, 8210–88, 'Report of the Council of the YCV of Ireland, 1912–13', Mercer, 'For King, Country and a Shilling a Day', p. 10 and Orr, *The Road to the Somme*, p. 49.
92 NAS, GD391/24/34, letter, Hubert Corry to John Stewart Peter, 12/12/1914, and W. J. Canning, *Ballyshannon, Belcoo, Bertincourt: The History of the 11th Battalion, the Royal Inniskilling Fusiliers (Donegal and Fermanagh Volunteers) in World War One* (privately published, Antrim, 1996), p. 15.
93 Simkins, *Kitchener's Army*, p. 71.
94 PRONI, D.1507/A/11/22, Carson papers, letter, Powell to Carson, 25/03/1915.
95 PRONI, D.1507/A/8/8, Carson papers, letter, Lieutenant General Sir George Richardson to Sir Edward Carson, 07/09/1914.
96 Crozier, *Impressions and Recollections*, p. 161.
97 TNA, WO339/14269, personal file of Captain G. R. Irwin and TNA, WO339/14333, personal file of Major A. P. Jenkins.
98 TNA, WO339/21314, personal file of Major C. F. Falls.
99 PRONI, D.1507/A/11/3 and 5, Carson papers, letters, W. Copeland Trimble to Carson, 15/01/1915 and 20/01/1915.
100 See, for example, TNA, WO339/14190, the personal file of Second Lieutenant J. A. Kelly.
101 See, for example, the personal files of TNA, WO339/16019, Lieutenant H. H. R. Dolling and TNA, WO339/21335, Second Lieutenant G. C. Wedgwood.
102 PRONI, D.1855/1, Leslie papers, UVF special order, 14/09/1914.
103 Beckett and Simpson, *A Nation in Arms*, p. 235.
104 On the war time record of the 36th (Ulster) Division see, Falls, *The History of the 36th (Ulster) Division*, Orr, *The Road to the Somme* and Bowman, *Irish Regiments in the Great War*.
105 PRONI, D.1507/A/29/30, Carson papers, letter, Richardson to Carson, 29/04/1919.
106 NAM, 5705–32, Richardson papers, UVF order 100, undated but May 1919.
107 PRONI, D.1507/A/29/51–52, Carson papers, letters, D. E. Lowry to Carson, 23/05/1919 and Carson to D. E. Lowry, 26/05/1919.

7

The revival and demise of the UVF, 1920-22

Standard works on the establishment of the Northern Ireland state tend to suggest that the re-establishment of the UVF in mid-1920 was short-lived as the force was quickly incorporated into the USC formed later that year.[1] However, the demise of the UVF was a much longer process than these accounts allow. Just as Carson's army did not seamlessly transform itself into the 36th (Ulster) Division in 1914, so it did not simply become the USC in 1920. In the period from 1920 to 1922 the UVF competed with the USC for recruits and, indeed, there was a wide number of other Loyalist paramilitary groups. One of these, the Ulster Imperial Guards, may even have eclipsed the UVF in terms of membership.

Despite Lieutenant General Sir George Richardson's resignation and the supposed disbandment of the UVF in early 1919, discussed in the previous chapter, RIC County Inspectors continued to send in returns on the strength of the UVF in their areas and UVF members who had retained their rifles throughout the 1914–19 period made no moves to surrender these to the police or military authorities, although there was no UVF activity as such throughout 1919.[2] This situation meant that UVF rifles and, to some degree, organisation were used in both the re-establishment of the UVF proper in mid-1920 and also in the formation of independent Loyalist paramilitary units. By November 1920 Sir Ernest Clarke was aware that six different, as he termed them, 'civilian forces' were operating in Dromore, Banbridge and Rathfriland in Co. Down and Maghera, Castledawson and Moneymore in Co. Londonderry. Some of these had been raised by individuals (those in Maghera and Castledawson had been formed by Colonel Chichester, formerly of the YCV) and others by committees. Clarke noted that these were mostly Vigilance Forces which were simply patrolling with the intention of reporting anything suspicious to the local RIC.[3] It also appears that the

Lord Mayor of Belfast had enrolled a guard of 20 ex-soldiers, who had mostly been former UVF members, to protect Belfast City Hall from a feared IRA raid in June 1920.[4] Two of the earliest and best documented vigilantee groups, in the context of the escalating Anglo-Irish War and the spread of IRA activity to Ulster, were Fermanagh Vigilance, formed by Major Sir Basil Brooke (later to be Prime Minister of Northern Ireland) and a so-called 'Protective Patrol' formed by John Webster in Armagh City.

Brooke seems to have been moved to form his Fermanagh Vigilance Force in June 1920 by witnessing the deteriorating security situation in Dublin while his wife was in hospital during March to May while expecting their first son.[5] In his own account of the formation of this force, Brooke stated that it was for three reasons:

1) I felt that the hotheads on the Ulstermen's side might take the matter into their own hands, if not organised.
2) The threat of raids was increasing.
3) There appeared to be a possibility that those of the Ulstermen who wished for a quiet life and finding no support elsewhere might turn to Sinn Fein.

Brooke went on to state that while he had used UVF rifles, which he had stored on his estate since 1914, to arm the force and followed the UVF style election of officers, he had not used the term 'UVF' as it seemed too 'political' and he had hoped to attract Catholic support for his cause. In the latter Broke felt that he had failed as while three Catholics initially joined, two had quickly withdrawn.[6]

Initially Brooke's force was, as with many of the UVF units of 1913–14, very feudal in character, being based on Brooke's estate at Colebrooke (itself situated in a small Unionist enclave in South Co. Fermanagh, adjacent to the Monaghan border) and enlisting its first 14 members among Brooke's estate workers. However, Brooke was soon organising patrols in the neighbouring area though it seems that he was reluctant to recruit more men into the force than he could arm with the limited amount of UVF rifles that he initially had available.[7]

In Armagh City, a force with similar aims was set up in April 1920 by John Webster, a local shopkeeper. Initially Webster's 'Protective Patrol' consisted of just ten men who patrolled the city, each member patrolling one night in every two. When these patrols started, their members armed themselves with whatever they had available: UVF rifles, shotguns or even sticks. Quickly a committee was formed which approached the

UUC for support and received 174 UVF rifles from Belfast to arm the rapidly growing force. Webster's patrol went on to be the basis on which the UVF was revived in Co. Armagh as a whole.[8]

While, infamously, at the traditional 'Twelfth' Orange Order demonstration in Belfast in July 1920 Sir Edward Carson had threatened to revive the UVF to secure fair treatment for Ulster Unionists, it seems that as early as March 1920 Carson had seriously advocated the re-establishment of the UVF.[9] However, as in 1912, it appears that it was the formation of independent Loyalist forces, along with the lobbying carried out by certain sections of the Ulster Unionist party, which lead to a centralised system being established, when the Standing Committee of the UUC revived the UVF on 25 June 1920. Unlike the situation in 1913–14, the revived UVF met with little support from Unionists in Great Britain. *The Times* was highly critical of Carson's speech, claiming that the British people would not accept counter provocation from the reformed UVF as a solution to IRA attacks.[10]

In early July 1920, Lieutenant Colonel Wilfrid Spender was appointed officer commanding the UVF, taking over from Major Horace Haslett who had been in command pending the appointment of a permanent officer.[11] Spender received his appointment from the UUC but this had the tacit agreement of the British government as Spender was given leave of absence from his post as 'Officers' Friend' at the Ministry of Pensions.[12] Why Spender was appointed is unclear; certainly he had been a key member of the original UVF staff and had served as GSO II in the 36th (Ulster) Division. However, Spender's connection with the 36th (Ulster) Division ended in July 1916 when he was promoted and moved to another division and it seems unlikely that Spender was well known in the Ulster of 1920 (he was, of course, living in London when he was offered the appointment). Indeed, it seems likely that F. H. Crawford, then a lieutenant colonel in the Royal Army Service Corps, was offered the post first but declined it as he held out some hopes of being retained in the post-war army.[13]

The UVF was theoretically reformed in July 1920, when announcements in Unionist newspapers called for former members to report for duty.[14] However, Spender's attempt to re-raise the UVF seems to have met with decidedly limited success. While the original 20 UVF battalions in Belfast had been revived they seem to have contained little more than 100 men each, meaning that they were under-strength companies in military terms.[15] Spender himself was concerned about the organisation in Co. Antrim and South Belfast and also noted that, 'In the doubtful districts the people will watch to see how things pan out before committing themselves'.[16] Thus the UVF of 1920 was, like that of 1914, and indeed like other Loyalist paramilitary forces formed in the 1920–22 period, recruiting heavily in the areas where it was least likely to be of any use.

The UVF seems to have failed to recruit well in 1920 for a number of reasons. Many men who had served in the Great War do not seem to have been keen to revisit a military lifestyle, even on a part-time basis. The Belfast and wider Ulster economy was experiencing a post-war boom into late 1920 which meant that unpaid evening and weekend duty was decidedly unappealing for many workers, who had the option of working overtime at high rates of pay. Potential recruits were deterred by a lack of both pay and, probably more importantly, an indemnity scheme which would cover them and their families in the event of their injury or death. Indeed it says much for the changed circumstances of 1920 compared to 1914 that there was no suggestion that the early voluntary indemnity scheme, outlined in chapter 5, should be re-activated. For extremists, the UVF held few attractions as the men were largely left unarmed and untrained (indeed it seems that in many areas the re-activation of the UVF entailed little more than taking a roll of possible members) while moderate Unionists felt that they had a claim on the services of the regular army and RIC for protection.

The reformation of the UVF was greeted with mixed emotions by senior military officers, which clearly affected its viability. General Sir Nevil Macready, long a critic of the UVF since his unhappy experiences in Belfast in 1914 as military governor in waiting, wanted any Loyalist forces raised in Ulster to be raised as SR battalions under clear military command (in a style curiously similar to the part-time battalions of the Ulster Defence Regiment raised in 1970) stating, 'the alternative, which appears to be either Special Constabulary or the Ulster Volunteers in its naked shape, would simply mean a body of undisciplined men over whom the Government would have no hold, and who would most assuredly paint the place red … I doubt whether most advanced Ulstermen would agree to the keeping of order in a Catholic County by the Ulster Volunteers under any guise'.[17] Field Marshal Lord French shared Macready's view that Loyalist forces should serve under military authority but continued, 'I think the Ulster Volunteer Force would prove a most useful and valuable contingent'.[18] Decisively though, Major General Guy Bainbridge, the officer commanding 1st Division, largely responsible for the security of Ulster, saw the UVF as part of the security problem rather than a security solution. He noted that the reformation of the UVF would, 'only lead to more trouble and excitement, more nerves and consequently more attacks on the part of the Catholic populations'.[19] Spender was also disappointed to find that few UVF leaders of 1913–14 vintage were prepared to take command of revitalised units and it seems that some of those who did answer his call, such as Major C. F. Falls and Brigadier General Ambrose Ricardo, were exhausted following strenuous war-time service. Having noted this, it is unclear why Brigadier General F. P. Crozier's services, offered in July 1920, were turned down and this does raise the possibility that Spender was uncomfortable working with those who had out-ranked him in the army.[20] Another problem for Spender was that some Orange Lodges had formed their own armed volunteers outside the UVF structure. Potential recruits to the UVF were also concerned that they would be placed under the control of Dublin Castle and sent anywhere in Ireland.

By early September 1920, Spender was admitting the limited military or police capacities of his force, stating, 'if the coal strike takes place [in Great Britain, necessitating the withdrawal of most British troops from Ulster] we shall have the most serious situation which we have ever had to confront and it is doubtful whether the UVF if called upon to help the Government at the last moment would be able to cope with it'.[21] The performance of the UVF as a security force had been very mixed in mid to late 1920. A Loyalist vigilantee group (distinct from either the Fermanagh Vigilance Force or UVF proper) in Lisbellaw, Co. Fermanagh, had prevented the IRA burning a number of buildings, including the courthouse on 8–9 June 1920.[22] Spender felt that the UVF had helped to restore order and confidence in Derry City by October 1920 and that the UVF had carried out useful intelligence work in Counties Fermanagh, Londonderry and Tyrone.[23] However, otherwise, the UVF seemed to have, as Bainbridge feared, contributed to security problems. The UVF or at least Loyalist gangs armed from UVF stocks of 1914, were implicated in serious trouble in Derry City in May and June 1920 when snipers operating from the city walls and Fountain area fired into Catholic areas, killing at least seven men.[24] While the UVF, as formed units, played no role in the serious disturbances in Belfast in 1920–22, as Alan Parkinson has noted, it must have been relatively easy for maverick Loyalists to arms themselves from UVF stocks.[25] As late as February 1921 the UVF was causing security problems, burning a number of homes in Rosslea, Co. Fermanagh, which lead to the murder of two USC sergeants in retaliation.[26] Important new work on the

Northern IRA suggests that, apart from refusing tamely to hand over its rifles, the UVF did little to prevent the growth or activities of the IRA in Ulster.[27] The irrelevance of the UVF in containing IRA activities is further demonstrated by the fact that Charles Townshend's standard work on the Anglo-Irish war makes no mention of the reformed UVF and Michael Hopkinson's new work on the war makes very limited reference to the force.[28]

Owing to the sluggish recruitment to and indifferent performance of the UVF, in September 1920 Sir James Craig urged the formation of a new force of Special Constabulary and Spender encouraged his men to enlist in this.[29] The basis of this force resolved some of the problems which had deterred Unionists from joining the UVF. The full-time 'A' section would be paid almost £4 per week with an annual bonus of £25 while the part-time 'B' section would receive an allowance of £10 per annum for performing one night's duty per week. Members of the USC would also receive the same indemnity payments as regular RIC officers.[30]

However, the newly raised USC did not subsume the UVF or, indeed, a number of other Loyalist paramilitary groups, until early 1922 and only when the USC had become a very different force from that originally envisaged. Initially the USC was to be fairly small in size, allowing for the continuance of the UVF. In November 1920 a USC force of just 910 'A' Specials and 12,000 'B' Specials had been proposed, although by February 1921 the USC establishment was fixed at 1,490 in 'A' Division, 19,500 in 'B' Division (of which only 15,000 had been recruited) with 4,000 recruited for 'C' Division, though it was noted that the authorised strength of this force was 'indefinite'.[31] In either case the numbers envisaged were far short of the UVF membership of 1914.

It is also noticeable that a number of personnel in the 'A' Division were not from Northern Ireland. Of the 623 recruited for Co. Fermanagh in 1920–22, 24 were from Great Britain, two from Co. Leitrim, and one each from Dublin and Co. Longford. What is most noteworthy though is that 46 of these men were from Counties Cavan, Donegal and Monaghan, suggesting that Loyalists in these areas preferred to enrol in Crown forces than re-establish UVF units in areas where they would be heavily out-numbered and out-gunned.[32] Unfortunately as a local force, in which officers and men knew each other well, the surviving paperwork on the 'B' Specials is very poor; crucially on enlistment men were not asked to give details of their employment or previous military experience, which makes it impossible to clearly assess the overlap between the UVF and USC in 1920–22.

In September and October 1921 it is clear that, despite the formation and expansion of the USC, the UVF was being reorganised.[33] Clearly this reorganisation was occurring against the backdrop of the Anglo-Irish Treaty negotiations, then being held in London, and dissatisfaction that the Northern Ireland government had not received full powers to administer law and order in Northern Ireland. Many men, who had not joined the USC, wanted to demonstrate their militant opposition to any settlement which would threaten the existence of the new six county Northern Ireland state. The *Northern Whig* noted:

> The reorganisation of the UVF is going on apace and before the winter is well under way there will be a body of from thirty to fifty thousand stalwart determined men, most of them possessing discipline and training, enrolled and ready to meet the menace which is confronting them now, just as the original members of the organisation nine years ago were prepared to meet the menace which confronted them then. As a fact it is the same old menace, although it approaches in a somewhat different form.[34]

The Unionist press, commenting on the reorganisation of the UVF, made much of the peaceable intentions of the force: 'The reorganisation of the UVF in the city and country throughout the Six Counties will, however, certainly not be made a means to annoy or interfere with any section of the peaceable inhabitants of that area. The force has a proud record in the past and it will be the aim of everyone associated with its reconstruction to maintain that record unsullied in the future'.[35] General Macready took a dim view of this latest resurrection of Carson's army, writing to James Craig, 'I have seen indications lately that certain steps have been taken by possibly irresponsible persons to revive the UVF If Martial Law is proclaimed [in the event of the breakdown of the truce] in Ulster the raising of troops as distinct from Police will be a matter for the Army Authorities'.[36]

In addition to the UVF a plethora of other Loyalist bodies, most of them apparently very short-lived, appeared in late 1921. The largest of these appears to have been the Ulster Imperial Guards. This organisation developed out of the Ulster Ex-Servicemen's Association with Mr Robert Boyd acting as secretary to both organisations.[37] The Ulster Ex-Servicemen's Association was formed very shortly after the end of the Great War and disappeared in the early 1920s as its members joined the then newly formed British Legion.[38] Like many of the short-lived veterans' organisations formed in this period the Ulster Ex-Servicemen's Association aimed both to provide financial help for veterans and their dependants and also to establish a labour bureau to aid ex-soldiers' efforts to find employment; the latter claimed considerable success in finding appointments in the 'A' Division of the USC for members of the organisation.[39]

While the Ulster Imperial Guards appear to have been formed in late August 1921, its first major public demonstration was not held until Armistice Sunday, 13 November 1921, when members of this force attended services at a number of Anglican, Methodist and Presbyterian Churches and the 'People's Hall' gospel hall in Belfast. It was claimed, at that time, that the organisation had 14,000 members, organised in nine battalions, and a press report went on to state:

> It is anticipated that within a fortnight or three weeks practically every able-bodied loyal man in Ulster will be recruited into the ranks. When thoroughly equipped and organised the forces will be offered to the Premier of Northern Ireland to safeguard the interests of his Parliament, to protect the Northern boundaries or to be used for such purposes as the Northern Cabinet may think necessary. The Guards are properly disciplined, a very large percentage of the members being ex-service men who before the war belonged to the Ulster Volunteer Force.[40]

The Ulster Imperial Guards was not a force on which the Northern Ireland government wanted to rely, in the event of an emergency. Macready was told by J. M. Andrews, the Northern Ireland Minister for Labour, in November 1921, that the Guards would require a long time in training before they were able to act against the IRA.[41]

There was a number of much smaller Loyalist organisations formed in this period. A Loyalist Association was created in Lisburn, which went on to form three 'Loyalist Battalions' under the ultimate command of Major Wilson with Captain Ensor, a veteran of the 36th (Ulster) Division, commanding one of the battalions.[42] It is unclear why so many small organisations flourished in this period with the USC and reorganised UVF both recruiting. It may be that in solidly Unionist areas the opportunities to serve in the USC were limited; conversely in such areas war veterans may have found the prospect of unpaid or poorly paid patrols and drills in the 'B' or 'C' Specials (the latter force not, it seems, being organised properly until 1922) decidedly unappealing, but wanted to make clear their determination to take military action in a serious situation. The serious riots in Lisburn in August 1920, when the town's first USC force evaporated in the face of unrest, some of them taking part in the riot, may have led to a reluctance by many Unionists there to enlist in the USC.

Certainly Sir James Craig and senior military figures were planning to make use of these various forces in the event of the Treaty negotiations breaking down in November and December 1921. Craig was planning to raise an additional 3,000 'A' Specials from them, in addition to the extra 700 'A' and 5,000 'B' Specials already earmarked for recruitment in late 1921 and early 1922.[43] Crucially the decision was made to arm the expanded USC with British army rifles in November 1921, ending the reliance of some USC units on former UVF rifles, a large number of which seem to have been held by the Ulster Imperial Guards at an armoury in Tamar Street, East Belfast.[44]

Macready seems to have thought that, in the event of the truce breaking down, the best solution in Northern Ireland would be to re-raise the Ulster Division with 12 battalions, each 1,000 strong, from loyalists in Ulster. He felt that this would prove a better disciplined and cheaper force than an expanded USC and would have the advantage that it could be used anywhere in Ireland.[45] However, Craig opposed Macready's suggestion, stating that it would be unpopular and it therefore seems that Craig's successful attempt to neutralise the various Loyalist paramilitary groups by enrolling them in 'C' Division of the USC was supported by the British government.[46] The incorporation of the UVF into the 'C' Specials was also supported by Lieutenant Colonel Fred Crawford who had succeeded Spender as commander of the force by late 1921.[47]

It should, of course, be recognised that the issue for Craig was more than just a security one. Craig wanted to ensure his political standing, and the expansion of 'B' and 'C' Divisions of the USC enabled him both to neutralise the political base of opponents like Boyd and to build up a useful patronage network. Indeed, it seems that in many areas the USC should be viewed as an instrument of Ulster Unionist patronage, rather than repression, with £10 per annum being paid to 'B' Specials and 'C' Specials, while unpaid, not having to pay £2 per annum for a firearms licence.[48] Indeed, when it was proposed to reduce or abolish the £10 payment to 'B' Specials each year, the Inspector General of the RUC wrote (in his capacity as head of the USC), 'The Co. Commandants all agree that to withdraw this wholesale will cause unrest and perhaps wholesale resignations. Everything depends upon how it is put to the men and what counter-advantages and privileges can be offered. Many are looking to their allowance to supply their Xmas dinner'.[49] The various Loyalist organisations also petered out in early 1922, partly as the Anglo-Irish Treaty signed in December 1921 was much more favourable to Ulster Unionists than they had imagined likely. With regard to the Ulster Imperial Guards, the major political figure involved in this was W. J. Twaddell, MP for the Belfast district of Woodvale in the Northern Ireland parliament.[50] It may be that his assassination on 22 May 1922 was connected with this and further lead to the demise of the Ulster Imperial Guards.

It is tempting, in a European context, to see the revived UVF and the USC as an Irish version of the German *Freikorps*. In proportional terms more Ulstermen were members of the USC (a maximum of one in six Protestant adult males in early 1922) than Germans were members of the *Freikorps*, which reached a maximum strength of around 400,000 men. In popular myth the *Freikorps* was a proto-Fascist force composed of ex-soldiers, which was prepared to operate against both internal dissent and external military threats.[51] In exploring this comparison it is worth emphasising that while no one would doubt the political leanings of the *Freikorps*, their age range was more diverse than popular accounts would suggest. Far from being Great War veterans, many *Freikorps* members were teenagers, who felt that they had missed their chance for adventure, with the end of the war. As Richard Bessel puts it, 'Those recruiting for the Freikorps often had better luck among school-leavers than among older men who had just returned from the senseless slaughter of the trenches'.[52] This certainly appears to have been the case in some units in the USC in Co. Tyrone where it is clear that when UVF veterans of 1913–14 vintage refused to enrol the local commander resorted to enlisting much younger and 'wilder' men.[53] While Ian Maxwell notes that 36th (Ulster) Division veterans were to be the 'backbone' of the revived UVF, it is unclear how many were actually involved.[54] The non-veteran age range is partly evident in the USC where, out of a sample of 244 men who enlisted in the 'B' Specials in 1920–22, 17 where under 20 years of age. More noticeable though is the role of this force as something of a Unionist patronage machine, as of these 244 men, 48 were aged 60 or above; the oldest being an 81 year old![55]

In political terms, the Northern Ireland government's relationship with Loyalist paramilitary groups was not entirely unlike the relationship between the Weimar government and the *Freikorps*. Macready felt that the Northern Ireland government was 'terrified of their own people' and wanted security to be handled by British regular troops, rather than having to rely on either the USC or Loyalist paramilitary forces.[56] This fear was expressed by Fred Crawford who wanted the old UVF re-established, 'with its old traditions + discipline, than have irresponsible individuals enlisting a lot of scallywags who will only be a menace + a danger to our cause'.⁵⁷ Meanwhile, Lieutenant Colonel G. C. Wickham (I.G., RUC) believed that Robert Boyd, the leader of the Ulster Imperial Guards, effectively forced Craig to incorporate his force into the USC. Brigadier General Cameron believed that the Ulster Imperial Guards posed a severe political threat to the Northern Ireland government, noting, 'Boyd is a regular kind of Bolshevist' who had threatened that his men would take over control of the USC.⁵⁸ However, unlike the Weimar government which had pitifully few regular forces to call on, the Northern Ireland government did have the services of both the British army and RUC, which both proved more reliable in restoring order than the Loyalist paramilitary groups or USC.

It should also be recognised that the political protests being voiced by many of these paramilitary groups were not against the Northern Ireland government *per se*, but rather against the British government's negotiations with Sinn Fein in 1921 and the failure of the British government to devolve security powers to the Northern Ireland government fully until early 1922. Certainly all of these forces seemed largely satisfied with the political leadership of Sir James Craig. The Lisburn Loyalist battalions sent a telegram of support to Craig, to which his private secretary, C. H. Blackmore, warmly replied by wire to Major Wilson, 'Will you kindly convey to the members of the 1ˢᵗ, 2ⁿᵈ and 3ʳᵈ Battalions the Prime Minister's sincere thanks for their kind telegram. It is just such messages of encouragement that nerve him to bear the heavy burden resting upon his shoulders at the moment'.⁵⁹ Similarly, the Ulster Imperial Guards eagerly participated in the monster Loyalist Demonstration held in central Belfast on 16 November 1921 and organised by the UUC, placing large notices in the Unionist press stating, 'It is most important that every Enrolled Member attend this Parade'.⁶⁰ Whatever Robert Boyd's attitude in private the Guards unhesitatingly placed themselves under the orders of Craig and the Northern Ireland cabinet in the event of an emergency.⁶¹ At this time though, Fred Crawford noted, 'My tigers [his own small paramilitary force formed in the Tiger's Bay district of Belfast] are very difficult just now to keep in hand in fact except the government (Ulster) does not get some force up to meet present emergency there will be trouble that they will not be able to cope with'.⁶² Crucially, while the *Freikorps* embarrassed the Weimar government through their actions in the Baltic states, Loyalist paramilitary forces did little to endanger the Anglo-Irish Truce of 1921, although incursions into Counties Cavan, Donegal and Monaghan, in support of their fellow covenanters of 1912, would have seemed a logical course of action for UVF units to have followed.

In conclusion it is therefore clear that Carson's army did not simply transform itself into Craig's militia on the formation of the USC in late 1920. The process was a much more gradual one and other groups competed for Loyalist support. The UVF provided something of a solution for the Northern Ireland government's security problems – a reservoir of trained men and a group which could make Craig's demands to the British government appear moderate. However, the UVF and other Loyalist paramilitary groups brought their own challenges, contributing in various ways to serious disorder in the new Northern Ireland state and souring relations between Craig, the Dublin Castle administration, the RIC and the British government. It is questionable the extent to which the UVF did actually reform in 1920, possibly the UVF proper amounted to little more than 3,000 men in this period and it is noticeable that the UVF never had a formal disbandment or even Home Guard style stand down at any stage; possibly so that attention would not be drawn to the extent to which the formation of 1920–22 was such a pale shadow of that of 1913–14. Having noted this, it is revealing that as late as May 1939, faced with a renewed IRA threat, sections of the Ulster Unionist Party wanted to re-establish the UVF as well as expand the 'B' Specials.[63]

Notes

1 Patrick Buckland, *The Factory of Grievances: Devolved Government in Northern Ireland, 1921–39* (Gill and Macmillan, Dublin, 1979), p. 181, Bryan Follis, *A State under Siege: The Establishment of Northern Ireland 1920–1925* (Clarendon Press, Oxford, 1995), p. 16 and Thomas Hennessey, *A History of Northern Ireland 1920–1996* (Gill and Macmillan, Dublin, 1997), p. 15.
2 'I. O.' [C. J. C. Street], *The Administration of Ireland, 1920* (Philip Allan & Co., London, 1921), p. 342
3 PRONI, D.1022/2/9/1, Clarke papers, 'Civilian Forces Already Formed – None Sworn In' by Clarke, ?/11/1920.
4 HLRO, LG/F/6/2/24a, Lloyd George papers, letter, Lord Mayor of Belfast to Carson, 17/06/1920.
5 Brian Barton, *Brookeborough: The Making of a Prime Minister* (Institute of Irish Studies, Queen's University of Belfast, 1988), p. 31.
6 PRONI, D.1022/2/3, Clarke papers, 'Fermanagh Vigilance' by Brooke.
7 Barton, *Brookeborough*, pp. 31–2.
8 PRONI, D.1290/6, Webster papers, notes on the formation of the 'B' Specials in Co. Armagh by John Webster.

9 PRONI, D.640/11/11, Colonel Fred Crawford's diary, entry for 17/09/1920.
10 *The Times*, 13/07/1920.
11 Ian Maxwell, pp. 115–16 and UVF HQ minute book, entry for 24/06/1920, UUC papers, PRONI, D.1327/4/2.
12 PRONI, D.1633/2/23, Lilian Spender's diary, entry for 16/07/1920.
13 TNA, WO339/23234, personal file of Lieutenant Colonel F. H. Crawford, 'Statement of Lt. Col. F. H. Crawford', 20/11/1920.
14 Maxwell, 'The Life of Sir Wilfrid Spender', p. 125.
15 PRONI, CAB5/1, 'UVF Papers', letter, Spender to Major General Bainbridge, 30/08/1920.
16 PRONI, CAB5/1, 'UVF Papers', letter, Spender to Craig, 09/09/1920.
17 IWM, HHW2/2A/49, Wilson papers, letter, Macready to Field Marshal Sir Henry Wilson, 01/09/1920. See also Sir Nevil Macready, *Annals of an Active Life* (Hutchinson & Co., London, 1924), vol. II, pp. 488–90.
18 IWM, JDPF8/3, French papers, letter, French to Walter Long, 01/07/1920.
19 PRONI, CAB5/1, 'UVF Papers', letter, Banbridge to Spender, 30/08/1920.
20 PRONI, D.1327/4/2, UUC papers, UVF HQ minute book, entry for 06/07/1920.
21 PRONI, CAB5/1, 'UVF Papers', letter, Spender to Craig, 09/09/1920.
22 Hezlet, *The 'B' Specials*, p. 11.
23 PRONI, CAB5/1, 'UVF Papers', letter, Spender to Blackmore, 01/10/1920.
24 Ronan Gallagher, *Violence and Nationalist Politics in Derry City, 1920–1923* (Four Courts Press, Dublin, 2003), pp. 25–7.
25 A. F. Parkinson, *Belfast's Unholy War: The Troubles of the 1920s* (Four Courts Press, Dublin, 2004), p. 32.
26 TNA, CO904/114, County Inspector's Report for Fermanagh, February 1921.
27 Lynch, *The Northern IRA and the Early Years of Partition, 1920–1922* and Fearghal McGarry, *Eoin O'Duffy: A Self-made Hero* (Oxford University Press, 2005).
28 Charles Townshend, *The British Campaign in Ireland 1919–1921: The Development of Political and Military Policies* (Oxford University Press, 1975) and Michael Hopkinson, *The Irish War of Independence* (Gill and Macmilan, Dublin, 2002), pp. 155–8.
29 PRONI, CAB5/1, 'Appreciation of the Situation in Ulster', 01/09/1920 and 'Suggested Steps for Government Action', 07/09/1920 both by Craig and 'Memorandum to O.C. Battalions, Belfast Regiment UVF' by Spender 29/10/1920.
30 TNA, HO351/176, 'Special Constabulary: Details of Conditions of Service, Equipment, etc.', n.d. but November 1920.
31 PRONI, USC/1/70A–C, USC archive, letter, Clarke to Sir John Anderson, 08/11/1920, and TNA, HO351/176, 'Special Constabulary – County Establishments', n.d. but February 1921.

32 PRONI, B.4267, USC archive, 'List of Special Constables (A) for Co. Fermanagh'.
33 *Northern Whig*, 18/10/1921, 25/10/1921 and 29/10/1921 and IWM, HHW2/2F/8, Wilson papers, letter, Macready to Wilson, 12/09/1921.
34 *Northern Whig*, 25/10/1921.
35 *Northern Whig*, 25/10/1921.
36 IWM, HHW2/2F/23, Wilson papers, Macready to Craig, 23/09/1921.
37 *Northern Whig*, 16/12/1921.
38 PRONI, D.1507/A/26/35, Carson papers, letter, Shannon Garvey to Carson, n.d. but 1919. On British veterans' organisations after the Great War see S. R. Ward, 'Great Britain: Land Fit for Heroes Lost' in S. R. Ward, *The War Generation: Veterans of the First World War* (Kennikat Press, London, 1975).
39 For a report of the annual meeting of the Ulster Ex-Servicemen's Association see *Northern Whig*, 16/12/1921.
40 *Northern Whig*, 14/11/1921.
41 IWM, HHW2/2G/4, Wilson papers, letter, Macready to Wilson, 26/11/1921.
42 *Northern Whig*, 19/11/1921 and 28/11/1921.
43 *Northern Whig*, 30/11/21 and IWM, HHW/2/63/5, Wilson papers, letter, Craig to Worthington Evans, 01/12/1921.
44 IWM, HHW2/2G/7, Wilson papers, 'Rifles for Special Constabulary', by IG Wickham, 28/11/1921.
45 IWM, HHW2/2F/26, Wilson papers, letter, Macready to Secretary, War Office, 17/10/1921 and IWM, HHW2/2F/35, Wilson papers, letter, Macready to Cameron, 24/10/1921.
46 IWM, HHW2/2F/37, Wilson papers, letter, Cameron to Macready, 28/10/1921, *Northern Whig*, 19/11/1921 citing the *Irish Bulletin* 18/11/1921. The Sinn Fein backed *Irish Bulletin* quoted extensively from a secret circular allegedly issued by the Divisional Commissioner's Office, RIC, Belfast, on this matter.
47 PRONI, D.640/11/1, Colonel Fred Crawford's diary, entry for 15/11/1921.
48 Walker, *A History of the Ulster Unionist Party*, p. 56.
49 PRONI, USC/1/70A–C, USC archive, letter, Wickham to Blackmore, 16/11/1921.
50 *Northern Whig*, 14/11/1921.
51 I am grateful to Professor Ian Beckett for suggesting this comparison.
52 Richard Bessel, *Germany after the First World War* (Clarendon Press, Oxford, 1993), p. 259. The standard account of the *Freikorps* remains, R. G. L. Waite, *Vanguard of Nazism: The Free Corps Movement in Postwar Germany* (Harvard University Press, Cambridge, 1952). See also A. D. Brenner, 'Feme Murder: Paramilitary "Self Justice" in Weimar Germany' in B. B. Campbell and A. D. Brenner (eds), *Death Squads in Global Perspective* (Palgrave Macmillan, Basingstoke, 2002), J. M. Diehl, *Paramilitary Politics in the Weimar Republic* (Indiana University Press, Bloomington, 1977) and R. M. Watt, *The Kings*

Depart: *The Tragedy of Germany: Versailles and the German Revolution* (Weidenfeld and Nicolson, London, 1969).
53 Wallace Clark, *Guns in Ulster* (privately published, Upperlands, 1963), p. 9.
54 Maxwell, 'The Life of Sir Wilfrid Spender', p. 123.
55 These figures are based on a sample of platoons in Co. Fermanagh from PRONI, B.4267, USC archive.
56 IWM, HHW2/2G/4, Wilson papers, letter, Macready to Wilson, 26/11/1921 and IWM, HHW2/2F/2, Wilson papers, letter, Macready to Wilson, 02/09/1921.
57 PRONI, D.640/11/1, Colonel Fred Crawford's diary, entry for 14/11/1921.
58 IWM, HHW2/2G/40, Wilson papers, letter, Cameron to Macready, 09/01/1922.
59 *Northern Whig*, 19/11/1921.
60 *Northern Whig*, 16/11/1921.
61 *Northern Whig*, 14/11/1921.
62 PRONI, D.640/11/1, Colonel Fred Crawford's diary, entry for 05/11/1921.
63 PRONI, D.1327/11/1/9, UUC papers, notes of a meeting between the executive committee of the Ulster Unionist Labour Association and the Prime Minister, 16/05/1939.

Conclusion

This study of the UVF has challenged a number of assumptions regarding the force. Particularly, its relationship with Ulster and British Unionist political leadership and the role of the force in serving as the basis for both the 36th (Ulster) Division and USC. This work has suggested that the UVF was better armed and worse financed than previous studies have allowed.

This work tends to support Alvin Jackson's attempt to discredit the so-called 'McNeill' thesis, first advanced by Ronald McNeill, which suggested that Unionist protest gradually and under central leadership progressed from the parliamentary arena to the populist and only, very reluctantly, to the paramilitary.[1] It is quite clear, as Jackson points out, that Unionist drilling started in 1910, before the Home Rule threat was at all significant. However, where this study does differ from Jackson's seminal work is to back date Unionist militancy. While Jackson sees 1905 as a crucial date, with the establishment of the UUC serving both to unify Ulster Unionism and to separate it from its Southern Irish and British varieties, it seems that the roots of Ulster Unionist militancy can be detected in 1893, if not 1886. From 1910 Ulster Unionists, many of whom had been involved in militant action in 1886 or 1893, were involved in importing firearms, drilling men or, at least, making the confused legal situation, which meant that neither activity was strictly illegal, clear to their fellow Ulster Unionists.

It is clear that the UVF was not simply a compliant party auxiliary and nor did its command structures follow the pyramid pattern expected in a strict military hierarchy. At the top of the UVF's command structure was Sir Edward Carson, but it is evident that his views on the organisation changed over time and he was, at various times, open to influence from both hawks and doves in the movement. Originally formed to maintain Unionist discipline and unity, the UVF soon served to threaten both.

During the height of the Third Home Rule crisis in July 1914, the UVF provided a forum for Ulster Unionists in the peripheral counties of Fermanagh, Tyrone, Cavan, Monaghan and Donegal to pressurise the Unionist leadership into the rejection of four county partition. The arming of the force in 1914 and the poor supervision of the rifles doled out by UVF HQ enabled the formation of a number of Unionist paramilitary groups in the 1920–22 period, one of which, the Ulster Imperial Guards, certainly caused concern to both the Ulster Unionist leadership and British military authorities. The UVF in the Edwardian period did at least serve largely to prevent Unionist protests from dissolving into rioting and, even in the face of considerable provocation, there is little evidence of UVF personnel causing damage to persons or property in 1913–14. The situation was, though, very different in 1920–22. While the UVF as a formed body was not involved in rioting, at the very least individuals armed from pre-war UVF stocks, if not UVF members, were involved in very serious disturbances in Belfast and Derry City, their actions causing a number of deaths.

UVF HQ did little to enforce its authority over most UVF units. Lieutenant General Sir George Richardson, appointed as the GOC of the force, was not the geriatric blimp-like figure that the Nationalist press portrayed, but neither was he a dynamic or especially active commander. Particularly in the period from August 1914 to April 1919 Richardson seems to have seen his UVF position as little more than a sinecure. Even at the height of the Third Home Rule crisis UVF HQ was inactive on many key issues. It reluctantly provided UVF units with firearms, but had made few preparations to provide food, clothing, accommodation or transport in the event of hostilities. Similarly, UVF HQ had engaged in little defence planning and seems to have functioned on the assumption either that British troops would never fire on UVF personnel (though as Lord Dunleath pointed out the reverse was also likely to be true) or that they would, in the finest traditions of the British armed forces, be able to 'muddle through' if the force did have to go into action.

As with the TF in Britain, the UVF's local organisation was based around county committees and locally based regiments. This attempt to replicate British military practice lead to some problems. In widely dispersed rural areas, the elaborate system of battalion and regimental command made little sense as UVF members rarely, if ever, saw their supposed battalion commander or county instructor. The regimental system brought in by Richardson in September 1913 also seems to have destroyed the early basis of the UVF formed around existing Orange

Lodges, Unionists Clubs and workplaces, replacing this simply by recruitment by area. The regimental system also did not allow for the system which soon evolved, of UVF members effectively defining their own commitment to the force. Battalions included men who had enrolled in the Special Service Sections, formed disproportionately from ex-servicemen who could be mobilised very rapidly and were committed to serve anywhere in Ulster; members of 'marching battalions' who were committed to serve at least in their own counties when mobilised; and those who were prepared to act as little more than sedentary guards, protecting their own homes and families. The county committees, which in the British Territorials were seen as centralising bodies, were considered to be decentralising in the UVF case. However, none had the finances required to redress the material shortages in the force and most seem to have fulfilled no particularly useful function. Most were simply compliant with the wishes of local regimental commanders, a serious problem in areas like Co. Cavan and North Antrim where local commanders (Colonel Oliver Nugent and Captain Arthur O'Neill, respectively) had effectively repudiated the control of UVF HQ. Nugent went to the extreme of renaming his force the Cavan Volunteer Force rather than the Cavan Regiment, UVF; emphasising that its role would be a purely police rather than military one in the event of conflict.

In terms of the social composition of the force, there is insufficient data surviving to enable definitive statements to be made about this, particularly as regards Belfast. However, it seems likely that the typical UVF member was male, urban based, in his twenties or thirties and either an unskilled or semi-skilled worker. Leadership tended to come from the local gentry, middle classes and, particularly in dispersed rural areas, the clergy. It therefore appears that the UVF was much larger and more accurately reflected the social composition of early twentieth-century Ireland than the IRA of 1919–21. In some rural areas UVF units had a definite feudal resonance (as, of course, did some amateur military units in Great Britain) and businessmen, especially those who effectively owned the industrial villages of Comber and Sion Mills, virtually conscripted their male workforces into the UVF units that they commanded.

Why men joined the UVF is similarly open to speculation. Some, apparently a very small minority, joined because their employer or landlord effectively forced them. For others the UVF provided an opportunity to engage in popular militarism, denied to most in Ulster as the TF had not been established there. Others saw their struggle as one for Empire or to uphold the British constitution against the actions of the Liberal government. What is clear is that UVF members agreed on relatively few issues. There was no general agreement over partition, especially where the new border should be made if it was implemented. Similarly, there were vast differences within the force over issues such as the labour question and the political role of women.

While historians considering other Irish paramilitary movements, such as the Fenians and Blueshirts, have argued, somewhat unconvincingly, that these were more important as social than military organisations, the same argument cannot be made for the UVF.[2] For most UVF members the only social activities associated with the force were marching and drilling. For many there were more military style activities, parades, camps and mock battles, but for only the small minority were there musical evenings, sporting events or magic lantern shows associated with the UVF. The truth was, of course, that the UVF was a military expression of Ulster Unionism, while pure social activities were generally carried out through membership of long-established Orange Lodges and Unionist Clubs.

Much has been made of the number of retired British army officers involved in the UVF. This study has tended to prove that while the numbers were significant, somewhere in the region of 140, many were unsuitable and others were involved on a very part-time basis, spending only a few weeks with UVF units as they were otherwise based in Great Britain. The number of British army officers available to the UVF was therefore considerably less than the number available to any of the Kitchener armies raised in 1914. Many UVF battalions were actually commanded by those with no military experience, a good example being A. P. Jenkins, who commanded the Lisburn Battalion largely as he was the owner of a large linen mill in the town.

The military efficiency of the UVF was far from uniform. While some units could draw on considerable professional military experience, others, especially in Belfast and Derry, could draw on very little. The instructors, training facilities and equipment available to UVF units varied enormously from place to place and over time, as did the commitment of UVF members with high absenteeism in many units. While previous authors have made much of the financial strength of the UVF it would appear that this was merely adequate, rather than generous. Finance was sufficient to provide the UVF (or at least sections of it) with reasonably modern firearms and barely sufficient ammunition, but it was not enough to provide uniforms or training camps for all members. It seems likely that some of the most efficient UVF units, in terms of training and equipment, were to be found in the Unionist heartlands of North Down and South Antrim, areas in which the UVF would have been least required in the event of civil war. The allocation of firearms and machine guns to UVF units was never worked out on a rational basis and the political pressure which individual UVF regiments or county committees could bring to bear on UVF HQ did much to decide what they received, in terms of both quality and quantity.

Of course the issue of military efficiency must be considered in the context of what the UVF would have been expected to do. Forced to defend the Ulster frontier against a determined attack by two British divisions and a naval landing on the shores of Belfast Lough the UVF would probably have collapsed quite quickly. If nothing else the ammunition supplies to the force would quickly have broken down. However, in the situation which was becoming increasingly likely after the Curragh Incident of March 1914, the UVF would have been perfectly capable of over-awing or militarily defeating the INV, RIC and small British military garrisons in Ulster, in the event of the Ulster Provisional Government declaring its governance of a nine county Ulster state. While a minority of UVF members could have been armed with modern rifles, probably 60,000 could have been armed with an assortment of rifles and most of the rest could have been armed with shotguns or revolvers, which were in plentiful supply in early twentieth-century Ulster. In other words the UVF was a poorly armed military force but a very well armed police force.

During the Great War the UVF played an important role in the formation of the 36th (Ulster) Division. Many, but by no means all, of the members of this formation had served in the UVF and a number of officers involved in the UVF went on to serve in the 36th (Ulster) Division. Some UVF commanders were to gain distinction in the war, the most noticeable being Oliver Nugent who started the war as a colonel and ended it as a lieutenant general. By contrast Colonel G. H. H. Couchman, given a brigade in the 36th (Ulster) Division at the start of the war, was quickly removed for incompetence. This raises interesting questions over how the Cavan Regiment, commanded by Nugent, and the Belfast Division, commanded by Couchman, would have performed in a civil war in Ireland.

In the 1914–15 period attempts were made to retain the UVF as a formed body. The Ulster Unionist leadership was conscious that Home Rule would be revisited at the end of the war and was reluctant to demilitarise their political army in this circumstance. However, as reservists returned to their British army regiments and enthusiasts volunteered for active service overseas, the UVF soon collapsed. By the time of the Easter Rising in 1916, the UVF was able to offer little more than 2,000 armed men to assist the British government. Following the Easter Rising, UVF HQ became concerned not with revitalising the force but with preventing its firearms falling into the hands of the Irish Volunteers. Richardson disbanded the UVF in May 1919.

With the escalation of the Anglo-Irish War in 1920, the UVF was reformed. However, while it is tempting to see a revolutionary force reforming as a counter revolutionary force, this was not the case. The UVF of 1920 was a pale shadow of that of 1914; its failure to recruit or reform in many areas resulting in the formation of the USC. The USC did not replace the UVF that quickly though. It appears that it was spring 1922 before the UVF and various other Loyalist paramilitary groups formed in 1920–21 were incorporated in the USC. In popular Unionist mythology the UVF was seen to have been effective in stemming the IRA in 1920–22, as shown by the proposal to reform the force in 1939, but this was simply not the case. The RUC, British army and 'A' Division of the USC proved much more successful in curtailing IRA activity. It is also clear that the 'B' Division of the USC, a part-time force, which does seem to have recruited a number of former UVF members, was as much an instrument of Ulster Unionist patronage as repression; recruiting many very elderly men and recruiting heavily in areas, such as North Down, where the IRA threat was negligible.

The UVF officially formed in 1913 can be seen to have disbanded in 1919, or at the latest, to have amalgamated into the USC by the end of 1922. Certainly Carson's army had no direct connection with the UVF formed in 1966, despite what many gable ends in Loyalist housing estates in Northern Ireland would have us believe.

Notes

1 Alvin Jackson, *The Ulster Party: Irish Unionists in the House of Commons, 1884–1911* (Clarendon Press, Oxford, 1989), pp. 284–321 and McNeill, *Ulster's Stand for Union*.
2 Comerford, *The Fenians in Context* and Cronin, *The Blueshirts and Irish Politics*.

Select bibliography

Primary sources

Archives

Bodleian Library, Oxford
Papers of Augustine Birrell and Sir Matthew Nathan.

Durham Record Office
Londonderry family papers

House of Lords Record Office
Papers of Lord Willoughby de Broke.
Papers of David Lloyd George.
Papers of Andrew Bonar Law.

Imperial War Museum (IWM)
Papers of Field Marshal Viscount French.
Papers of Field Marshal Sir Henry Wilson.

National Archives, Dublin
Chief Secretary's Office Registered Papers, 1910–21.

National Archives of Scotland
John Stewart Peter papers, GD391.

National Army Museum (NAM)
5705 – 32 Papers of Lieutenant General Sir George Richardson re. to Ulster.
8210 – 88 Documents relating to the Belfast Young Citizen Volunteers, 1912.

National Library of Ireland (NLI)
Breenan papers, Moore papers, Redmond papers.

Nuffield College, Oxford
Mottistone papers.

Public Record Office of Northern Ireland (PRONI)
CAB5/1, 'UVF Papers'.
D.640, Papers of Colonel F. H. Crawford.
D.845, Jenkins papers re. Lisburn UVF.
D.1022, Sir Ernest Clarke papers.
D.1132, R. T. G. Lowry papers re. UVF in Co. Tyrone.
D.1191, Papers re. North Londonderry Regiment, UVF.
D.1414, Papers re. 1st Tyrone Regiment, UVF.
D.1238, O'Neill Papers of the North Antrim Regiment, UVF.
D.1295, Papers of Sir Wilfrid Spender.
D.1327, Ulster Unionist Council papers, including records of UVF HQ.
D.1507, Papers of Lord Edward Carson.
D.1518, Lyle papers.
D.1889, Papers of Colonel R. H. Wallace.
D.1263, Forde Papers re. Seaforde Company, 1st South Down Regiment, UVF.
D.1267, C. F. Falls Papers re. 1st Fermanagh Regiment.
D.1327, Ulster Unionist Council papers.
D.1498, Papers of Lieutenant General Sir George Richardson.
D.1527, Accounts of the Young Citizen Volunteers of Belfast.
D.1568, Papers of the Young Citizen Volunteers of Belfast.
D.1633, Lady Lilian Spender papers.
D.1855, Leslie papers re. Monaghan Regiment.
D.1939, Papers of the Earl of Erne re. the UVF in Fermanagh.
D.3054, Harvey papers re. Derry City UVF.
D.3692, Papers re. 2nd West Belfast Regiment, UVF.
D.3835, Farren Connel papers, papers of Lieutenant General Sir Oliver Nugent re. Cavan Regiment, UVF.
T.1784, Papers re. 1st North Down Regiment, UVF.
T.2615, Papers re. Enniskillen Horse, UVF.
USC archive (only partially catalogued at the time of writing).

The National Archives (TNA) (formerly Public Record Office), Kew

CO904, Various RIC County Inspectors reports, 1910–22.
CO904/182, 'Prosecution for Illegal Drilling in June 1886'.
CO904/28/1, '1886–1913 Arms Importation + Distribution'.
CO904/29, 'Arms and Ammunition for Volunteers, Correspondence 1914 and 1915'.
CO904/27/1, 'Enniskillen Horse'.
PIN15/3590–3591, Papers regarding the UVF hospital.
PRO30/57/60, Papers of Field Marshal Lord Kitchener.
WO32/9515, 'Administration of D.O.R.A. in Ireland'.
WO141/26, RIC reports on officers and former other ranks involved in training the UVF.
WO162/3, 'New Armies Organisation, 1914 and 1915'.
WO339, Officers' personal records.

The Royal Inniskilling Fusiliers Museum

Papers regarding the recruitment of UVF personnel into the 9th Royal Inniskilling Fusiliers.

The Royal Ulster Rifles Museum

Anon., 'Historical Records of the 13th Service Battalion of the Royal Irish Rifles' and Membership roll for 14th Royal Irish Rifles, 1914–15.

Official publications

Census of Ireland, 1911. Province of Ulster. Summary Tables (1912/13, XCV, Cd 6051).
Irish Land Acts, 1903–09. Reports of the Estates Commissioners for the years 1912–13 (1914, XXXVI, CD. 7145).
The Monthly Army List, 1900–1919.
Northern Ireland House of Commons Debates.
Northern Ireland Senate Debates (Belfast, 1926).
Report of the Public Accounts Committee (Belfast, 1928).
'Statement giving particulars regarding men of military age in Ireland', xvii, [8390], H.C. 1916, 581.
War Office, *Army List* (HMSO, London), 1900–22.

Newspapers

Belfast News Letter
Belfast Evening Telegraph

Devon and Exeter Gazette
Donegal Vindicator
Fermanagh Times
Impartial Reporter
Irish News
Irish Times
Northern Whig
The Times
Ulster Gazette
Wiltshire Gazette

Secondary sources

Books

Adams, R. J. Q., *Bonar Law* (John Murray, London, 1999).

Adgey, R. J., *Arming the Ulster Volunteers 1914* (privately published, Belfast, n.d.).

Alexander, Yonah and Alan O'Day (eds), *Ireland's Terrorist Dilemma* (Kluwer Academic, Lancaster, 1986).

'An Irishman', *Is Ulster Right? A Statement of the Question at Issue between Ulster and the Nationalist Party and of the Reasons – Historical, Political and Financial – Why Ulster Is Justified in Opposing Home Rule* (John Murray, London, 1913).

Anon., *Standing Orders of the 14th (County of London) Battalion, the London Regiment (London Scottish)* (McCorquadale & Co. Ltd, London, 1912).

Anon., *The Volunteer Force during the Great War: Official Record of the Central Association Volunteer Regiments* (P. S. King and Son, London, 1920).

Augusteijn, Joost, *From Public Defiance to Guerrilla Warfare: The Experience of Ordinary Volunteers in the Irish War of Independence 1916–1921* (Irish Academic Press, Dublin, 1996).

Augusteijn, Joost (ed.) *The Irish Revolution, 1913–1923* (Palgrave, Basingstoke, 2002).

Bartlett, Thomas and Keith Jeffery (eds), *A Military History of Ireland* (Cambridge University Press, 1996).

Barton, Brian, *Brookeborough: The Making of a Prime Minister* (Institute of Irish Studies, The Queen's University of Belfast, 1988).

Barton, Brian and Michael Foy, *The Easter Rising* (Sutton, Stroud, 1999).

Select bibliography 215

Beckett, I. F. W., *Riflemen Form: A Study of the Rifle Volunteer Movement 1859–1908* (The Ogilby Trusts, Aldershot, 1982).
Beckett, I. F. W. (ed.), *The Army and the Curragh Incident 1914* (Army Records Society and the Bodley Head, London, 1986).
Beckett, I. F. W., *The Amateur Military Tradition, 1558–1945* (Manchester University Press, 1991).
Beckett, I. F. W. and Keith Simson (eds), *A Nation in Arms: A Social Study of the British Army in the First World War* (Manchester University Press, 1985).
Beckett, J. C., *Confrontations: Studies in Irish History* (Faber and Faber, London, 1972).
Bessel, Richard, *Germany after the First World War* (Clarendon Press, Oxford, 1993).
Bew, Paul, *Ideology and the Irish Question: Ulster Unionism and Irish Nationalism 1912–1916* (Clarendon Press, Oxford, 1994).
Birrell, Augustine, *Things Past Redress* (Faber and Faber, London, 1937).
Blackstock, Allan, *An Ascendancy Army: The Irish Yeomanry 1796–1834* (Four Courts Press, Dublin, 1998).
Bond, Brian, *The Victorian Army and the Staff College 1854–1914* (Eye Methuen, London, 1972).
Boulton, David, *The UVF 1966–73* (Torc Books, Dublin, 1973).
Bowman, Timothy, *Irish Regiments in the Great War: Discipline and Morale* (Manchester University Press, 2003).
Boyce, D. G., Robert Eccleshall and Vincent Geoghegan, *Political Thought in Ireland since the Seventeenth Century* (Routledge, London, 1993).
Boyce, D. G. and Alan O'Day (eds), *The Making of Modern Irish History: Revisionism and the Revisionist Controversy* (Routledge, London, 1996).
Boyce, D. G. and Alan O'Day (eds), *Defenders of the Union: A Survey of British and Irish Unionism since 1801* (Routledge, London, 2001).
Boyce, D. G. and Alan O'Day (eds), *The Ulster Crisis 1885–1921* (Palgrave Macmillan, Basingstoke, 2006).
Bruce, Steve, *The Red Hand: Protestant Paramilitaries in Northern Ireland* (Oxford University Press, 1992).
Buckland, Patrick, *Irish Unionism 2: Ulster Unionism and the Origins of Northern Ireland, 1886–1920* (Gill and Macmillan, Dublin, 1973).
Buckland, Patrick, *Irish Unionism 1885–1923: A Documentary History* (HMSO, Belfast, 1973).

Buckland, Patrick, *The Factory of Grievances: Devolved Government in Northern Ireland, 1921–39* (Gill and Macmillan, Dublin, 1979).
Buckland, Patrick, *James Craig* (Gill and Macmillan, Dublin, 1980).
Campbell, B. B. and A. D. Brenner (eds), *Death Squads in Global Perspective* (Palgrave Macmillan, Basingstoke, 2002).
Campbell, Colm, *Emergency Law in Ireland 1918–1925* (Clarendon Press, Oxford, 1994).
Campbell, Fergus, *Land and Revolution: Nationalist Politics in the West of Ireland 1891–1921* (Oxford University Press, 2005).
Canning, W. J., *Ballyshannon, Belcoo, Bertincourt: The History of the 11th. Battalion, the Royal Inniskilling Fusiliers (Donegal and Fermanagh Volunteers) in World War One* (privately published, Antrim, 1996).
Choille, Breandan MacGiolla (ed.), *Intelligence Notes, 1913–16* (State Paper Office, Dublin, 1966).
Clark, Wallace, *Guns in Ulster* (privately published, Upperlands, 1963).
Coleman, Marie, *County Longford and the Irish Revolution 1910–1923* (Irish Academic Press, Dublin, 2003).
Colles, Ramsay, *The History of Ulster From the Earliest Times to the Present Day* (Gresham Publishing Co. Ltd, London, 1920).
Colley, Linda, *Britons: Forging the Nation, 1707–1837* (Yale University Press, 1992).
Colvin, Ian, *The Life of Lord Carson* (Victor Gollancz Ltd, London, 1934).
Comerford, R. V., *The Fenians in Context: Irish Politics and Society 1848–82* (Wolfhound Press, Dublin, 1985).
Cooper Walker, G. A., *The Book of the Seventh Service Battalion, the Royal Inniskilling Fusiliers* (Brindley & Son, Dublin, 1920).
Crawford, F. H., *Guns for Ulster* (Graham & Heslip, Belfast, 1947).
Cronin, Mike, *The Blueshirts and Irish Politics* (Four Courts Press, Dublin, 1997).
Crossman, Virginia, *Politics, Law and Order in 19th Century Ireland* (Gill and Macmillan, London, 1996).
Crozier, F. P., *A Brass Hat in No Man's Land* (Gliddon Books, Norwich, 1989).
Crozier, F. P., *Impressions and Recollections* (T. Werner Laurie Ltd, London, 1930).
Cunningham, Hugh, *The Volunteer Force: A Social and Political History, 1859–1908* (Archon Books, Hamden, 1975).
Dane, Mervyn, *The Fermanagh 'B' Specials* (Impartial Reporter, Enniskillen, 1970).

Denman, Terence, *Ireland's Unknown Soldiers: The 16th (Irish) Division in the Great War 1914–18* (Irish Academic Press, Dublin, 1992).

Dennis, Peter, *The Territorial Army, 1907–1940* (Royal Historical Society and The Boydell Press, Woodbridge, 1987).

Devine, T. M., *The Scottish Nation 1700–2000* (Allen Lane, Harmondsworth, 1999).

Diehl, J. M., *Paramilitary Politics in the Weimar Republic* (Indiana University Press, Bloomington, 1977).

Dooley, Terence, *The Plight of Monaghan Protestants, 1912–1926* (Irish Academic Press, Dublin, 2000).

Dooley, Terence, *The Decline of the Big House in Ireland: A Study of Irish Landed Families, 1860–1960* (Wolfhound Press, Dublin, 2001).

Dudley Edwards, Ruth, *The Faithful Tribe: An Intimate Portrait of the Loyal Institutions* (Harper Collins, London, 2000).

English, Richard and Graham Walker (eds.), *Unionism in Modern Ireland: New Perspectives on Politics and Culture* (Gill and Macmillan, Dublin, 1996).

Ervine, St. John G., *Sir Edward Carson and the Ulster Movement* (Maunsel & Co. Ltd, London, 1915).

Ervine, St. John, *Craigavon: Ulsterman* (George Allen & Unwin Ltd, London, 1949).

Ewart, Wilfrid, *A Journey in Ireland 1921* (G. P. Putnam's Sons, London, 1922).

Falls, Cyril, *The History of the 36th (Ulster) Division* (McCaw, Stevenson and Orr, Belfast, 1922).

Farrell, Michael, *Northern Ireland: The Orange State* (Pluto Press, London, 1980).

Farrell, Michael, *Arming the Protestants: The Formation of the Ulster Special Constabulary and the Royal Ulster Constabulary, 1920–27* (Pluto Press, London, 1983).

Farry, Michael, *The Aftermath of Revolution: Sligo 1921–1923* (University College Dublin Press, 2000).

Fergusson, Niall (ed.), *Virtual History: Alternatives and Counterfactuals* (Picador, London, 1997).

Fitzpatrick, David, *Politics and Irish Life 1913–1921: Provincial Experience of War and Revolution* (Gill and Macmillan, Dublin, 1977).

Fitzpatrick, David (ed.), *Revolution? Ireland 1917–1923* (Trinity History Workshop, Dublin, 1990).

Fitzpatrick, David, *The Two Irelands, 1912–39* (Oxford University Press, 1998).

Fleming, N. C., *The Marquess of Londonderry: Aristocracy, Power and Politics in Britain and Ireland* (Tauris Academic Studies, London, 2005).
Follis, Bryan, *A State Under Siege: The Establishment of Northern Ireland 1920–1925* (Clarendon Press, Oxford, 1995).
Foster, R. F., *Modern Ireland 1600–1972* (Allen Lane, London, 1988).
Fraser, T. G. (ed.), *The Irish Parading Tradition: Following the Drum* (Macmillan Press, Basingstoke, 2000).
French, David, *Military Identities: The Regimental System, the British Army and the British People c. 1870–2000* (Oxford University Press, 2005).
French, David and Brian Holden Reid (eds), *The British General Staff: Reform and Innovation, 1890–1939* (Frank Cass, London, 2002).
Gallagher, Ronan, *Violence and Nationalist Politics in Derry City, 1920–1923* (Four Courts Press, Dublin, 2003).
Garnham, Neal, *Association Football and Society in Pre-Partition Ireland* (Ulster Historical Foundation, Belfast, 2004).
Gatrell, V. A. C., Bruce Lenman and Geoffrey Parker (eds), *Crime & The Law: The Social History of Crime in Western Europe since 1500* (Europa Publications, London, 1980).
Gibbon, P., *The Origins of Ulster Unionism: The Formation of Popular Protestant Politics and Ideology in Nineteenth-Century Ireland* (Manchester University Press, 1975).
Gleichen, Count, *A Guardsman's Memories* (William Blackwood and Sons, London, 1932).
Green, E. H. H., *The Crisis of Conservatism: The Politics, Economics and Ideology of the British Conservative Party, 1880–1914* (Routledge, London, 1995).
Grieves, Keith, *The Politics of Manpower, 1914–18* (Manchester University Press, 1988).
Gwynn, Dennis, *The Life of John Redmond* (G. G. Harup, London, 1932).
Gwynn, Stephen, *John Redmond's Last Years* (Edward Arnold, London, 1919).
Harkness, David, *Northern Ireland since 1920* (Gill and Macmillan, Dublin, 1983).
Harrison, John, *The Scot in Ulster: Sketch of the History of the Scottish Population of Ulster* (William Blackwood, Edinburgh, 1888).
Hart, Peter, *The IRA and its Enemies: Violence and Community in Cork, 1916–1923* (Clarendon Press, Oxford, 1998).

Hart, Peter, *The I.R.A. at War 1916–1923* (Oxford University Press, 2003).

Hennessey, Thomas, *A History of Northern Ireland 1920–1996* (Gill and Macmillan, Dublin, 1997).

Hennessey, Thomas, *Dividing Ireland, World War I and Partition* (Routledge, London, 1998).

Heslinga, M. W., *The Irish Border as a Cultural Divide* (Van Gorcum Assen, The Netherlands, 1979).

Hezlet, Sir Arthur, *The 'B' Specials: A History of the Ulster Special Constabulary* (Tom Stacey Ltd, London, 1972).

Holmes, Richard, *The Little Field Marshal: Sir John French* (Jonathan Cape, London, 1981).

Hopkinson, Michael (ed.), *The Last Days of Dublin Castle: The Diaries of Mark Sturgis* (Irish Academic Press, Dublin, 1999).

Hopkinson, Michael, *The Irish War of Independence* (Gill and Macmillan, Dublin, 2002).

Howe, Stephen, *Ireland and the Empire: Colonial Legacies in Irish History and Culture* (Oxford University Press, 2000).

Hume, David, *'For Ulster and Her Freedom': The Story of the April 1914 Gunrunning* (Ulster Society, Lurgan, 1989).

Hyde, Hugh Montgomery, *Carson: The Life of Sir Edward Carson, Lord Carson of Duncairn* (William Heinemann, London, 1953).

'I. O.' [C. J. C. Street], *The Administration of Ireland, 1920* (Philip Allan & Co., London, 1921).

Jackson, Alvin, *The Ulster Party: Irish Unionists in the House of Commons, 1884–1911* (Clarendon Press, Oxford, 1989).

Jackson, Alvin, *Sir Edward Carson* (Historical Association of Ireland, Dublin, 1993).

Jackson, Alvin, *Ireland 1798–1998: Politics and War* (Blackwell, Oxford, 1999).

Jackson, Alvin, *Home Rule: An Irish History 1800–2000* (Weidenfeld and Nicolson, London, 2003).

Jalland, Patricia, *The Liberals and Ireland: The Ulster Question in British Politics to 1914* (Harvester Press, Brighton, 1980).

Jeffery, Keith (ed.), *'An Irish Empire'? Aspects of Ireland and the British Empire* (Manchester University Press, 1996).

Jeffery, Keith, *Ireland and the Great War* (Cambridge University Press, 2000).

Jeffery, Keith, *Field Marshal Sir Henry Wilson: A Political Soldier* (Oxford University Press, 2006).

Johnstone, Tom, *Orange, Green and Khaki: The Story of the Irish Regiments in the Great War, 1914–18* (Gill and Macmillan, Dublin, 1992).
Kelly's Handbook to the Titled, Landed and Official Classes, 1914.
Kendle, John, *Walter Long, Ireland and the Union, 1905–1920* (McGill-Queen's University Press, Dun Laoghaire, 1992).
Kennedy, Liam and Philip Ollerenshaw (eds), *An Economic History of Ireland 1820–1939* (Manchester University Press, 1985).
Kenny, Kevin (ed.), *Ireland and the British Empire* (Oxford University Press, 2006).
Keown-Boyd, Henry, *Soldiers of the Nile: A Biographical History of the British Officers of the Egyptian Army 1882–1925* (Thornbury Publications, Thornbury, 1996).
Lee, Janet, *War Girls: The First Aid Nursing Yeomanry in the First World War* (Manchester University Press, 2005).
Lee, J. J., *Ireland 1912–1985* (Cambridge University Press, 1989).
Leslie, Shane, *The Irish Tangle for English Readers* (Macdonald, London, 1946).
Lewis, Geoffrey, *Carson: The Man Who Divided Ireland* (Hambledon and London, London, 2005).
Londonderry, Marchioness of, *Retrospect* (Frederick Muller, London, 1938).
Lynch, John, *A Tale of Three Cities* (Macmillan, Basingstoke, 1998).
Lynch, Robert, *The Northern IRA and the Early Years of Partition 1920–1922* (Irish Academic Press, Dublin, 2006).
McAnnally, Sir Henry, *The Irish Militia 1793–1816* (Eyre and Spottiswoode, London, 1949).
McBride, L. W., *The Greening of Dublin Castle: The Transformation of Bureaucratic and Judicial Personnel in Ireland, 1892–1922* (Catholic University of America Press, Washington D.C., 1991).
McCartney, H. B., *Citizen Soldiers: The Liverpool Territorials in the First World War* (Cambridge University Press, 2005).
McColgan, John, *British Policy and the Irish Administration 1920–22* (George Allen and Unwin, London, 1983).
McDowell, R. B., *The Irish Administration 1801–1914* (Routledge and Kegan Paul, London, 1964).
McFarland, Elaine, *Protestants First: Orangeism in 19th Century Scotland* (Edinburgh University Press, 1990).
McGarry, Fearghal (ed.), *Republicanism in Modern Ireland* (University College Dublin Press, 2003).

McGarry, Fearghal, *Eoin O'Duffy: A Self-made Hero* (Oxford University Press, 2005).
Mackenzie, S. P., *The Home Guard: The Real Story of 'Dad's Army'* (Oxford University Press, 1995).
McNeill, Ronald, *Ulster's Stand for Union* (John Murray, London, 1922).
Macready, Sir Nevil, *Annals of an Active Life* (Hutchinson & Co., London, 1924).
Malcolm, Joyce Lee, *Guns and Violence: The English Experience* (Harvard University Press, London, 2002).
Maxwell, Henry, *Ulster Was Right* (Hutchinson, London, 1934).
Megahey, Alan, *The Irish Protestant Churches in the Twentieth Century* (Macmillan Press, Basingstoke, 2000).
Middlemass, Keith (ed.), *Thomas Jones, Whitehall Diary: Volume III Ireland 1918–1925* (Oxford University Press, 1971).
Miller, D. W., *Queen's Rebels: Ulster Loyalism in Historical Perspective* (Gill and Macmillan, Dublin, 1978).
Mitchinson, K. W., *Defending Albion: Britain's Home Army 1908–1919* (Palgrave Macmillan, Basingstoke, 2005).
Morgan, Austen, *Labour and Partition: The Belfast Working Class 1905–23* (Pluto Press, London, 1991).
Morrison, H. S., *Modern Ulster: Its Character, Customs, Politics and Industries* (H. R. Allenson Ltd, London, 1920).
Muenger, E. A., *The British Military Dilemma in Ireland: Occupation Politics, 1886–1914* (Gill and Macmillan, Dublin, 1991).
Murphy, Desmond, *Derry, Donegal and Modern Ulster 1790–1921* (Aileach Press, Londonderry, 1981).
O'Halpin, Eunan, *The Decline of the Union: British Government in Ireland 1892–1920* (Gill and Macmillan, Dublin, 1987).
Orr, Phillip, *The Road to the Somme: Men of the Ulster Division Tell Their Story* (Blackstaff Press, Belfast, 1987).
Parkinson, A. F., *Belfast's Unholy War: The Troubles of the 1920s* (Four Courts Press, Dublin, 2004).
Patterson, Henry, *Class Conflict and Sectarianism: The Protestant Working Class and the Belfast Labour Movement 1868–1920* (Blackstaff Press, Belfast, 1980).
Patterson, J. H., *The Man-Eaters of Tsavo* (Macmillan, London, 1907).
Patterson, J. H., *With the Zionists in Gallipoli* (Hutchinson, London, 1916).
Patterson, J. H., *With the Judians in the Palestine Campaign* (Hutchinson, London, 1922).

Patterson, R. J., *Catch-my-pal: A Story of Good Samaritanship* (privately published, London, 1912).
Peel, George, *The Reign of Sir Edward Carson* (P. S. King & Son, London, 1914).
Probert, Belinda, *Beyond Orange and Green: The Political Economy of the Northern Ireland Crisis* (Zed Press, London, 1978).
Roebuck, Peter (ed.), *Plantation to Partition: Essays in Ulster History in Honour of J. L. McCracken* (Blackstaff Press, Belfast, 1981).
Rosenbaum, S. (ed.), *Against Home Rule: The Case for the Union* (Frederick Warne, London, 1912).
Ryan, A. P., *Mutiny at the Curragh* (Macmillan, London, 1956).
Samuels, A. W., *Home Rule: What Is It?* (Hodges Figgis, Dublin, 1911).
Scott, Brough, *Galloper Jack: A Grandson's Search for a Forgotten Hero* (Macmillan, London, 2003).
Seley, J. E. B., *Adventure* (William Heinemann, London, 1930).
Simkins, Peter, *Kitchener's Army: The Raising of the New Armies, 1914–16* (Manchester University Press, 1988).
Smith, Jeremy, *The Tories and Ireland 1910–1914: Conservative Party Politics and the Home Rule Crisis* (Irish Academic Press, Dublin, 2000).
Spiers, E. M., *Haldane: An Army Reformer* (Edinburgh University Press, 1980).
Stewart, A. T. Q., *The Narrow Ground: The Roots of Conflict in Ulster* (Faber and Faber, London, 1967).
Stewart, A. T. Q., *The Ulster Crisis* (Faber and Faber, London, 1967).
Strachan, Hew, *The Politics of the British Army* (Clarendon Press, Oxford, 1997).
Street, C. J. C., *Ireland in 1921* (Philip Allan & Co., London, 1922).
Streeter, Patrick, *Mad for Zion: A Biography of Colonel J. H. Patterson* (The Matching Press, Harlow, 2004).
Townshend, Charles, *The British Campaign in Ireland 1919–1921: The Development of Political and Military Policies* (Oxford University Press, 1975).
Townshend, Charles, *Political Violence in Ireland: Government and Resistance since 1848* (Oxford University Press, 1984)
Townshend, Charles, *1916: The Irish Rebellion* (Allen Lane, London, 2005).
Trimble, W. C., *The History of Enniskillen with References to Some Manors in Co. Fermanagh and Other Local Subjects* (William Trimble, Enniskillen, 1919–21).

Turner, John (ed.), *Britain and the First World War* (Unwin Hyman, London, 1988).
Urquhart, Diane, *Women in Ulster Politics 1890–1940* (Irish Academic Press, Dublin, 2000).
Urquhart, Diane (ed.), *The Minutes of the Ulster Women's Unionist Council and Executive Committee 1911–40* (The Women's History Project in association with Irish Manuscripts Commission, Dublin, 2001).
Waite, R. G. L., *Vanguard of Nazism: The Free Corps Movement in Postwar Germany* (Harvard University Press, Cambridge, 1952).
Walker, Graham, *Intimate Strangers: Political and Cultural Interaction between Scotland and Ulster in Modern Times* (John Donald Publishers, Edinburgh, 1996).
Walker, Graham, *A History of the Ulster Unionist Party: Protest, Pragmatism and Pessimism* (Manchester University Press, 2004).
Ward, Paul, *Britishness since 1870* (Routledge, London, 2004).
Ward, S. R., *The War Generation: Veterans of the First World War* (Kennikat Press, London, 1975).
Watt, R. M., *The Kings Depart: The Tragedy of Germany: Versailles and the German Revolution* (Weidenfeld and Nicolson, London, 1969).
Wheatley, Michael, *Nationalism and the Irish Party: Provincial Ireland 1910–1916* (Oxford University Press, 2005).
Wheeler-Bennett, J. W., *John Anderson, Viscount Waverly* (Macmillan, London, 1962).
White, S. N., *The Terrors, 16th. (Pioneer) Battalion, Royal Irish Rifles* (Somme Association, Belfast, 1996).
Whittam, John, *The Politics of the Italian Army 1861–1918* (Croom Helm, London, 1977).
Wichert, Sabine (ed.), *From the United Irishmen to Twentieth Century Unionism: A Festschrift for A. T. Q. Stewart* (Four Courts Press, Dublin, 2004).
Wicks, Pembroke, *The Truth About Home Rule* (Pitman & Sons, London, 1913).
Williams, T. Desmond, *Secret Societies in Ireland* (Gill and Macmillan, Dublin, 1973).
Wingfield-Stratford, Esme, *Home Rule and Civil War: An Appeal to the British People* (Bell & Sons, London, 1914).
Wood, I. S., *God, Guns and Ulster: A History of Loyalist Paramilitaries* (Caxton Editions, London, 2003).

Woodburn, J. B., *The Ulster Scot: His History and Religion* (H. R. Allenson, London, n.d. but 1913).

Articles

Beckett, I. F. W., 'Aspects of a Nation in Arms: Britain's Volunteer Training Corps in the Great War', *Revue Internationale d'Historie Militaire*, 63, 1985.

Beckett, Ian and Keith Jeffery, 'The Royal Navy and the Curragh Incident', *Bulletin of the Institute of Historical Research*, 62, 147, 1989

Bowman, Timothy, 'The Ulster Volunteer Force and the Formation of the 36th (Ulster) Division', *Irish Historical Studies*, 32, 2001.

Boyle, J. W., 'The Belfast Protestant Association and the Independent Orange Order 1901–1910', *Irish Historical Studies*, 13, 50, 1962.

Campbell, Fergus, 'The Social Dynamics of Nationalist Politics in the West of Ireland 1898–1918', *Past and Present*, 182, 2004.

Fitzpatrick, David, 'The Logic of Collective Sacrifice: Ireland and the British Army, 1914–18', *The Historical Journal*, 38, 4, 1995.

Fitzpatrick, David, 'The Orange Order and the border', *Irish Historical Studies*, 33, 129, 2002.

Foy, Michael, 'Ulster Unionist Propaganda against Home Rule 1912–14', *History Ireland*, 6, 1, 1996.

Gailey, Andrew, 'King Carson: An Essay on the Invention of Leadership', *Irish Historical Studies*, 30, 17, 1996.

Green, E. H. H., 'The Strange Death of Tory England', *Twentieth Century British History*, 2, 1985.

Jackson, Alvin, 'Irish Unionism and the Russellite Threat 1894–1906', *Irish Historical Studies*, 25, 100, 1987.

Jackson, Alvin, 'Unionist Politics and Protestant Society in Edwardian Ireland', *Historical Journal*, 33, 4, 1990.

Jackson, Alvin, 'Unionist Myths, 1912–1985', *Past and Present*, 136, 1992.

Jackson, Alvin, 'Larne Gun Running, 1914', *History Ireland*, 1, 1, 1993.

Jackson, Alvin, 'Unveiling Irish History', *Journal of Contemporary History*, 40, 4, 2005.

Jackson, Dan, '"Friends of the Union": Liverpool, Ulster and Home Rule, 1910–1914', *Transactions of the Historic Society of Lancashire and Cheshire*, 152, 2004.

Loughlin, James, 'Northern Ireland and British Fascism in the Inter-war Years', *Irish Historical Studies*, 29, 116, 1995.

Murphy, R., 'Faction and the Conservative Party and the Home Rule Bill', *History*, 71, 1986.

Osbourne, J. M., 'Defining Their Own Patriotism: British Volunteer Training Corps in the First World War', *Journal of Contemporary History*, 23, 1988.

Perry, Nicholas, 'Maintaining Regimental Identity in the Great War: The Case of the Irish Infantry Regiments', *Stand To!*, 52, 1998.

Phillips, G., 'Lord Willoughby de Broke and the Politics of Radical Toryism', *Journal of British Studies*, 20, 1980.

Rodner, W., 'Leaguers, Covenanters, Moderates: British Support for Ulster, 1913–14', *Eire-Ireland*, 17, 1982.

Stubbs, J. O., 'The Unionists and Ireland, 1914–18', *Historical Journal*, 33, 4, 1990.

Theses

Foy, M. T., 'The Ulster Volunteer Force: Its Domestic Development and Political Importance in the Period 1913 to 1920', Ph.D. thesis, The Queen's University of Belfast, 1986.

Marsano, Viviana, '"Those Who Wish for Peace Must Prepare for War." The Ulster Volunteer Force and the Home Rule Crisis of 1912–14', Ph.D. thesis, University of California, Santa Barbara, 1997.

Maxwell, Ian, 'The Life of Sir Wilfrid Spender, 1876–1960', Ph.D. thesis, The Queen's University of Belfast, 1991.

Mercer, Eric, 'For King, Country and a Shilling a Day: Recruitment in Belfast during the Great War, 1914–18', MA dissertation, The Queen's University of Belfast, 1999.

Smyth, P. D. H., 'The Volunteer Movement in Ulster: Background and Development, 1745–85', Ph.D. thesis, The Queen's University of Belfast, 1974.

Index

absenteeism in UVF 8, 76, 88, 101–3, 208
accidental death 127
Acheson, Viscount of 57, 96
Adair, W. T. 47, 64, 84, 85, 96, 99, 100, 102, 103, 104, 128, 138, 142, 171
Adgey, R. J. 1, 140, 141, 143, 144, 146, 151, 152, 155
aeroplanes 84
age profile of UVF 46–7, 54–7
Aghadowey 33, 84
Alexander, A. M. 32
Allom, H. M. 62
American Civil War 68
American War of Independence 68
Andrews, J. M. 49, 197
Andrews Mill 6, 49
Anglo-Irish War (1919–21) 1, 148, 191–201, 210
Anglo-Irish Treaty (1921) 196, 198
Annalong 167
Antrim Castle 124
Armagh City, parades in 31, 119
Armagh City 'Protective Patrol' 191–2
arming the UVF 138–46
armouries 140, 146, 155, 198
arms dealers 141
Army Pensioners 50
artillery 84
Asquith, H. H. 8, 106

athletics clubs 61
Augher Castle 126
Aughnacloy 86, 118
Australia 151

Bainbridge, Guy 193–4
Ballycastle, 88, 124, 168
Ballymena 84, 120
Ballywalter 21, 23, 35–6
Balmoral (Belfast) 21, 97, 118, 131
Banbridge 156, 190
bands 9, 125
Bangor, Co. Down 120, 124, 139, 141–3, 148
Bangor, 6th Viscount of 86
bank holidays 126
Bann, River 93
Barbour, J. Milne 49
Baronscourt 52, 104, 105, 129, 136
Bates, R. Dawson 149, 152, 153, 170
Bective, Countess of 121
Belfast Cathedral 121
Belfast Chamber of Commerce 30
Belfast Citizens' Association, 25
Belfast City Corporation 30
Belfast City Hall guard 191
Belfast Defence Corps 170
Belfast dock strike (1907) 27
Belfast Harbour Board 30
Belgian army 146
Belgium 151

Index

Bernard, H. C. 165
Best, Edwin 17
Birney, Lily 118, 123
Birrell, Augustine 34, 36, 37, 136
Blacker, S. W. 181
Blackmore, C. H. 200
Blueshirts 116, 208
Boyd, Robert 196, 200
Boyne, Battle of (1690) 67, 118
Boy Scouts 25, 26, 31, 36, 66
Boys' Brigade 16, 25, 26, 27, 31, 66
British army
  officers in UVF 6, 7, 10, 46, 57–60, 94–7
  response to UVF 91–4, 106
British army formations
  Battalions
    14th London (Scottish) Regiment 28, 53
    28th London (Artists' Rifles) Regiment 53
    2nd Manchester Regiment 59
    5th Royal Fusiliers 58
    7th Royal Fusiliers 99
    38th Royal Fusiliers (Jewish) 60
    2nd Royal Inniskilling Fusiliers 32
    9th Royal Inniskilling Fusiliers 171, 177, 178, 181
    10th Royal Inniskilling Fusiliers 173, 177, 181
    11th Royal Inniskilling Fusiliers 177, 179, 180, 181
    3rd Royal Irish Fusiliers 32
    4th Royal Irish Fusiliers 78
    9th Royal Irish Fusiliers 177, 180, 181
    3rd Royal Irish Rifles 80
    5th Royal Irish Rifles 58, 81
    8th Royal Irish Rifles 165, 177, 181
    9th Royal Irish Rifles 59, 175, 177, 180, 181
    10th Royal Irish Rifles 165, 177, 181
    11th Royal Irish Rifles 177, 181
    12th Royal Irish Rifles 177, 178, 180, 181
    13th Royal Irish Rifles 164, 177, 178, 180, 181
    14th Royal Irish Rifles 59, 177, 179, 180, 181
    15th Royal Irish Rifles 165, 177, 181
    16th Royal Irish Rifles 177, 181
    19th Royal Irish Rifles 156
    14th Royal Warwickshire Regiment (1st Birmingham) 175
    3rd Somerset Light Infantry 58, 164
  Brigades
    107th 99, 165, 176–7, 182
  Divisions
    51st (Highland) 176
    10th (Irish) 173
    16th (Irish) 175
    14th (Light) 182
    36th (Ulster) 10, 46, 62, 98, 99, 100, 146, 156, 163–83, 198, 199, 205, 209
    38th (Welsh) 59, 175
  Regiments
    3rd Dragoon Guards 60
    4th Hussars 58
    10th Hussars 58
    21st Lancers 58
    Army Service Corps 173, 192
    Connaught Rangers 165
    Devon Militia 59
    Dorsetshire Regiment 59
    Down Militia 24
    East African Rifles 59
    East Kent Yeomanry 50, 97
    Fermanagh Militia 17
    Hampshire Regiment 81

Index

Irish Guards 173
King's African Rifles 59
King's Royal Rifle Corps 57
Leicestershire Yeomanry 50, 97
London Regiment 28, 30
North Irish Horse 25, 32, 58, 63, 66
Queen's University of Belfast OTC 96
Royal Army Medical Corps 168
Royal Artillery 80, 84
Royal Fusiliers 60, 63, 99
Royal Horse Guards 25, 47, 164, 165
Royal Inniskilling Fusiliers 18, 37, 53, 57, 58, 63, 66
Royal Irish Fusiliers 63, 66
Royal Irish Regiment (post 1991) 3
Royal Irish Rifles 58, 63, 66, 105
Royal Munster Fusiliers 165
Royal West Kent Regiment 59
Thorneycroft's Mounted Infantry 59
Trinity College Dublin OTC 170
Ulster Defence Regiment 3, 193
University of Edinburgh OTC 53, 96
Warwickshire Yeomanry 172
West African Frontier Force 59
Wiltshire Yeomanry 78
Yorkshire [sic] Yeomanry 50, 97
Zionist Mule Corps 60
British League for the Support of Ulster and the Union 6, 53, 57, 59, 61–2, 65, 77, 96, 98, 99, 172, 179
British Legion 196
Broke, Lord Willoughby de 6, 77, 172
Brooke, Basil (1st Viscount Brookeborough) 4, 10, 58, 191
Bull, William 139, 141

camps of instruction 8, 76, 81, 97, 100–1, 104–5, 127, 128, 136, 153–4, 208
Canada 59
Canadian Expeditionary Force 173
Canadian Militia 99
Cantrell and Cochrane's Ltd. 31
Carlingford Lough 167
Carrowdore 23, 120
Carson, Edward (Baron Carson)
  and arming of UVF 76, 77, 138–9
  and command of the UVF 3, 7, 66, 76, 78, 82, 85, 105–6, 166, 205
  and fears of rioting 77
  and formation of UVF 22, 47, 79, 85–6
  and propaganda 60, 125, 129
  and revival of UVF (1920) 192
  and UVF finance 9, 122, 155–6
  at UVF parades 24, 67, 78, 79, 98, 117–20, 124, 126
Carson Unionist Defence Fund 122, 155–6
Castle Blayney 168
Castlecaulfield 21, 67
Castlecoole 24, 83
Castle Irvine 17, 23
Castlereagh, Lord (later 7th Marquess of Londonderry) 7, 47, 53, 97, 164
Castleton Pipe Band 19
Catch my Pal Temperance Society 6
Catholics
  as minority in N. Ireland 11, 193–4
  and Unionist Clubs 20
  in UVF 65
  in YCV 31
  cavalry 84
Cavan Volunteer Force 207
Chamberlain, Joseph 118, 124
Charlemont, 8th Viscount of 50
Chartists 35
Chichester, R. Spencer 29–31, 105, 190

China 80, 151–2
Church Lads' Brigade 25, 26, 31, 66
Churchill, Winston 65
'Civilian Forces' (1920) 190
Clandeboye 105
Clanwilliam, 5th Earl of 164, 165
Clark, George 97
Clarke, Ernest 7
clergy 6, 50, 65, 67, 121–3
Clough 119
Clyde Valley, S. S. 142–3
Coastguards 142–3
Coates, H. V. 97
Colebrooke 124, 191
Coleraine 18, 33, 37, 65, 120
colours, presentation of 100–1
Colt machine guns 124
Comber 6, 120, 207
command structures 76–88
concerts 128–9, 156, 208
conscription 5, 6, 27, 47, 101
Conservative Party 3, 76, 94, 205
contingency plans 10, 90–4
Couchman, G. H. H. 8, 99, 142, 164, 165, 182, 209
county committees 7, 22, 47, 85–7, 106, 139, 144, 146, 206, 207, 209
Craig, James (1st Viscount Craigavon)
   and arming of the UVF 138–9, 141
   and disposal of UVF rifles 152
   and formation of the USC 148, 195, 198, 200
   and formation of the UVF 32
   his military career 58, 80, 165
   as Prime Minister of N. Ireland 198, 200
   and revival of the UVF (1920) 148, 196, 198
   and role of the UVF 93, 94
   and 36th (Ulster) Division 165, 171, 174, 182
   and UVF finance 155
Craigavon (Belfast) 15, 16

Crawford, F.H.
   and 'Crawford's Tigers' 10
   as Director of Ordnance 80
   and disposal of rifles 150–3
   and guerrilla warfare 93
   and gunrunning 7, 138, 139, 140–3,
   his memoirs 1
   his military career 80
   and reformation of UVF (1920–22) 192, 199–200
   and Ulster Imperial Guards 148
   and USC 198
   and YCV 25
   and Young Ulster 5, 17–18
Crawford, R. Sharman 140, 155
Crichton, Viscount of 25, 48, 66, 67
Crom Castle, 23, 101, 104
Cromwell, Oliver 68
Crozier, F. P. 1, 59, 89, 98–9, 100, 166, 180, 194
Cunningham, J. Lennox 96, 97
Curragh Incident 8, 20, 105, 106, 120, 138, 209
Cushendall 93
Cushendun 93
Customs Laws Consolidation Act (1876) 137

Davis, H. O. 81
Davis, Robert 80
Derry, Bishop of 67
Derry, Siege of (1689) 67, 118
Devlin, Joseph 53
discipline (UVF) 24, 27, 46, 77, 85, 88–90, 101, 105, 126, 193, 196, 199
dismissal 88–9
Donaghadee 120, 139, 141–3
Down, W. L. 164
Downshire, 6th Marquess of 48
drilling
   (1886) 17, 34–5
   (1893) 17

Index   231

(1910–14) 3, 5–6, 15, 16, 18, 21, 23, 32, 34–8, 47, 48, 55, 57, 58, 78–9, 88, 101, 103, 104, 106, 117, 128, 205, 208
   legality of 34–8, 136–7, 205
Drogheda 127
Dromore 19, 125, 156, 190
Dublin Castle, Administration 4, 22, 34, 85, 144, 172, 183, 194
Dublin Metropolitan Police 136
Dufferin and Ava, 2nd Marquess of 120
Dundalk 168
Dungannon 47, 68, 97
Dunleath, 2nd Baron of 23, 86, 94, 106, 121, 206
Dunleath Arms Hotel 35
Dunville's Distillery 28–9
Durham Constabulary 140

Easter Rising 4, 10, 12, 147, 168–9, 210
economic concerns 68, 91, 193
election of officers 82, 83
Edwards, Joseph 79
Egyptian Army 63, 80
Empire Day 118
Enniskillen Horse
   age profile of 56
   assimilation into UVF 24
   election of CO 83
   formation of 24
   incorporation into 6th Inniskilling Dragoons 181
   military expertise in 50, 97, 100
   military role 25, 84
   North Irish Horse personnel in 63
   officers of 50
   parades of 24, 100, 117, 126
   social composition of 45–6, 51, 54
   and Territorial Force 66–7
Enniskillen, Siege of (1689) 67
Ensor, C. H. 197
Erne, 4th Earl of 23, 25, 81
Ethiopia 148

Falls, C. F. 98, 181, 194
Fanny, S. S. 141–3
Farnham, 11th Baron of 48, 97, 139
Fanu, V. P. Le 36
Fenian movement 116, 208
Fermanagh Unionist Association 155
Fermanagh Vigilance 10, 191, 194
'Feudal' units 4, 6, 23–4, 32, 47–9, 69, 96, 191, 207
field days 100, 103, 116, 120
films 117
finance 9, 27, 79, 84, 87, 88, 105, 135, 154–7, 208
firearms (see also gunrunning, machine guns, revolvers, rifles, shotguns)
   disposal of 148–53
   issuing of 90
   legislation concerning 33, 37, 135–8, 150
   and Loyalist formations (1920) 148
   numbers in UVF possession 144–5
   seizure of 10
Firearms (Amendment) Act (Northern Ireland) (1926) 150
Florencecourt 48
foodstuffs 154, 206
football 116–17
Forde, W. G. 23, 48, 49
Forth River Football Grounds 122
Fortwilliam Unionist Club (Belfast) 19–20
Freikorps 3, 199–200
French, John D. P. (1st Earl of Ypres) 147, 193

Gallaher's Tobacco 28
German naval raid, threatened 166, 167
George, David Lloyd 175
Glasgow 19
Glasslough 20, 35
Gleichen, Count 81, 84, 144

Index

Glentoran Football and Athletic Club 121
Gordon, A. R. G. 152
Gordon, J. F. 20, 150
Gough, Hubert 120
Gough, John 120
Gray, Betsy 120
Great War 1, 11, 53, 62, 81, 99, 146, 163–84, 193, 209–10
Greer, T. MacGreger 50
Greyabbey 7, 23, 96
guerrilla warfare 93, 106, 157
gun licences 21, 37, 135–6
Gun Barrel Proof Act (1868) 138
Gun Licence Act (1870) 136
Gunmakers' Company 138
gunrunning 2, 7, 8, 17, 20, 33, 76, 85, 137–44, 155
  at Larne 8, 9, 20, 76, 85, 106, 139, 141–3, 155

Haldane, R. B. 5, 25, 26, 66, 101
half day holidays 126
Hall, Frank 22
Hall, Roger 86
Hall-Thompson, S. H. 86
Hamburg 33
Hamilton, Robert 18
Hammersmith 138, 140, 141
Harrell, David 34, 85
Harris, Percy 169–70
Harrods Department Store 141
Haslett, Horace 192
Hastings, T. E. 53, 96
Healy, Cahir 152
Herdman, E. C. 47, 49, 83
Herdman's Mill 6, 83
Hickman, T. E. 63, 80, 100, 139, 165, 181
Hilden 49
Hillsborough Castle 125
Hill-Trevor, A. 128
Holywood 117, 142

home defence plans (1914–15) 146, 166–8
Home Guard 90, 148, 153, 201
Home Office 151
Home Rule
  First Bill (1886) 3, 5, 16, 122, 140
  Second Bill (1893) 3, 5, 16, 17, 122, 140
  Third Bill (1912) 1, 15, 16, 32, 33, 64, 90, 146, 175, 206
Horend, W. R. 151
Horner, A. L. 67
Hungerford, Wilson 152
Hunter, J. R. 35
Ford-Hutchinson, G. H. 165

ideology 63–9
Imperial identity 7, 12, 27, 67, 122, 167, 178, 207–8
Imperial Service 176
Imperial Yeomanry 5, 32, 60
Indemnity Fund 156, 193
India 60, 61, 80
Indian army 165
Inglis's Bakery 28
intimidation 97
Irish Convention (1917–18) 155
Irish National Volunteers 7, 8, 10, 88, 90, 93, 147, 156, 169, 173, 183
Irish Parliamentary Party 169, 174–5
Irish Republican Army 1, 53–4, 55, 69, 157, 169, 184, 191, 192, 194, 195, 197, 207, 210
Irish Volunteers (1777–92) 3, 16, 68
Irish Volunteers 145, 183, 210
Irvine, D'Arcy 17, 21, 23
Irvine, Gerald 17
Irvinestown 23
Italian army 144

Jameson, Eustace 169
Jenkins, A. P. 82, 97, 181, 208

Killylea 16
Kilrea 88
Kinahan, R. H. 27
King's Regulations 4, 36–7, 46
Kitchener, H. H. (1st Earl Kitchener) 167, 171–2, 174

Lack 32, 37
Land Acts 23, 47, 50, 68
landlords 4, 5, 6, 23, 24, 32, 47–9, 69, 96, 191, 207
Land War 47
Landwehr 27
Lanesborough, 7th Earl of 48, 141
Law, A. Bonar 3, 64, 77, 139
Leitrim, 5th Earl of 139, 181
Leslie, John 48, 55, 168
Leslie, Lionel 55
Leslie, Shane 48
Liberal government 67, 106, 116, 138
Lincoln, Abraham 68
Linen Thread Company 49
Lisbellaw 194
Lissanoure Castle 105
Lisburn 5, 10, 18, 49, 97, 124, 148, 181, 197
Lisburn Loyalist Association (1921) 197, 200
Liverpool 61, 179
Local Defence Volunteers (1940) 82, 153
London 9, 62
Londonderry, 6th Marchioness of 121
Londonderry, 7th Marquess of 7, 47, 53, 97, 164
Long, Walter 77, 78, 120, 139
Lonsdale, J. B. 31, 119
Lord Primate of Ireland 122–3
Loyalist forces (1920–22) 190–201, 210
Lyle, H. T. 93, 102, 165

McCallum, Charles 34

McCammon, T. V. P. 32, 58, 80, 81, 90, 100, 105, 129, 139
McCauley, David 55
McMeekin, Alexander 48
McMenemy, William 97
McMordie, R. J. 25, 26, 29, 30, 118, 123
Mackie, James 25
Macready, Nevil 193, 196, 198, 199
McVicker, Leon 31
machine guns 124, 141, 145, 151, 209
Madden, Gerald 62, 65, 94, 97, 137, 168
Madden, J. C. 20, 48, 88, 97, 137
magic lantern shows 117, 129
Magill, A. P. 172–3
Magill, W. A. 152
Mahon, Bryan 147
'marching battalions' 90–1, 144, 207
Martin, W. F. 50
Massereene and Ferrard, 12th Viscount of 150
Maxim machine guns 124, 171
May, F. W. L. 29, 30
Medical Board (UVF) 78, 80, 128
Metropolitan Police 140
Meyer, Robert 30
Midland Gun Company 18
Military Council (UVF) 78
military intelligence 4
Militia 4, 16, 17, 28, 58, 59, 103, 170
Mitchell, Robert 34
mobilisation plans 87, 104, 127
mock battles 126–7
Montgomery, W. E. 7, 23–4, 96
Moore, Maurice 7
Moore, R. L. 63
Moore, William 37
morale 103, 116, 138
Morrison, H. S. 45, 65
Moss Brothers Ltd. 171
Mountstewart 47, 97
Murlough House 48

Narrow Water Castle 120
Nathan, Matthew 169
Nationalists 64, 90, 91, 93, 116, 126, 170
National Registration Bill (1915) 168
National Reserve 46, 62
National Rifle Association 21
National Service League 5, 66, 101
Nazism 3
Nelson, Thomas 16
Newcastle upon Tyne 6, 61, 141
Newry 78, 124, 167
newspapers 5, 46, 103
Newtownards 21, 97, 120
Newtownbutler 23, 48
North Down Voters' Association 20
Northern Banking Co. Ltd. 29
Northern Ireland government 149, 196, 197, 199, 200
Northland, Viscount of 47, 57, 88–9, 96, 164
North of Ireland Rifle Club 18
North Tyrone Unionist Association 83
Nugent, Oliver 7, 57, 64, 99–100, 139, 207, 209

O'Connell, W. A. 35
officer corps 57–60, 179–181
Officer Training Corps 95, 96, 170, 174, 180
O'Leary, Michael 155
Old Town Hall (Belfast) 76
Olympic Games 26
Omagh 5, 37, 79, 122, 124
O'Neill, Arthur 81, 90, 100, 105, 153, 164, 207
Orange Order
 and formation of UVF 5, 22, 61, 62–3, 67
 drilling by (1910–13) 15–16, 18–19, 23, 32, 33, 35, 38, 78
 parades by 9, 16, 31, 90, 117–19, 192
 and Unionist Clubs 19–21

 unwillingness to join UVF in some areas 78–9, 194
Ormerod, G. S. 165, 180
Orr, R. C. 58, 164

Pain, G. W. Hacket 58, 63, 80, 82, 90, 128, 139, 144, 165
Painter, H. E. 142
Pakenham, H. A. 67, 105, 153, 181
'Pals' battalions 62, 175, 178
parades (UVF)
 attendance at 8, 102–3, 118–19
 commemorative 118
 and enlistment for 36th (Ulster) Division 166, 178
 funeral 118, 123–4
 HQ involvement in 90, 116, 125
 interference with military training 100
 musical accompaniment of 125
 and presentation of colours 117, 121–3
 and religious services 65, 67, 119, 121–3
 rifles carried at 124
 role of 8–9, 100, 116, 131
 venues held at 120–1
Paris 9
partition of Ireland 6, 65, 69, 77, 196, 206
Patriotic Fund 154, 156
Patterson, J. H. 60, 99
Pau (France) 171
Peace Preservation Act (Ireland) (1881) 136
Pearson, Edward 15–16
Penny, A. F. 58, 99
Personnel Board (UVF) 78
Plunkett, Horace 66
Pole-Carrew, Reginald 61
Pollock, H. M. 149
Pomeroy, 104
Portadown 33

Index 235

Portaferry 20
Porter-Porter, J. 142
Pountney, F. S. 149
Powell, C. H. 96, 99, 164, 165, 179
Pratt, Audley 88
Proctor, J. C. B. 96
proficiency, certificates of 89, 102
propaganda 9, 19, 23, 60, 116, 124, 127
PRONI 4, 5, 8, 45

Queen's Island (Belfast) 53
Queen's University of Belfast, The 63, 171
Quicke, Frank 62
Quinn, S. Blacker 98, 121, 154

Railway Board 78
railways 92
rank structure 82–3
Rathfriland 124, 165, 190
recruitment to the British army 172–82
Red Cross 61
regimental system 11, 82, 83–4, 90–1, 144, 174, 206–7
religion 6, 9, 16–17, 116, 121–3
Repington, C. a la C. 45, 53, 54–5, 67–8, 86–7
revolvers 18, 33, 34, 144
Ricardo, Ambrose 57, 100, 171, 178, 182, 194
Richardson, George
  appointed GOC 7, 58, 78, 80
  and arming of the UVF 124, 139
  and Great War 99, 164, 168–70, 176–7, 180, 182
  institutes regimental system in UVF 62, 83, 121, 206–7
  military experience of 80
  present at parades 7, 117–18, 119, 120, 127
  resignation of 10, 148, 182–3
  role of 7, 76, 78, 82, 105–6, 125, 164, 184, 206

salary of 9, 155
Richill 17, 35, 124
rifle clubs 5, 21, 22
rifles
  disposal of 147–53, 168, 190
  distribution of 20, 34, 85, 143–6
  dummy 17, 31, 124, 170
  importation of 33, 138, 141–3
  issued to Loyalist groups (1920) 190, 191–2, 206
  issuing of 90, 124, 140
  Lee Metford 144, 153
  loaned to 36th (Ulster) Division 171
  Mannlicher 152
  Martini Enfield 141, 143
  Martini Henry 18, 140, 144
  Mauser 67, 103, 144, 151, 152
  protection of 147–8, 168
  purchase of 9, 18, 29
  seizure of 138, 141
  stealing of 143
  Steyr 144, 151
  Vetterli 139, 144
  Winchester 18
Rifle Volunteers 23, 27, 28, 54, 66, 69, 82
rioting 34, 77, 88, 118, 197, 206
Roberts, F. S. (1st Earl Roberts) 66, 80
Royal Irish Constabulary
  political sympathies of 4, 34
  reports on UVF enlistment in the British army 172–3
  reports of UVF parades 118, 126
  and rioting 88
  seizure of rifles 136, 142
  surveillance of the arming of the UVF 17, 18, 32–3, 79, 140–3, 145
  surveillance of British army officers 57
  surveillance of UVF drilling 17, 18, 19, 21, 23–4, 33, 35, 36, 137

UVF plans regarding 92–4, 106, 156, 209
  views of military capabilities of UVF 126
Royal Navy 93, 106, 138, 209
Royal School Armagh 119
Royal Ulster Agricultural Society 118
Royal Ulster Constabulary 149, 198, 200, 210
rugby 62, 116–17
Russell, T. W. 77

Saintfield, Battle of (1798) 16
Samuels, A. W. 170
Saunderson, Edward 78
Scriven, J. B. 58, 60
Sea Cadets 153
Seaforde 21, 23
Sears, Jack 50–1, 55, 101, 102, 104
Seely, J. E. B. 37, 66, 123
shipyards 53, 62, 83, 183
shooting competitions 21, 78, 129, 168
Shortt, Edward 147
shotguns 3, 34, 145, 191, 209
Simon, John 136
Sinn Fein 147, 191, 200
Sion Mills 6, 57, 83, 207
Sirocco Engineering Works 125
Smith, F. E. 119
Smith, T. J. 21
smoking concerts 19
Smyth, Ross 96, 100
social activities 128–9
social composition 6, 24, 45–64, 68–9, 130, 207
socialism 11
Society of Miniature Rifle Clubs 21, 22
Solemn League and Covenant 37, 46, 47, 64, 65, 67, 94, 118, 125, 130
Somerville, A. A. 62
Somme, Battle of (1916) 4
Somme Hospital 171
songs 128, 129–31

South African War (1899–1902) 59, 60, 62, 80
South Tyrone Unionist Association 67
Special Reserve 57, 58, 63, 66, 96, 193
Special Service Force 8, 89, 97, 125, 180, 207
Spender, Lilian 53, 60, 61, 65, 94, 99, 119, 120, 127, 165
Spender, W. B. 11, 60, 80–1, 85, 91, 94, 120, 139, 146, 152, 165, 192–8
sports 30, 62, 116–17, 128, 129, 156, 175, 208
Sprucefield 149–53
Stack, W. A. 50
Staff College 80
Stewart, H. H. 32
suffragettes 64, 126
Supply Board 78

tarrif reform 68
temperance movement 21
Templetown, 4th Viscount of 19
Territorial Force 5, 10, 25, 26–7, 28, 30, 46, 50, 54, 66, 84, 86, 87, 89, 96, 101, 105, 146, 163, 169, 176, 206, 207
Thompson, S. E. 98
Trade Unions 64, 68
training 84, 100–6
Transport Board 78, 84
Trimble, W. C. 24–5, 50, 66, 83, 96, 117, 181
Trinity College Dublin 170
Twaddell, W. J. 199
Twelfth of July celebrations 118, 192

'Ulster Day' 24, 118, 130
Ulster Ex-Servicemen's Association 196–7
Ulster Hall 68, 128
Ulster Home Guard 153
Ulster Imperial Guards 10–11, 131, 148, 196–201, 206

Ulster Provisional Government 78, 81, 85, 92, 106, 151, 209
Ulster Scots 64
Ulster Special Constabulary 3, 10, 11, 148, 153, 190, 195–201
Ulster Tower (Thiepval) 156
Ulster Unionist Council 9, 19, 46, 47, 127, 154, 166, 192, 200, 205
Ulster Women's Unionist Council 9
uniforms 125, 153, 171, 206, 208
Unionist Clubs
  activities of 19–21, 22, 79, 128
  arming of 20, 21, 103
  continuing military role (1913–14) 78–9
  drilling by 5–6, 15, 16, 18, 19, 20, 21, 23, 38, 48, 62
  formation of 19, 20, 22–3, 47, 117
  and formation of UVF 7, 22, 67, 79, 85
  Fortwilliam Unionist Club 19
  membership of 20–1
  numbers of 19–20
  outside Ulster 19
  and propaganda 19
  unwillingness of some to support UVF 7, 22–3

Unionist Party (Irish/Ulster) 2, 58, 76–7, 91, 94, 148, 174, 179, 205
UVF formations
  Battalions
    1st Armagh Regiment 181
    Ballymoney Battalion 120
    1st Donegal 100
    1st East Belfast Regiment 156
    3rd East Belfast Regiment 98
    5th East Belfast Regiment 121
    2nd East Down Regiment 121
    1st Fermanagh Regiment 6, 49, 50, 51, 54, 56, 98, 101, 102, 104
    2nd Fermanagh Regiment 104
    3rd Fermanagh Regiment 104, 181
    Lisburn Battalion 208
    1st North Antrim Regiment 105, 164
    2nd North Antrim Regiment 102, 105, 124, 167, 178
    1st North Belfast Regiment 121
    6th North Belfast Regiment 121
    1st North Derry Regiment 96
    2nd North Derry Regiment 96, 104, 127
    3rd North Derry Regiment 96
    1st North Down Regiment 121
    2nd North Down Regiment 97, 121
    Queen's Island Battalion 121
    1st South Antrim Regiment 121, 124
    6th South Belfast 63, 96
    1st South Derry Regiment 96
    2nd South Derry Regiment 96, 97
    2nd South Down Regiment 126–7
    3rd South Down Regiment 165
    1st Tyrone Regiment 47, 83–4
    2nd Tyrone Regiment 122
    3rd Tyrone Regiment 118
    4th Tyrone Regiment 164
    5th Tyrone Regiment 49, 50, 52, 54, 126, 147
    1st West Belfast Regiment 121
    2nd West Belfast Regiment 98, 121
  Companies
    'A' Company, 2nd North Antrim Regiment 101, 102
    Aughnacloy Company 118
    Bellisle Company 124
    'C' Company, 6th North Belfast Regiment 128
    'C' Company, 2nd North Antrim Regiment 173

'C' Company, 2nd West Belfast Regiment, 54
Castlecaulfield Company 67
Clough Company 122
Greenisland 128
'H' (Seaforde) Company, 1st South Down Regiment 45, 48, 49, 52, 56
'J' Company, 4th (Dungannon) Tyrone Regiment 57, 88, 101–2
'J' Company, 2nd Tyrone Regiment 128
Leitrim Company 61
Lisnaskea Company 122
Loughgall Company 127
Newbliss Company 124
Richill Company 127
Corps
  Motor Car Corps 85
  Nursing Corps 61, 84, 123, 124
  Ulster Signalling and Dispatch Rider Corps 84, 154
Divisions
  Belfast 52–3, 59, 97, 99, 118, 126, 167, 209
  North Down 164
Headquarters
  and arming of the UVF 138–40, 144, 153, 206
  composition of 58, 59, 79–82
  contingency planning by 90–3, 167–8
  establishment of 67, 85
  finances of 105, 135, 156
  and formation of 36th (Ulster) Division 46, 166, 182
  military expertise of 58, 59, 79–82, 85
  provision of equipment 84–5, 87, 91, 153–4, 157
  relationship with local units 7, 45, 76, 78, 83, 90–1, 125, 127, 129, 165, 184, 206, 207, 209
  role of 81–2, 83, 87, 88, 116, 169
Hospital 171
Regiments
  Armagh Regiment 127
  Cavan Regiment 88, 97, 100, 207, 209
  Central Antrim Regiment 91, 93, 102
  Derry City Regiment 6, 45, 53, 55, 83, 100, 101, 123
  Donegal Regiment 165
  Dublin Regiment 6, 61, 143
  East Belfast Regiment 103, 127, 128
  East Down Regiment 121
  Fermanagh Regiment 81, 103
  Monaghan Regiment 55, 65, 93, 94, 120, 168
  North Antrim Regiment 82, 85, 89, 90, 93, 105, 120, 164, 207
  North Belfast Regiment 53, 55, 97, 121, 168
  North Down Regiment 105, 120, 154, 165
  North Londonderry Regiment 100, 120
  South Antrim Regiment 91, 93, 127, 153–4
  Tyrone Regiment 83, 96, 100, 104, 128
  West Belfast Regiment 6, 53, 60, 89, 98, 99, 119, 180
  Young Citizen Volunteers (see separate entry)

Vickers machine guns 141
Vigilance Forces (1920) 190
Volunteer Act (1868) 170
Volunteer Advisory Board (UVF) 78
Volunteer Training Corps 10, 163, 169–70, 182, 183

Wake, C. St. A. 59, 99

Index

Walker, Samuel 35
Wallace, R. H. 18, 32, 58, 78, 79, 139
Wansey, Hugh 50
Waring, Holt 86
War Office 5, 27, 30, 66, 149, 153, 169, 170, 171, 174, 175
Webster, John 191
Weimar Germany 199–200
Wickham, G. C. 200
William Ewart and Sons Ltd. 28
Wilson, Henry 68
Wimborne, 1st Viscount of 169
Witherow, W 122
Wolverhampton 63, 80
women 60–1, 84, 124
Workman and Clark shipyard 25, 29, 58, 97
Workman, Frank 25, 27, 29, 30–1
Workman, W. E. H. 58

Yeomanry (1796–1834) 16, 17, 22

York Street Flax Spinning Company 28
Young Citizen Volunteers
   assimilation into UVF 24, 30–31
   Catholic membership of 5, 65
   CO of 29–30
   Constitution of 25–6
   financial difficulties of 28–9
   formation of 5, 24, 25
   and formation of 14th Royal Irish Rifles 177, 179, 180
   and Lord Mayor of Belfast 24, 26
   membership costs of 28
   planned revival of (1919) 183
   social activities in 30, 128
   social composition of 53
   and Territorial Force 25, 26–7, 30
   uniform of 26, 125
   and youth movements 25
Young, Osbourne 5, 32
Young Ulster 5, 17–18

Lightning Source UK Ltd.
Milton Keynes UK
UKOW07f0706160115

244548UK00001B/26/P

9 780719 073724